PADRES

The National Chicano Priest Movement

†

RICHARD EDWARD MARTÍNEZ

UNIVERSITY OF TEXAS PRESS

AUSTIN

First edition, 2005

Requests for permission to reproduce material from this work should
be sent to Permissions, University of Texas Press, P.O. Box 7819, Austin,
TX 78713-7819.

⊗The paper used in this book meets the minimum requirements
of ANSI/NISO Z39.48-1992 (R1997) (Permanence of Paper).

Library of Congress Cataloging-in-Publication Data

Martínez, Richard Edward, 1968–
PADRES : the national Chicano priest movement /
Richard Edward Martínez.— 1st ed.
p.   cm.
Includes bibliographical references and index.
ISBN 0-292-70644-8 (alk. paper) —
ISBN 0-292-70678-2 (pbk. : alk. paper)
1. Padres Associados para Derechos Religiosos, Educativos y
Sociales—History.   2. Civil rights workers—United States—Histroy—
20th century.   3. Political activists—United States—History—
20th century.   4. Priests—United States—Political activity—
History—20th century.   5. Catholic Church—United States—Clergy—
Political activity—History—20th century.   6. Mexican Americans—
Civil rights—History—20th century.   7. Civil rights movements—
United States—History—20th century.   8. Mexican Americans—Social
conditions—History—20th century.   9. Church and social problems—
Catholic Church—History—20th century.   I. Title.
E184.M5M387   2005
267'.24273'0896872—dc22
2004026227

CONTENTS

†

PADRES

ONE

INTRODUCTION

†

Areview of the major works on the Chicano Movement[1] reveals the expected: people struggling for political rights, better education, land, and labor rights. It is rare to find any mention of the Catholic Church, which is rather striking given that more than 90 percent of Mexican Americans are Catholic. The lack of attention suggests that the church had no significant role during the Chicano Movement era, which is far from true. This book seeks to place the Catholic Church in the historical context of the Chicano era. It shows that the church played a role in the movement and that Chicano priests were not mere bystanders.

The church is currently undergoing change and acknowledging the horrible things it has done in the past.[2] The story told in these pages shows that the church has not always acted in the best interests of Mexican Americans. In fact, this relationship has been oppressive in many ways. The church was made aware of this in one of the most controversial (albeit largely unknown) battles of the movement—a battle waged by laypersons but primarily by two internal church groups. One of these groups was PADRES, a national activist Chicano priests' organization that was formed in 1969 and lasted until 1989. PADRES, Spanish for "priests," is an acronym for Padres Asociados para Derechos Religiosos, Educativos y Sociales, or Priests Associated for Religious, Educational, and Social Rights. In 1971 Las Hermanas (The Sisters), a national organization of activist Chicana/Latina nuns, was established; and it is still active. Through sustained agitation, often in collaboration, these groups resisted more than one hundred years of institutional racism, discrimination, and neglect of Mexican Americans at the hands of the U.S. Catholic Church. They challenged the oppressive cultural practices that defined this relationship, and the ideology that supported it. They also pressured the church to become more involved in the struggles of their people for social justice in the United States. Many were directly involved at the grassroots level as activists and organizers.

Together, PADRES and Las Hermanas formed the first wave of organized resistance from within the church aimed at institutionalizing a Latino-specific agenda. In large part as a result of their efforts, the 1970s and 1980s witnessed an increase of activity by Mexican American and Latino Catholics across the nation and especially in the southwestern United States where Mexican Americans were concentrated. Thousands of Latino laypersons became involved at the local level in parish councils, thousands of others participated in the national Encuentros (Encounters, or conferences), the Spanish language became more common in formal church practices, the first Chicano and Latino bishops were appointed, many local parishes became sites where class struggles were waged, and the dominance of white priests and nuns in Latino Catholic ministry was greatly diminished. Moisés Sandoval refers to these changes as the "Latinization" of the U.S. Catholic Church and rightly gives credit to PADRES and Las Hermanas.[3] Ana María Diaz-Stevens and Anthony M. Stevens-Arroyo, who also credit PADRES and Las Hermanas, argue that this movement started in the Catholic Church but spread to Protestant and Pentecostal denominations to create a larger movement called "the Latino Religious Resurgence in the U.S."[4] Are these changes token, or are they meaningful? This is an important question, but before it can be answered, we must take a close look at PADRES and Las Hermanas.

This is the first book dedicated entirely to the investigation of the PADRES movement.[5] It began as a way to obtain my Ph.D. from the University of California, Los Angeles. It ended up as a way to honor what these Chicano priests tried to do. To be sure, this is but one book. Many more could be written. And I encourage others to do so.

This book, which is based heavily on oral histories of PADRES' founding members, presents a brief history of PADRES and an analysis of its emergence. Chapter 2 reviews the Mexican American Catholic experience. Chapter 3 describes the historical context from which PADRES emerged. Chapter 4 describes the first two official PADRES meetings, the way in which PADRES became an exclusively Chicano organization, the organization's goals, and the initial reception by white priests and bishops. Chapter 5 highlights PADRES' major battles, and Chapter 6 describes its demise.

Chapter 7 addresses the question, how and under what conditions did PADRES emerge? I answer this question by first assuming that

PADRES was a social movement that emerged within an established organization with the goal of liberating its oppressed membership. I analyze its emergence using a social-psychological framework called the "insurgent state of being," which refers to an action-oriented state of being among movement participants comprising their thoughts, emotions, and identities. The development of these elements over time is influenced by specific direct experiences within three interdependent dimensions: inside the formal organization, outside the formal organization within the oppressed community, and inside small isolated groups. These experiences increase the likelihood that the elements will develop.

THE MEXICAN AMERICAN
CATHOLIC EXPERIENCE

†

The Mexican American Catholic experience cannot be appreciated without an understanding of the historical implications of the imposition of particular foreign social structures. Since the sixteenth century Spanish Catholicism dominated religion in Ibero-America. Until the mid-nineteenth century in the Southwest territory the membership and leadership of the Catholic Church was predominantly Spanish and Mexican. Churches were governed by the hierarchy in Mexico.

In 1848 the signing of the Treaty of Guadalupe Hidalgo made official the violent imperial seizure of half of Mexico's northern territory, which then became the U.S. Southwest. Institutions throughout this territory were colonized by the United States, including the Catholic Church.[1] The Mexican Catholics who refused to leave were subjected to a European form of Catholicism[2] and a church that was often openly racist.[3]

During the late nineteenth and early twentieth century, large waves of Catholics immigrated to the United States from Ireland, Italy, Germany, and Poland. Each group arrived with its own priests and religious leaders who established parishes, schools, and hospitals, which serviced the respective ethnic enclaves.

By contrast, the large numbers of Mexican immigrants who came to the United States during and after the Mexican Revolution arrived without benefit of their own clergy. The Euro-American Catholic clergy ministered to Mexican immigrants in ways that were culturally foreign to them. Significantly, this new church-parishioner relationship occurred in a context of popular anti-Mexican sentiment, which was highly institutionalized in the political and social arenas.

Fr. Edmundo Rodríguez, a PADRES cofounder and former Jesuit provincial, argues that the resulting oppression by the church stemmed from a cultural misunderstanding: "Obviously, the practices and style were vastly different between the two traditions, and they clashed in the Southwest as Catholic peoples from Mexico and Catholic clergy from the northern European traditions attempted to continue to foster Catholicism in the United States. It is out of this clash that many mistakenly label what was happening in the southwestern church as discrimination and injustice."[4]

Nevertheless, it is widely acknowledged that during the period between 1848 and 1960, the church effectively functioned as a partner in the colonization process by helping to maintain the racial and capitalist order in the Southwest.[5] This was accomplished in part by the infliction of daily indignities, the administration of bourgeois theology, cultural oppression, and the elimination of native Mexican American clergy. Gilbert R. Cadena gives an exemplary illustration of the second-class treatment accorded Mexican Americans in a story about Mexican American Catholics in Riverside, California, in the mid-1800s told by Fr. Roger Luna at a Western Vocation Directors Association conference in 1980.

> Chicano Catholics were only allowed to attend the 8:00 A.M. Sunday Mass at St. Francis de Sales Catholic Church. Before Mass, Chicanos had to wait outside until the Anglo parishioners sat down and then they could occupy the last few rows. According to Fr. Luna, one Sunday the Zúñiga family, a new family to Riverside, attended the 10:00 Mass when the Irish priest went down the aisles asking all Mexicans to leave. A few weeks later, while the Mexicans were celebrating the December Mass of Our Lady of Guadalupe, the service took a little longer than usual and went into the Anglo Mass. The pastor became very angry and told the Mexican parishioners never to come back. The Zuniga family and others organized and went to the diocese of Los Angeles to get permission to make their own Church. After lengthy negotiations the bishop allowed them to build the Church themselves, with the stipulation that they not name it after the Virgin de Guadalupe, the patron saint of Mexico. The bishop named it St. Francis of Assisi, which meant there were two "St. Francis" Churches in Riverside. It took over 30 years before the parishioners were able to rename it the Santuario (Shrine) of Our Lady of Guadalupe, their original choice.[6]

During the first half of the twentieth century, de facto segregation of Mexican Americans existed.[7] Large towns commonly had a "Mexican" church and a "white" church. The Mexican church was usually more rundown than the white church, and it was common for Mexicans to be denied access to white Masses or to be relegated to the back pews. Where only one church existed, separate Masses were often held for Mexicans. My father, Fred Martínez Jr., recalls that in the 1950s in Floresville, Texas, where there was only one Catholic church, the Masses themselves were segregated. Mexicans sat on one side and whites on the other. The homily was partially bilingual, fifteen minutes in English and five minutes in Spanish. In addition, throughout the Southwest it was common for Catholic clergy to publicly express anti-Mexican attitudes and for Mexicans to be denied access to white cemeteries.[8] It was not unheard of for a Mexican Mass to be held in the church basement.[9]

Blanca García, PADRES secretary at the national headquarters in San Antonio from 1972 to 1976, had this to say:

> I was exposed to discrimination, and you never guess from where: from my grade school. And I went to a Catholic school. The nuns showed me what discrimination was. And I guess I didn't realize it until I became a grownup, what these women were doing. They were supposed to be religious women, they were supposed to have seen all the children as children of God and they didn't. Because when we were the last ones in line to eat, when we were the last ones in line to go down the fire escape, when we always sat at the back of the class, when we were always the last to have them help us, we were the last ones they called for an answer when we had our hands up, and all of this came back when I started working for PADRES. And maybe a lot of people were like me. Not the Church, the Church is supposed to be holy.[10]

The theology that the church generally promoted emphasized the spiritual dimension and deemphasized the material dimension, which is the dimension in which people actually live. What is more, the two dimensions were kept largely separate. So, for instance, the life of Jesus Christ was not related to the lives of the poor, who nevertheless held a token position of honor in the church: they were blessed. This is radically different from liberation theology, which makes connections between spirituality and material conditions for purposes of resistance. The result was a church that glorified poverty and reproduced acquiescence among its members who were oppressed by the larger society.[11]

A number of recent attempts to create a distinct Chicano theology in the tradition of Latin American liberation theology reflect the seriousness of this matter.[12] James H. Cone points out similar experiences in his critique of the black American church:

> [O]ne of the greatest failures of the church is its failure to teach its members the theological reasons for their existence. Theology is the critical side of faith. It provides a critical test for the church so as to determine whether its life and work are consistent with the person and work of Jesus Christ. . . . When one's Christian identity is ahistorical and thus exclusively spiritual or otherworldly, then it is possible, perhaps necessary, to separate the gospel from the fight for political justice. White churches make the separation between faith and justice only when their own sociopolitical interests are not at stake, but never when they are.[13]

Through these historic relations the Catholic Church was complicit in the larger white supremacist process that continued to foster dependency, passivity, and intellectual immaturity among Mexican Americans.[14] Several informants agree. PADRES founder Fr. Ralph Ruiz said:

> To me the Church is a paradoxical thing. Although the Church considers itself our Mother, it has acted more like our stepmother, treating us like stepchildren. The Church has always seen Mexicanos, especially in Texas, as incompetent, dependent, ignorant, and docile people. And so we became exactly that. In fact, we are still suffering from that conditioning. The Church has been a top-down institution, with the pope, the bishops, and priest on top. They have the authority. We, the people, have been the sheep. They, the hierarchy, have been the shepherds. All of this has been a process of subjugation. We have been conditioned by the Church for ages and ages to be docile, to be fatalistic, to be dependent. We have been told that it's God's will. And I say, "But these people are poor." And the Church says, "Blessed are the poor." The reality is that poverty is not a virtue. It's a damnable economic condition. I think the Chicanos have been the bastard sons of the Catholic Church and we needed to change that. The Church was not helping the Chicano; it was helping the oppressors by reproducing and conditioning a childlike mentality in the Mexican Catholic. The Church had given preferential treatment for the rich and not for the poor. PADRES was saying, "We are not going to take this bull crap from you anymore. You come to us as our friend, but in fact you are keeping us enslaved. You continue to condition us to remain inane, dwarfed, impotent socially in terms of leadership. No more."[15]

Roberto Piña, a longtime teacher at the Mexican-American Cultural Center, added:

> The church socialized us to be docile, simple, and reverent of the church so the idea of the church as the oppressor was not thought of, but it was true. We [the Mexican American laity] were taught that you pray, pay, and obey. But you cannot take on leadership. The church has been like an abusive mother. But they kept trying to put us on guilt trips. . . . The migrant trail, when farmworkers would go to a certain city and then they'd go to church to the parish and the people would know that they're farmworkers, they'd literally tell them your service is in the basement or the church hall. They couldn't go to the regular church with the rest of the people. There were so many abuses that went on. And what bewilders me is we were asked to forgive, love our enemy.[16]

Regarding the issue of cultural oppression, Lara Medina states, "[E]xamples of institutional efforts to strip Mexican Americans of their cultural . . . identity abound."[17] Indeed they do. An early compelling example is the story of Bishop Jean-Baptiste Lamy of New Mexico.[18] When Bishop Lamy, a Frenchman, began his work in northern New Mexico in 1850 he immediately set out to Americanize the Mexicanos, whom he viewed with great distaste. He suppressed the Spanish language, imposed new architectural standards, and destroyed what he viewed as "grotesque" native religious art. This process was continued by the four French bishops who followed Lamy.[19]

The period between 1940 and 1960 can be characterized as one of heightened Americanization efforts by the Catholic Church.[20] By "Americanization," I mean the process by which people were encouraged to adopt dominant cultural traits and lose traditional cultural traits. These efforts, which coincided with a remarkable level of popular nativism in the United States, were facilitated by, for instance, the establishment of youth clubs and the building of parochial schools that outlawed the speaking of the Spanish language in barrios after World War II.[21]

With Americanization the formal goal of youth clubs and parochial schools, which were undoubtedly white run, the Catholic Church sought to make "Mexican Catholics good American Catholics [and therefore] . . . better citizens."[22] In return, the church gained a measure of social legitimacy after many decades of anti-Catholic sentiment in the Protestant-dominated U.S. society.[23]

But for Mexican American Catholics, Americanization by the Catholic Church equaled a war against their culture. The cultural suppression

practiced in the youth clubs and parochial schools mirrored the cultural and linguistic suppression Mexican Americans faced in the larger church and society. As a consequence, Americanization caused cultural denigration and stigmatization of Mexican Americans.[24] The frustration that this caused was noted by the late César Chávez: "Everywhere we went: to school, to church, to the movies, there was this attack on our culture and our language, an attempt to make us conform to the 'American Way.' What a sin!"[25]

According to Cadena, the Americanization policies can be characterized as pastoral paternalism.[26] And Jeffrey Burns writes that the church often did this "without a sufficiently critical attitude toward the American society of which they wanted the Mexican to become a part and without a sufficiently appreciative attitude toward the culture brought by the Mexican immigrant."[27] Furthermore, this lack of cultural ownership of the church by the Mexican American functioned as an obstacle to such processes as organizing for change and the development of a positive Mexican American identity. This structural disadvantage of the Mexican American sharply contrasts with the advantage enjoyed by African Americans in many African Methodist Episcopal (AME) churches.[28]

By the late 1960s and early 1970s, sharp criticism of the church's Americanization policies and their effects became more common among Mexican American Catholics. An especially articulate statement against Americanization appears in a report by the Subcommittee for the Spanish-speaking of the Minorities Committee of the Los Angeles Priests' Senate in 1971:

Many of our people are being driven to anger, frustration, and even to despair because the Church has not made sufficient efforts to understand their culture, their traditions, and their needs. Without realizing it, the Church reflects the majority culture, the typical American middle-class mentality which is basically racist. Moreover, the Church in the Southwest has a unique cultural problem. It has not only lost its historical Hispanic traditions, but has also acquired a strong Irish tradition. This tradition, coupled with the racist undercurrents of the majority culture, have made the Church in the Southwest insensitive to the culture, traditions and character of the Mexican-American people.[29]

Cultural oppression has been studied by such scholars as Amílcar Cabral and John Gaventa. Cabral argues that culture is important because it is essential. It comprises our very core. To oppress one's culture is to oppress one's essence. To oppress one's essence is to dominate the individual. This is why the struggle to save one's culture from colonial repression is so important.[30]

Gaventa illustrates how the positive institutionalization of the culture of the dominant group and the simultaneous silencing of the culture of the minority helps to maintain the acquiescence of the latter. Names of streets and buildings, iconography, architectural style, and in general things associated with the dominant group are imprinted on the built environment. This validates the dominant group in the minds of both the dominant class and the subordinate class. Those from the subordinate class, especially those who grow up in such an environment, develop over time the fraudulent idea of the superiority of the dominant group and—because their cultural attributes are not glorified but rather stigmatized—of their own inferiority.[31]

Cadena writes that "immediately after the Treaty of Guadalupe Hidalgo was signed in 1848, the Catholic Church quickly sought to eliminate indigenous Mexican clergy and imposed European bishops and priests."[32] One of these was Bishop Lamy. On his arrival in New Mexico, he wrote, "I pray that these Mexican clerics would leave soon, and the sooner the better."[33] In time, he excommunicated one and disciplined, jailed, suspended, and transferred others and replaced them with European clergy.[34] In the years that followed, the church kept the number of U.S.-born Mexican American priests at a very low level. The result was a "legacy of more than a hundred years of discouraging Spanish-speaking leadership."[35]

By 1970 this legacy remained dramatically evident. Out of a total U.S. Catholic population of 47.8 million, Latino Americans constituted 27 percent. Out of this 27 percent, Mexican Americans constituted about 19 percent.[36] Yet there were only 200 native-born Mexican Americans out of 54,000 U.S. Catholic priests, or 0.37 percent.[37] This disparity was pronounced in areas with high concentrations of Mexican American Catholics. In 1970 in the diocese of Los Angeles there were approximately 25 Mexican American priests to serve well over 500,000 Mexican American parishioners. In 1970 the diocese of El Paso, where 75 percent of the Catholics were Mexican American, had 12 Mexican American priests. In 1969 in San Antonio, there were only eight Mexican American priests to serve almost 400,000 Mexican American Catholics, four of whom were on loan from other dioceses.[38] In addition, in 1969 there were no Latino Americans among 275 U.S. bishops.[39] Furthermore, no Latino American had ever held an Episcopal seat in U.S. Catholic history. Meanwhile, the Irish were overrepresented. In 1970 approximately

17 percent of the U.S. Catholic population was Irish American, while 56 percent of U.S. Catholic bishops were of Irish decent.[40] Together, Irish and Germans made up 81 percent of the church hierarchy.[41]

The historically low number of U.S-born Mexican American clergy had profound impacts on the Mexican American peoples. Luciano C. Hendren suggests that this served an important function in the process of Americanization: "Once the native clergy ceased to be (there was an occasional and rare native ordained who 'qualified') the people could be handled with ease, and the American dream of 'achievement' could be realized."[42] Organic leadership within the church that could have organized the masses was largely absent. The implications of this can be appreciated by comparing the Mexican American situation with that of African Americans. As both Cone and Douglas McAdam suggest, a key contribution of the black church to the black civil rights movement is the long tradition of developing native black leadership.[43] Clearly, the same cannot be said about the Catholic Church and the Mexican American people. In addition, the few native-born clergy and the absence of native-born bishops combined to give credence to the argument that between 1848 and 1970 Latino Americans had effectively no voice in the policy-making circles of the U.S. Catholic Church.[44]

Cadena neatly summarizes the historic relationship between the Mexican American and the Catholic Church: "The Catholic Church has largely reflected the ethos of U.S. colonialism: manifest destiny, Anglo-racism, anti-Mexican sentiment, influence of wealthy laity. . . . Moreover, the Southwest Catholic Church has a mentality of 'European superiority' and was not willing to adapt to Mexican culture."[45] This sentiment is affirmed in PADRES member Fr. Alberto Carrillo's appropriately titled essay, "The Sociological Failure of the Catholic Church towards the Mexican-American."[46] Carrillo writes, "On the one hand, the Church cannot be criticized for being human and reflecting the society it serves; but on the other, it must be pointed out that while becoming a member of the Anglo-American society, she reflects all the same biases and prejudices of that majority society."[47] Moreover, abundant evidence exists to support the argument that up to 1970 the church had generally neglected the Mexican American's struggle for justice and equality.[48] Theologian and PADRES member Fr. Virgil Elizondo states, "The church is an institution that can either inhibit or facilitate activism. And it has done both. But in fact it has done more to inhibit than to promote it."[49]

To be fair, the church did not completely fail Mexican American Catholics. It aided considerably in the establishment of many Mexican

American communities. For instance, it established parishes that provided a terrain for social interaction and some semblance of stability and cohesion, in addition to recreation, education, and religiosity. The church also assisted in the administration of much-needed social services.[50] A notable example is the Bishops' Committee for the Spanish Speaking, which was started by Archbishop Robert E. Lucey in 1945. The committee was responsible for constructing medical clinics, settlement houses, community and catechetical centers in Los Angeles, Santa Fe, Denver, and San Antonio.[51] Yet, while these efforts undoubtedly produced considerable good, the motivation underlying these efforts went beyond social welfare. The church was also attempting to frustrate Protestant proselytizing and promote Americanization.[52] Thus, these efforts were no more than a "secondary mission."[53] Further, typically, these institutions were not under the leadership of Mexican immigrants or Mexican Americans.[54]

As Alfredo Mirandé states, "while the church has typically served as an instrument of colonization and domination in . . . the United States, individual priests have not infrequently resisted colonization and subordination."[55] This is indeed true, and it would be easy to draw up a list of progressive priests who fought individual battles on behalf of and with Mexican Americans.[56] But this resistance had never been articulated the way it was in October 1969, when a small army of courageous Chicano priests formed PADRES.

THREE

THE ORIGINS OF PADRES

✝

PADRES emerged after years of slow, steady agitation punctuated by many significant events and the experiences and ideas of the men who started it. I am reminded of an interview that I conducted with a PADRES founder and the organization's first national chairman, Fr. Ralph Ruiz. He asked me to "be true to the spirit of the times" in my telling of their story.[1] He was talking about the 1960s, years of social ferment and militancy and years that reflected the spirit that gave birth to PADRES.

THE SEMINARY

The courageous and prophetic Mexican American priests who founded PADRES were typically born into materially poor but culturally rich families that instilled respect for their heritage and knowledge of the Spanish language. But when they left home for the predominantly white seminaries, often as young as fourteen, their lives dramatically changed. Most entered the seminary during the early 1950s. Like all seminarians, they were subjected to as many as twelve years of highly structured living. As Father Ruiz, who was ordained in 1965, recalls, "You are behind walls. Imaginary walls, but walls. And you're being conditioned day after day from 5:30 in the morning until 10:30 at night when they turn off the lights. You are what they formed you to be. They have the model; and they want everyone to conform to that model, a one-sized shoe."[2] But for these young Mexican American seminarians, the structured environment was a small matter compared to the personal challenges they faced. Typically, there were few other Mexican Americans in the seminary.

Father Ruiz was the only Mexican American in his class. Although there were others initially, he said, "they didn't last."[3] Fr. Alberto Carrillo of the Redemptorist order was ordained in 1959. When he left the seminary, he was one of only two Mexican Americans in a class of one hundred fifty.[4] Fr. Roberto Peña of the Oblate order was ordained in 1955. He reported: "I was the first Mexican American in the seminary after the Oblates had been one hundred years here in San Antonio."[5] Fr. Lonnie Reyes of the Austin, Texas, diocese, who was ordained in 1969, said: "I think as I recall there were three of us Mexicanos out of about 120 or 130 seminarians."[6] And Fr. Juan Romero of the Los Angeles diocese, who was ordained in 1964, said: "[There were] [v]ery few. The proportion in my day was very small. There were my two brothers, myself and a couple of other guys."[7]

Understandably, many complained of feeling alienated due to what Father Peña explained as "not seeing more brown people around."[8] In addition, Mexican American seminarians were subjected to cultural whitewashing, which caused many to lose touch with their culture. Some even lost the ability to speak Spanish. According to Father Peña, "[The seminary was] not sensitive to having another culture there."[9] Fr. Patricio López of Albuquerque said:

> When I was a boy I grew up thinking I was Chicano. At home we didn't speak Castilian Spanish, we spoke Mexican. When I went to the seminary, they told me I was Spanish and tried to force me to forget the Spanish I spoke at home. It was crazy.[10]

Similarly, Fr. Edmundo Rodríguez of the Jesuit order, who was ordained in 1966, said:

> I remember people in the Jesuits telling me, "Oh, you're not Mexican. You're Spanish." And I kept saying, "No, you see, my father was born in Mexico and he wasn't born in Spain and I was born on the border," and so on, "so I'm not Spanish." And they kind of kept on trying to make me Spanish, and I kept resisting that.[11]

In addition, Mexican American seminarians typically experienced outright bigotry. The following testimonies from my interviews are illustrative.

> There was [discrimination against Mexican Americans]. Certainly there was. You could feel it. (Fr. Ramon Aragón, Santa Fe diocese)

There were some guys who were just racist, no doubt about it. I didn't feel inferior or discriminated against by the faculty. I didn't think in those terms. But there was definitely the racism there among some of my colleagues, some of my classmates. I became dean of my class and there were some guys in my class that just couldn't stand it. A couple of times there were almost fistfights. (Fr. Ralph Ruiz)

I came with a lot of Anglo guys from Texas into the Jesuit society and they always let me know that I was one of those Mexicans. Sometimes they called me names like some movie star kind of guy who had a Spanish name. Not Chico. It will come to me. (Fr. Edmundo Rodríguez)

There was separation, division, isolation. We had to kind of stick to each other, get together often because we were called spik, mix, dirty Mexicans, and if we spoke Spanish it was worse. When we would play basketball or football we were always chosen last, and we knew why. It was known. It was understood. And some of the seminarians were worse than others. Not all of them were that way. And we thought, well, going to the seminary, that's going to end it. Seminarians don't do that. In some instances it was even worse because we were isolated and there were so few of us. The difference between the majority and the minority just became even more accentuated. And of the five Mexicans, two were ordained. (Fr. Roberto Flores, Franciscan, ordained 1965)

Greasers. That's the word that was used often, often. Even in our seminary. Greasers, Mex, and it was frustrating, it was hurtful for us to be called that way. [In minor seminary in Chicago] one of the priests, he didn't like us because we had accents. A lot of our guys were kicked out because they had accents. Five my year. Seven the following year. Nine the following year. They were all kicked out. How I ever made it I don't know. (Fr. Albert Gallegos, Servite, ordained 1964)

I'd have to say I didn't [experience discrimination] in any explicit way that I was aware of. But don't forget, I was sheltered with a kind of naiveté. An innocence. But I suppose we were assimilated enough, the New Mexico thing, there's no accent, not heavily Mexicano. (Fr. Juan Romero)

Despite the oppression, however, the PADRES founders felt their seminary experience was largely positive. All said something similar to this, from Father Ruiz: "Aside from all that, it was just hard work, studies, never a boring moment. I enjoyed my seminary life. I had friends. After vacation, I could hardly wait to get back to the seminary."[12] And indeed they had friends, many if not most of whom were white. Further, many owe their vocations to kind white priests who encouraged them when they were young.

SOCIAL JUSTICE TEACHINGS

For many PADRES founders, the seeds of social activism were planted in part through contact with progressive thinkers while they were in the seminary. Father Ruiz and Fr. Henry Casso, both of the San Antonio diocese, said they were inspired by the progressive teachings of Archbishop Lucey. And Father Gallegos mentioned progressive teachers such as Dominic Crossin and Hugh McElwain:

> I think we had some priests who were terrific theologians. They had a good sense of social justice. Some came from Ireland, and they knew about the trouble in Ireland, and they knew about the oppression that they as Catholics had, and in a very real sense they conveyed that to us. And I saw the kind of compassion that these Irish had. It was a wonderful thing. They had compassion for their fellow human beings.[13]

Father Romero added:

> The idea of social advancement was certainly the spirit of the times, and I knew it was fundamental to our Catholic social teachings. I also was aware of the labor priests in the 1930s, of the priests who basically were with their people. These were the immigrants, they were the Irish priests, usually of the same racial stock. So it was easy for me to feel blood kinship with César Chávez in the struggle as well as *movimento la causa* and the theological underpinnings which were very strong.[14]

Fr. Manuel Martínez of the Franciscan order, who was ordained in 1966, said:

> I think in terms of social thought it came from the church itself. From the encyclicals and from the pope and the unions and defending the unions. I think no one brought it up in our terms today, but with the Franciscans it was an emphasis on serving the poor and being with the poor and favoring the poor. So in that sense the whole emphasis and focus was on that.[15]

For others, the seeds of activism were planted through direct action during their years in the seminary. Fr. Edmundo Rodríguez helped to integrate the Jesuit high school in New Orleans, which was closed to blacks. He reported that the experience was "very tense and very difficult."[16] Fr. Vicente López, a Carmelite ordained in 1968, spoke of his experience:

> We studied in Washington, D.C., which was not exactly the hotbed of Hispanic movements in those days. But we were very involved in the black civil rights movements. Stokely Carmichael, SNCC [Student Non-Violent Coordinating Committee], they all had meetings in our place. We loaded the buses with seminarians and went down to whatever kind of demonstration. When the city burned in '68 we helped the people who had been burned out in the black ghetto and we were intimately involved and saw that as part of our pastoral formation, our priestly service in the civil rights movement. Because of that we were also involved in conscientious objection in the war in Vietnam, and so I was down at the Lincoln Memorial and the various marches and we had a leadership role as seminarians and it was seen as integral to our formation as priests. All in the name of the renewal of Vatican II. We were not isolated. We were not apart from the breathing living experience of the downtrodden or the poor at that time between 1965 and 1969, which was when I was studying in Washington, D.C. And so when the Chicano Movement—the Brown Berets and the whole Chicano movement in the States—began I remember right off I called myself a Chicano priest.[17]

VATICAN II

At the time of Vatican II, between 1962 and 1965, the Mexican American priests who founded PADRES were either newly ordained or seminarians in their final years of study. Vatican II influenced them in a variety of ways. For some, it affirmed already existing, or developing, progressive beliefs. Father Rodríguez explained:

> Already before Vatican II, many of us were having "dangerous thoughts" about what we as Christians should be doing. There were many of us who already in the 1950s and 1960s were engaged in combating racism in society, who knew the plight of the migrant workers, who were aware of the dominant society's fears of immigrants and read works like *Social Order*, a little magazine put out by the Jesuits of St. Louis University and *Christ's Blueprint for the South*, published by Loyola University of

New Orleans. We felt that the whole church needed to engage the justice issues of secular society. Vatican II, in the document, *Gaudium et Spes,* affirmed this stance. Long before PADRES was formed or Vatican II was "implemented," I was already engaged in forming lay leaders to develop cooperatives and fight *caciquismo* in Central America. This was done through a program sponsored by Loyola University of New Orleans headed by Louis J. Twomey, S.J. So, to be brief, the thrust of Vatican II came as a surprise and a change of direction for many in the church, but for those of us who already had a notion of where the church should be regarding social justice and poor, it was an affirmation of what we were already doing rather than a change in direction.[18]

For others, Vatican II created a spirit of openness to change within the church.

The church was opening its doors and we were thinking, okay, since the church has changed from the vernacular, since there's an emphasis of increasing the awareness of the laity, well, this is a perfect way for us to start making the move for them to be aware of the Hispanic community and how the Hispanic community can take care of itself. Latinos and Mexicanos are capable of taking care of themselves if they give us the opportunity. But they wouldn't give it to us. The whole theological atmosphere at that time, if you would take it from a sociological point of view, religion was changing, religion was in turmoil. The Church was no longer top to bottom. There was a bottom to top. The faithful have a right to their positions within the church and they are the church. And having that happen and the resistance from the administration and the hierarchy—they hated to be reminded by the clergy, especially the Chicano clergy. "What do they know about theology?"[19] (Fr. Roberto Flores)

I was in the seminary when Pope John was selected. It was a very wonderful thing because of his spirit and then what he immediately wanted to do and what we saw, at least those of us in the seminary, we could see how the church needed to change, the seminary structure needed to change, the mentality of Rome that governs everything. We were excited. In the seminary we were having debates and talking about changes in the church that were needed. Perhaps at the time we didn't realize how many changes were really needed but at least the spirit, the spirit of the time of openness, with the liturgical movement, changing Latin to the vernacular, these were in many ways small changes but big because after so many years of having that. I felt excited and encouraged about it.[20] (Fr. Manuel Martínez)

For some, like Father Ruiz, Vatican II created a climate of freedom that facilitated criticism:

> With PADRES it was first and foremost Vatican II, because it was the spirit of Vatican II that gave us a sense of liberation. It inspired freedom of expression. We no longer felt paralyzed with fear. With Vatican II many of us priests felt that we could take more chances and not be "yes men" to the structure but instead to differ with the structure without considering ourselves heretics. This sense of liberation was very important because the priests who work at the grassroots, as opposed to those in the high towers, become instrumental in liberating those whom they lead.[21]

By contributing to an atmosphere of ideological openness and affirmation, Vatican II created a political opportunity that motivated critical thought and made collective action more feasible. The experience of Father Romero is a dramatic illustration of the way in which exposure to progressive thinkers and Vatican II while in the seminary brought about an activist mind-set among some founders. Father Romero experienced what he calls a coming-of-age in terms of church politics in the late 1950s. When he was a senior year in high school, a priest named John Cofield came to speak about the Young Christian Students (YCS). That summer, the young Romero attended a YSC summer conference.

> It was a major conversion experience for me because here I was a senior in high school about to begin college and there they were—young high school people, sophomores, juniors, and seniors, who were much more enthusiastic about their faith and about changing the world. And here we were in the seminary just studying Latin, history, English composition, math, just normal subjects. It was very structured, but it wasn't really involved with what was going on in the world. And these young men and women were, with a sense of enthusiasm, interested in the Mass, the liturgy, full participation, the theology of the mystical body, the whole question of race relations, ecumenism, the church in the world. And I said, my gosh, and it was a real revelation that these kids were my age and they were interested in things that we should be talking about in the seminary, it seemed to me.[22]

In 1957, during his first year in college, Father Romero's philosophy developed further when he was working on a research paper on the lay apostolate using examples in Europe during the 1940s and 1950s. Father Romero said: "I became intellectually convinced about what was going on, and said this is the future of the Church. It has to be. The role of the lay person, a transformation of the world and all my idealism were kind of encapsulated, and I was fired up with a sense of zeal."[23] But in 1959, the year Romero entered the major seminary in Los Angeles, his idealism was shattered:

> A labor union guy spoke to the high school students about right to work laws and how they were really right to wreck labor unions. And some student mentions it to her father, who was an antiunion Republican who heard that his daughter was getting brainwashed with all this union stuff [and he] complained to Cardinal McIntire, who was a very conservative pro-business guy who effectively killed the Young Christian Students. And I said, how could this be? I was naive. You know, this was a very good thing. I know it is because I've experienced it and I've seen what it has done to young high school students, the zeal it brings in living out our Catholic values. We had studied already in the seminaries the labor encyclicals, and this to me was just one way of putting this into social action. So this was a major block and I said, something was happening. It was a moment of serious depression for me as a third-year college guy.[24]

Soon after, Pope John XXIII was elected, and the process of Vatican II began. This gave Romero hope and affirmation: "I began to breathe, saying, 'You know, there are going to be some important changes coming soon.'"[25] Romero decided to remain patient during his seminary years and waited with great anticipation for his ordination so that he could actualize his idealism through activism:

> I began to prepare for it in my head and in my heart, and I lived in it as it was unfolding. I knew it was going to mean new pastoral life in the church. In the initial years, I tried to interpret the documents in a way that could be translated into our parish life. It served as a guideline and support.[26]

Some PADRES founders did not have such life-changing experiences. For instance, most of those who were ordained before the 1960s said their seminaries were orthodox and therefore did not provide progressive instruction. Father Carrillo said: "We were Council of Trent. That's all we knew. That was our theological training. When we got out it was 'Dominus Vobiscum' up to the shoulders. And, you know, like a kid coming out of West Point, we followed the line."[27] But in the long run it did not seem to matter. For if they were not activists at the time of their ordination, this mind-set developed when they became directly involved with poor and working-class Mexican Americans. Again, Father Carrillo: "[After ordination] you see reality and you see the world. Once you see the needs of the people firsthand and you see people and you see starving farmworkers and you see people dying because they can't get a job that gives health care—that's when you have to do something."[28] Father Casso, who was ordained in 1957, said, "Was I formally made aware of the social doctrines? I don't think so. Not so much in the church. I think I was thrown into it. I got thrown into a very impoverished, economically depressed area. That's how I began to realize the need."[29]

DIRECT SOCIAL ACTION DURING THE 1960S

Ordination, the triumphant last step in the manufacturing of a priest, came for the vast majority of PADRES founders by the mid-1960s. With noble enthusiasm and youthful vigor, they proudly donned their standard black uniforms and stiff white collars and set out across the country to serve the people. Many found themselves working directly with the Mexican American poor and working class in the southwestern United States where these groups were concentrated. In 1960 there were roughly 3 million Spanish-surnamed persons of a total population of 29 million in the Southwest.[30] Roughly 79 percent of these Spanish-surnamed persons lived in urban areas.[31] Life for the vast majority was hard. Among Spanish-speaking families, 35 percent lived in poverty, as compared to 16 percent of whites.[32] Racism in the educational system made schools a terrain of injustice.[33] Labor exploitation and workplace discrimination impeded advancement.[34] Politically, Mexican Americans lacked power at the local, state, and national levels.[35]

The great social ferment of the 1960s was picking up steam. The black civil rights movement was intensifying, and others emerged: the free speech movement, the anti–Vietnam War movement, the poor people's movement, and the American Indian movement.[36] On the international scene, liberation movements in Cuba, Vietnam, and Africa gave rise to new ideologies.

Meanwhile, many Mexican Americans grew increasingly frustrated by their second-class treatment. Gómez-Quiñones writes: "[W]ithin the

ferment created by changes in the ideological climate and material conditions of the early 1960s, there arose a variegated burst of activity
loosely identified as the Chicano movement."[37] This "activity" refers
to the rise in insurgency among Mexican Americans throughout the
Southwest who struggled for political, economic, educational, cultural,
and basic civil rights. Literature on this activity is rich and plentiful.[38]
Some of the more dramatic efforts are the United Farm Workers movement, the Alianza, the Brown Berets, and the Crusade for Justice, as well
as various student movements. In addition, the Political Association of
Spanish-Speaking Organizations (PASSO) and the Mexican-American
Youth Organization (MAYO) were formed at this time.[39]

While working directly with the Mexican American poor and working class, Mexican American PADRES founders, to quote a letter from
Father Ruiz to Archbishop Furey of San Antonio, "experienced firsthand the social, economic and religious isolation forced on these communities by a majority which has not accepted racial and cultural difference."[40] This led them to become directly involved in the social justice
movement.

After ordination in 1966, Father Rodríguez began his first year as a
priest in his hometown of El Paso, Texas. It was not long before he got
into trouble with the local political establishment and the diocese:

> I was working with high school kids in the poor sections of El Paso,
> doing some pretty important work. . . . I had already gotten into trouble
> in El Paso with the diocese and some other people because I'd wrote an
> article that was published in the *Ave Maria Magazine*. It was the cover
> article, and what I did, I described the situation in El Paso. I called it the
> invisible poor. The Chicanos in El Paso. I had taken pictures of the ter-
> rible tenement situation there. The editor of the newspaper was one of
> the owners of the tenements and the newspaper never covered the terrible
> conditions. And I also described what different churches were doing, like
> the Methodists had a health clinic on the southside and the Lutherans had
> a language school, and I also said what the Catholic Church was doing.
> And so we basically had like a little trial. At the chancery I was asked
> about this and I told them, "You tell me what the Catholic Church is do-
> ing besides what I said in the article. Five years ago you promised certain
> projects and none of this has come to pass." So they finally said, "we'll
> table this." But I knew I was in trouble.[41]

Father Rodríguez was exiled to San Antonio, which he was not happy
about. He believes he was sent away in part because of his activism.

"But," he said, "it was a very providential move because all kinds of stuff began to happen there."[42] In San Antonio, he soon became involved in the Coalition Against Police Brutality:

> There were ten young Chicanos that had been gunned down, mostly from the back because they were running away. They were killed by the police in ten months. And this just became an outrage. I don't think any of them had been armed, and they were just running away from whatever they were trying to be arrested for. . . . So we formed a coalition with lawyers and other people in the community and we negotiated with the police chief to take some of those policemen off the street and put them on desk jobs. There were big protests and marches.[43]

Father Casso was active in a number of progressive projects during the 1960s. As a parish priest in a tough barrio in San Antonio, he organized youth sports and coached. In time, he coordinated the conversion of empty fields into ballparks for kids and called it the St. John Bosco Youth Center. He later became executive secretary of the Bishops' Committee for the Spanish Speaking, and was a founding board member of the Mexican American Legal Defense and Educational Fund (MALDEF) in 1967. When the War on Poverty monies became available, Father Casso was one of the lead organizers of a coalition that successfully pressured a very conservative city hall to accept the funds. In addition, he was involved in early organizing efforts at Kelly Air Force Base, where Mexican Americans were being discrimated against in the workplace.

Fr. Roberto Peña spent most of the 1960s in rural South Texas working with Mexican immigrant and Mexican American farmworkers. He said:

> My concern was the farmworker situation, the border situation. Because they could get people from Mexico to come work for less. Can you imagine working for less than 35 cents an hour? I saw the reality of the farmworkers in the valley. No fresh water. No rest rooms. No living wage. I had [i.e., ministered to] eleven ranches. Two-thirds of my collection was $63.50 a week. Three sisters and a priest tried to live on $63.50 a week from the collection.[44]

Father Peña helped to establish a variety of programs for farmworkers, such as health clinics, clean water, and affordable housing.

In 1967, two years after his ordination, Father Ruiz became director of San Antonio's Inner City Apostolate, a ministry under the auspices of the archdiocese located on the near westside that worked with the poorest and most politically disenfranchised Mexican Americans in the city. Father Ruiz and his staff began to distribute food and clothing to meet immediate needs. Though Father Ruiz had been born and raised in these same neighborhoods, he soon realized he had a lot to learn:

> When I first came to the Inner City I was disturbed by the suspicion with which I was greeted. But after having established who I was, I still was not able to communicate with the people. After four months, I finally got the message: I was a real phony! I came there with an affluent middle-class gospel and stood and watched all anguish of life in the Inner City but was unwilling to jump in and be human. I could no longer stand on the bank of the world in the safety of my own church and throw life rings out to drowning people, hauling them into the security of the church where I stood untouched. These people are poor, hungry, sick, filled with mental anguish, and the medication I brought was as inadequate as a band-aid on a gaping wound.[45]

In time, Father Ruiz realized that Inner City had a duty to enable the poor to fight against the root causes of their misery so that they could mature personally and socially and progress economically. This enabling would not come from pious sermons but from organizing and consciousness raising. The development of self-awareness, self-worth, and cultural pride was necessary. Building unity and self-reliance followed. The area was divided into blocks consisting of about three dozen families. Through house-to-house contact, each block was organized, and the people elected their own leaders. Inner City then provided the leaders with guidance. Father Ruiz reflected on this period:

> The Inner City Apostolate experience was very important to PADRES because it became an example of the kind of grassroots activity every PADRES member should have been involved in, as they dedicated their lives to the people of God. What we saw in the inner city was the kind of lifestyle we did not want for our people any longer. We had a powerful institution which could change all that—the Catholic Church. We were hoping that PADRES could become a more effective advocate within the church for Latinos and reverse the process of conditioning dependency, which the church structure had started in the first place. We wanted to correct the kind of preaching that held that suffering and being poor was

a virtue. "Suffer with patience," we were told, and we kept responding, "Bull." Poverty is not a virtue. It is a damnable condition that needs to be eradicated.[46]

In September 1967 Inner City hosted the Hunger Hearings Conference, which was sponsored by Citizens' Crusade Against Poverty, a group of professionals from throughout the United States. In May 1968 Father Ruiz and San Antonio's poor were featured in the nationally televised CBS documentary, "Hunger in America." The controversial documentary was narrated in part by Father Ruiz. In addition, Inner City aided in the formation of the Mothers Welfare Rights Organization to resist civic officials' harsh treatment of the poor. Also, voter registration drives made considerable gains.

It was during these struggles that Father Ruiz began to use a new vocabulary to refer to the oppressed. The third-person pronoun *they* became the first-person plural *we:* "It was no longer 'they' who were suffering, but I was suffering too, because it impacted me as well. 'We' were suffering."[47]

Because of his advocacy and exposure, Father Ruiz became a marked man. He was ridiculed and slandered privately and publicly. Some of the poor people he worked with were targeted as well. According to Father Ruiz, the FBI sent agents to the area in search of the names of those who had testified in the Hunger Hearings and who appeared in the documentary. Many people became frightened. Father Ruiz expressed his outrage before the Commission on Civil Rights in 1968, and the FBI subsequently discontinued their investigation.

At one point, Father Ruiz received word that Archbishop Furey had fired him from his position at Inner City. He speculated that the archbishop was responding to pressure from local white political elites, which was not implausible since Furey was rumored to have had close personal ties with the conservative Republican mayor, Walter McAllister. But Father Ruiz and his local clerical allies—who were still energized by the ousting of the autocratic and repressive San Antonio archbishop, Lucey, by organized clerics of the archdiocese in October 1968—would have none of it. Acting on Father Ruiz's behalf, fellow clergy fired telegrams and letters at Archbishop Furey, demanding confirmation of the firing and threatening to call a press conference. Furey immediately backed down and denied that he had fired Father Ruiz. Soon after, Father Ruiz was accused by Auxiliary Bishop Levin, assistant to Furey, of desecrating the Mass. As punishment, he was exiled for several weeks to nearby Sacred Heart Church. There Father Ruiz said Mass and was confined to his quarters and prevented from contact with his people. The accusation was challenged and eventually proven fraudulent. Father Ruiz speculated that these events reflected an effort by the local hierarchy to avert another clerical rebellion. Despite the extreme pain and stress, a determined Father Ruiz persevered.

At the May 1968 Poor People's March on Washington Father Ruiz confronted black organizers, which further tested his tenacity. While the event was being planned, he accompanied a delegation from San Antonio to Atlanta, where he met Dr. Martin Luther King Jr. After King was assassinated, Ralph Abernathy took over, and the event went ahead as scheduled. Father Ruiz was to attend the march as a member of a delegation of poverty advocates from San Antonio. But as the event was about to take place, he was prevented by Archbishop Lucey from leaving San Antonio. Disappointed, he was forced to stay behind as the delegation went to Washington without him. Soon after the delegation reached Washington, Father Ruiz received a call from one of the delegates, Texas state senator Joe Bernal. He recalls the event as follows:

"You need to come to D.C. immediately, because the Hispanics are being treated terribly." I told Joe I needed to get permission from Archbishop Lucey, but Archbishop Lucey was out of town. I could not disobey his orders. However, I felt that if the archbishop knew the urgency of the situation he would have given me permission. Based on that assumption, I left. I arrived in Washington. It had been raining. The tent city was all muddy. Some of the blacks were staying there. The Hispanics were taken to Hawthorn High School. At the time we had few Mexican American leaders. Reyes Tijerina from New Mexico and Corky González from Denver were the two Chicano leaders at Hawthorn. Reyes went around with his bodyguards wearing bandannas and being nasty to his own delegation. Corky was a far more responsible, level-headed, and caring leader. Food was in short supply. They were eating Spam and crackers. That's all they had to eat. There were children there, and they didn't have the appropriate diet. And then at night, five, six, seven big black guys would come in and push people around and intimidate them. It was a terrible situation. I suggested to Corky that we needed to do something about this. He said, "We have no resources, the blacks control everything. All the assistance and donations go through their hands." I said, "Corky, this is not acceptable. Let's raise hell. Let's call Abernathy to meet with us in order to correct this situation." We called and asked Abernathy to meet with us the following morning and we said this was serious.[48]

The next morning, just before the meeting was about to take place, Father Ruiz succeeded in persuading Reyes to keep his bodyguards outside the room in which they were to meet:

At 10:30 the next morning, here comes Abernathy, Andrew Young, and Jesse Jackson and a couple of more black men. Corky, Reyes, and I were sitting at a round table eating saltines and Spam because that's all we had to eat. They sat down at the table. Young sat next to me, Jackson sat next to Reyes, and Abernathy sat next to Corky. There were a few other black guys standing around and about fifty *mexicanitos* standing around the table watching. All of a sudden Abernathy reached out into Corky's plate, grabbed the Spam and saltines, and shoved them into his mouth, the crumbs falling onto the table. Corky said nothing. I think he was shocked. Then this guy Jackson does the same thing with Reyes. When Andrew Young reached out to my plate, I grabbed my fork and told him, "If you take my Spam I'll stab your hand." He left my Spam alone. The tense silence around the table was broken by an outburst of cheers from the Mexican Americans. It was obvious that these black folks were there to intimidate us, but we told them that we wanted a room full of provisions and medications by two o'clock in the afternoon. We gave them a list of demands. We told them that if we did not receive the goods by 2:00 P.M., we would call an international press conference and tell the whole world how the black leadership, who claimed to be victims of oppression, had become subjugators themselves. By one o'clock that afternoon, most of our demands were met. Tijerina, however, called a press conference where he blasted the blacks. He broke the rules. Two nights later we met at a huge black church. Corky and Abernathy sat at center stage while Reyes sat in the corner not to be seen. It was incredible.[49]

During the early 1960s, Fr. Alberto Carrillo and fellow Redemptorist Fr. Vincent Soriano visited about twenty parishes per year throughout the Southwest and gave objectives in Spanish. This lasted for about three years, and eventually the two began working at the Inner City Apostolate in Tucson, an organization very similar to Father Ruiz's apostolate in San Antonio in terms of its mission and activism. In the evenings, Masses were held in people's homes with captive audiences of fifty or more. Other sacraments such as first communion, baptism, and marriage validation were performed. According to Father Carrillo, "It turns out statistically we proved to the bishop that we had more Mass attendance, marriage validations, and first communions and confirmations than all the parishes in the westside of town."[50] During the day, they were involved in prison ministry, Model Cities programs, and community organizing.

By the mid-1960s this Tucson barrio was organized into four cells and a massive telephone tree established. According to Father Carrillo, on more than one occasion, several thousand people packed city hall on twenty-four hours' notice:

> One time we did this when we found out that some of the city councilmen had a dummy corporation, and down in the poorest barrio of town they were changing the zoning laws and not telling the people. The taxes go up, they take over the property, their dummy corporation gets the profit. Soriano discovers this, and this law student, a little Jewish guy who was in the domestic peace corps, VISTA, does the research. We go to city hall and we pack it with people and talking very polite, please rescind the tax, and the people make their pleas, please rescind the tax, it's unfair. And, no, no, no. And so we say okay we want an executive session and there Soriano says okay we know about your dummy corporation, we know who it is, we got it researched. Soriano says here's the stuff in this envelope and by the way there's also an envelope at the post office. If anything happens to any one of us we'll blow it. So they came out and they rescinded the tax. And the people never knew. Well, that day one of our cars was stolen and shot up and driven a couple of miles down the road and got blown up. A couple of shots were taken at the rectory.[51]

In terms of community organizing, Fr. Huey Elford worked among the Yaqui Indians, Father Soriano dealt with the problems of poverty housing, and Father Carrillo was spending much of his time on education issues in the barrio. As Father Carrillo recalls, it was a baptism by fire:

> When the kids walked out of L.A. with their famous walk-outs, not much longer after that they walked out of Tucson. All the kids from the westside came marching to our rectory. I didn't know anything about public education. And they said you got to come with us, father, the police are going to—okay, so I end up going with them to the park where they were going to meet and here we got about a thousand, two thousand Chicano kids who just walked out of school. I ended up on the podium, the TV on me.[52]

Father Carrillo soon learned that Mexican Americans faced racism in the schools and dropped out at an alarming rate. When challenged, the school board refused to listen and denied that they had statistics on dropout rates. Father Carrillo continued:

[W]e went back to the rectory and had a meeting with an organization called The Forum made up of some of the young college kids, MEChA [El Movimiento Estudantil Chicano de Aztlán], but it wasn't called MEChA yet, Mexicano bankers, teachers, lawyers, laborers, etc. We got together at least twice a month to say what are the problems and what can we all do together and we formed a coalition. The education kids said, "Hey, we can get you the records." So we said go for it. We didn't know they were going to break in, get the records, Xerox them, which was new at the time, put them all back, lock them, boom, and nobody ever knew. So then the educators get down and start counting the records and we find out that the dropout rate is in excess of 60 percent. So we go back to the school board and very politely say, "We challenge you. We believe the dropout rate is in excess of 60 percent." "No, no, no." So we say, "Let us look at your records." "No, no, we can't do that because they'll get lost." And I said, "Let's do it this way. You don't trust me, let the bishop be present, the superintendent of schools be present, and then get somebody to open up the records and keep score." And they wouldn't do it. So I drove to see —— at the civil rights commission office in L.A., and I told them what was going on and they say we'll send an investigator. HEW [Department of Housing, Education, and Welfare] comes and does a complete investigation. The way the report's done, they send it to the senator first and then he gives it to the district. Well, the senator was [Barry] Goldwater. He wouldn't release it. This is about a year later now. He still wouldn't release it and we're bugging ——. So one night at midnight I get a call. Meet me at such and such a bar. I go and there's —— and he buys me a drink and we're talking. And it's one o'clock. The bar was closing in Tucson so we didn't have much time. And he said, "Well, I'm going to go to bed." He was staying at the hotel. And I said, "It was good talking to you." And he says, "You forgot something." And I said, "No, I didn't bring anything." I see a brown envelope on the table. He says, "You forgot something." I said, "I didn't bring anything." He says, "You forgot something! That's yours. I didn't give it to you." It was the HEW report. So I took it to the rectory and after much consideration, do we release it? Do we not and use it as a bargaining tool? We were outvoted by the kids, who said let's release it. So we Xeroxed it and passed it out on the westside after all the Masses. And then the parents could see that their kids were being screwed.[53]

Soon after, HEW officials came to Tucson, and Father Carrillo, the educators, and the superintendent negotiated a host of reforms, including
bilingual education.

The social change in which these clerical guerrillas engaged was a
logical extension of how they came to define their priesthoods. For
them, being a priest meant that if the need presented itself, social justice
activism was necessary. As Father Ruiz explained, "I saw from the very
beginning, the mission of priesthood and the role of the priest in justice,
in social issues, they go hand in hand."[54]

In addition, being a priest meant solidarity with the poor.

> I was in league with the poor. I could not separate evangelization from
> what the poor were going through. (Fr. Roberto Peña)

> My awareness was: I'm a priest but I'm a priest because I'm for the people
> and not to subjugate the people. And I wanted to be a part of the move-
> ment that would be the priesthood for the people and not just the hierar-
> chical church. (Fr. Roberto Flores)

Together, these meanings comprised an activist priest identity that was
common among founding members.

Direct contact between PADRES founders and the Mexican American poor and working class was not limited to social justice struggles.
Founders also enjoyed day-to-day contact with the spiritual lives of the
people. A shining example is their involvement in the Cursillo movement. The Cursillo is a three-day retreat for laypeople that was introduced in the United States in the late 1950s and eventually spread
throughout the country. The retreat emphasized renewal and spiritual
discipline and was held in English and Spanish. In the 1960s Cursillos
became popular in Mexican American communities in Texas and in the
rural Southwest. According to Fr. Edmundo Rodríguez, it gave Mexican American Catholics a new sense of purpose and involvement in the
church.[55]

Though the Cursillo was presented as a religious rather than a social
action movement, it nevertheless motivated many Mexican Americans
to become actively involved in the pursuit of social justice.[56] Thus it
functioned as a leadership school. This informal function was facilitated by the fact that for many Mexican Americans, the Cursillos validated the Spanish language and nurtured a sense of cultural pride. Many
Mexican American lay leaders of the 1970s went through the program
in the 1960s. Among them was César Chávez and Archbishop Patrick

Flores. While a parish priest in Texas in 1962, Father Flores participated in a Cursillo and soon after became a Cursillo coordinator.

The power of the Cursillo to motivate Mexican Americans is illustrated by the story of Genaro García:

> Genaro García of San Antonio, who was president of FAMA (Federation for Action by Mexican Americans) in the turbulent 1960s and early 1970s, says that the *Cursillo* helped him to recover his language and his cultural heritage. The methodology of the *Cursillo*, which gave him a way of looking at issues and immersed him in a community of people who could share both aspirations and the concerns of their lives, helped him to develop an awareness of social issues affecting the Chicano people of San Antonio's Westside. The result was a commitment on his part to work on specific issues like the need to remove the welfare assistance ceiling set by the Texas State Constitution, job discrimination, school-funding disparities, and the selection of Mexican Americans on grand juries, among others.[57]

The development of these Mexican American leaders began a new tradition of native leadership. Because of this, many people began to think of themselves as agents of change. For many, this was radical thinking.

The Cursillo was not accepted everywhere, however. Many priests and bishops were unsupportive because of their anti-Spanish-language bias[58] and precisely because the program radicalized Mexican American laity. The success of the Cursillo therefore varied. Nevertheless, what is significant here is that many PADRES founders in the 1960s were involved in the Cursillo as both participants and coordinators. This involvement, as well as their daily interaction with Mexican American Catholics, helped them to reconnect with their culture and gain firsthand knowledge of the special spiritual and material needs of their people. In addition, the valuable leadership and organizing skills they acquired would become useful during PADRES's agitation within the church and during its grassroots organizing efforts in the Mexican American community.

While in the trenches, PADRES founders privately began to think seriously about the role of the church in the lives of Mexican American Catholics. They thought that the ideal church should attend to both the spiritual and the material needs of the people. In attending to the spiritual needs of the people, the church should be culturally relevant and respectful. And it should liberate the consciousness of the people, not subjugate it. In attending to people's material needs, the church should engage substantively and forthrightly in the social struggles of people in need and give preferential treatment to the poor. But, as PADRES founders learned, the church was far from this ideal.

THE CONTRADICTORY CHURCH

Second-Class Treatment

Interviews with PADRES founders reveal numerous examples of second-class treatment of Mexican American Catholics in the church. As we have already seen, Spanish-language Masses were permitted but were often held in the church basements rather than in the sanctuaries. Several PADRES founders presided over such Masses. Fr. Albert Gallegos, for example, reported that he did so "many times": "[In Chicago] there were concentrations of Hispanics in parishes, and they never had a Mass. I started to say Mass in a Polish church, but the pastor would not allow us to say Mass at the main church. We had to go into the basement and the place was full with Hispanics."[59]

A large number of informants said priests from Spain tended to treat Mexican American Catholics badly. For example, Father Gallegos said: "We had a couple of Spanish priests in Chicago, they would go to the Chicano communities and call them stupid from the pulpit. They really were conquistadors in their attitude."[60] And Balthasar "Balty" Janacek of the San Antonio diocese said that it was completely misguided for the church to assume that Spaniards and other foreigners would be appropriate priests for Mexican Americans: "The Spanish missionary tended to be totally paternalistic in his approach to the Mexican Americans during the mission itself, while he was preaching the mission. It was obvious."[61]

When he was a young priest in Houston, Archbishop Patrick Flores was prohibited from hearing confessions in Spanish or communicating in Spanish with parishioners who could not understand English. He was not permitted to speak to his own mother in Spanish in the parlor of the rectory.[62] At one point in the mid-1960s, Flores felt so hurt and frustrated that he contemplated leaving the priesthood. It was Father Janecek, who would later become a strong supporter of PADRES, who talked him into staying. Archbishop Flores said:

> There was injustice in the sense that there was neglect. Also on the part of some who said, "They're in America, we have to do everything in English." And we used to say, "That's not what the Germans and the

Italians and the Polish did when they came. . . . They used their language; they had separate churches to use their language." I'm all for people here learning English and getting educated, but we have to give them time. And I thought there were injustices in the way people were being neglected because they didn't know English and sometimes because they were not "acting like Anglos."[63]

Father Juan Romero recalled his days as a young priest in the Los Angeles diocese during the mid- and late 1960s:

Eighty percent of people who came to me in confession in this parish, which liked to consider itself an English-speaking parish, spoke in Spanish. Well, 80 percent of those in their language of prayer conversed in Spanish, and I was not permitted to preach in Spanish because all the Masses were in English. . . . It bothered me and it helped radicalize me so by the time I heard about PADRES it was like it fit right, like a glove.[64]

This negative attitude toward Spanish-language Masses was widespread. According to Archbishop Flores, "In many places Hispanics were either uneducated or newly arrived from Mexico or other Hispanic countries. They did not know English and hardly any of these parishes had Spanish services. The Protestants seemed to be doing things in Spanish, but we were not."[65] Father Alberto Carrillo, who recalled seeing German-language Masses, said:

Our Redemptorist parishes in Chicago were founded to take care of German immigrants. By the 1960s there were very few. I have no objection to taking care of the little old German ladies. I mean, that was the function of the Redemptorists, to take care of immigrants. So we were just saying, "Hey, let's do it for the Mexicans."[66]

And Father Romero added:

It wasn't fair that there were no Masses in Spanish in parishes with such high percentages of Latino Catholics. And if there was one in Spanish, the dignity of Mexican American Catholics was not respected by having Mass at such a late or inconvenient hour or in the cellar. It's a second-class Catholic citizenship and that's not just. There must be cultural expression. Gringo priests must learn to do a *quinceanera* [celebration of a girl's fifteenth birthday] if people are asking for it. It's a legitimate request.[67]

Father Romero described with great emotion his observations of Spanish-language prejudice in a letter to Bishop Sylvester Trinan of Idaho in 1972:

> Yesterday I returned to San Antonio from a parish in the diocese of San Angelo where I helped in a mission in honor of Our Lady of Guadalupe. San Angelo diocese is one of the largest in area in the country, and one with a very high percentage of Spanish speaking people. What a tragedy that there is not one native Spanish speaking priest there from the diocese! There I met two priests, both young, whose divergent attitudes towards people of Mexican descent reminded me of the reality we face in the American Church. One made no secret that he has made no effort to learn Spanish and expected everyone to converse with him only in English. He was obstinately imposing his Irish cultural and thought patterns identifying them with the Gospel—on the people he was supposed to be serving. The attitudes he manifested were offensive and the saddest thing is that he may not even have been aware of it.[68]

Father Janacek supported these views:

> Mexican American peoples, their culture wasn't respected by the official church. Where I grew up in a very rural part of South Texas, Mexican Americans had the *pastorela* [pastoral play] for years and years, twenty-five miles away from the parish church. The parish considered them separate from the Anglos. . . . The systems were death to them.[69]

Second-class treatment of Mexican American Catholics by the church was due in part to its Americanization policies. It was also due to the racism directed against Mexican Americans that dominated the church. This racism made the minuscule number of Mexican American priests, despite the considerable number of Mexican American Catholics, seem almost natural. Further, it justified what effectively amounted to a "brown-out" in seminaries. As Fr. Virgil Elizondo accurately stated, "The Catholic Church was not allowing us into seminaries. And in many ways it had kept us out. And yet the vast majority of Latinos were católicos."[70] Father Ruiz added:

> The mentality of the Church—certainly in San Antonio—was that Mexican Americans were not ready to become priests. That, as a people, we were not mature enough to be entrusted with this office. So rather than foster native vocations, the church preferred to support seminaries and

recruit seminarians from Ireland and then import the average priest to San Antonio.[71]

For PADRES founders, the second-class treatment of parishioners was difficult enough without the added aggravation of being treated like second-class priests. After ordination, the discrimination and bigotry they had experienced in the seminary became magnified to a remarkable extent. A PADRES founder who wished to remain anonymous told me, "As soon as I got into ministry, I experienced a lot of racism and just plain ignorance from white Catholics in my parish."[72] Fr. Lonnie Reyes said:

> Early on in my personal experience, my first assignment, I was really involved in the Chicano community in Waco, Texas. Being a predominantly Anglo upper-middle-class church, that caused a lot of problems. And then on the other side, the bishop [Riecher of Austin, Texas] and the pastor tried to get me out of there, and then the Chicanos really got upset and met with the bishop and apparently he said that wouldn't happen but he sent me a letter of transfer anyway and of course that thing blew up. Definitely the church had been a tool for the rich. I think this is where PADRES was a big help.[73]

When Fr. Roberto Flores was appointed by the Franciscan provincial to represent the province at the national level, a group of Anglo priests successfully agitated against it. "But that was happening all over," Father Flores said. "Priests were appointed and as soon as the Anglos would find out that a Mexican had been appointed they would do everything to get that appointment changed."[74]

When asked if he thought many PADRES would have been promoted to the church hierarchy had they not been Mexican Americans, Father Gallegos said, "Yes. No doubt about it. If we were Irish we would have. Absolutely. Absolutely. Many of us were teachers. We were at the universities. We were getting big degrees. But it was ignored."[75] Father Flores reported:

> I would see how we were put into leadership positions in the community but not given the responsibility of leadership. We were like puppets. Just for show. It was like crumbs for the people so they would keep coming into the church. . . . They [white priests] would come in and change the devotional fermentation of the people. They were taking away the devotions to Our Lady of Guadalupe, the life of the people. You don't take

away devotions to Our Lady, and you don't take the pictures of the saints off the walls. Color of skin is a tremendous factor in this whole thing even among ourselves as Chicano PADRES priests. The darker ones, how they had the poorer parishes because they were dark complected and the guys that were light complected were living in the richer parishes. And the bishops were following it.[76]

Blanca García, PADRES secretary from 1970 to 1975, said:

A lot of the priests that I knew personally, and they were of Hispanic background, I recognized their talent. I recognized their ambition. And a lot of the priests that came out of the Oblates, that came out of the Jesuits, these priests of Hispanic backgrounds, were well educated. And during my time with PADRES I saw how the church would reprimand them. The church would reprimand them in the sense that the promotions, the advancements, the nominations were not there. Through my association with PADRES, I became very aware of the fact that a lot of these priests were well educated, they were qualified and yet they were being passed by. Now it wasn't on account of education. It wasn't on account of leadership. So what else is there? Discrimination.[77]

Negligence

By the mid-1960s tension developed between Mexican American lay Catholics involved in the emerging Chicano Movement and the Catholic Church.[78] By the late 1960s this tension erupted into direct and often heated conflict. In Mission, Texas, on the Sunday after Christmas in 1969, about one hundred Chicanos painted the statue of the Virgin Mary brown.[79] This tension continued into the early 1970s. In Brighton, Colorado, in 1974, members of the Brown Berets seized a church and pressured the pastor to offer a Mass in Spanish each weekend.[80] Many also became critical of the church's failure to involve itself in the struggle for social justice and equality.[81] As Chicano insurgency increased, the church's lack of involvement became more apparent, and the gap between effort and need exacerbated tensions. A classic example of this conflict is the emergence in 1969 of Católicos Por La Raza (CPLR).

CPLR was a group of activist Chicana/o Catholic laity that pressured the Catholic Church in San Diego and Los Angeles to stop neglecting Mexican Americans' need for social justice. They argued that while Mexican Americans made up the majority of the church's membership, the church, one of the wealthiest institutions in the world, was doing very little for them.[82] According to Raoul Isais-A., the group wanted to bring local and possibly national attention to the fact that the church in the Southwest had ignored Mexican Americans.[83]

The emergence of CPLR was facilitated in part by several visible contradictions. These contradictions were visible in Los Angeles, where "Chicanos were asking why the Archdiocese chose to close a high school in the barrio due to lack of funds, but could still afford to build a three million dollar cathedral in downtown Los Angeles."[84] Pope Leo XIII's encyclical *Rerum Novarum* (published in 1891) gave the church the authority to support the rights of farmworkers to unionize, fight oppression, and so on. But as strike activity intensified, the hierarchy vacillated, with some clergy in support but most opposed. It is believed that one of the reasons for the lack of support was fear of losing growers' money.[85] The priests who supported movement activity were criticized by fellow priests and by bishops. It was not until 1973 that the American Catholic Church extended its support to California farmworkers—and then in part as a result of pressure by PADRES. But, interestingly, each Catholic bishop was allowed to interpret the farmworkers' rights within his own diocese.[86]

Because of its lack of commitment to the farmworkers, many urban Chicano Catholics saw the church for the first time as socially irresponsible. Some began to ask why the church hierarchy was not doing more to aid the Chicano struggle for social justice in the city. The church began to be viewed by more and more people as an obstacle to the Chicano struggle for social, political, and economic independence. Many thought the church must be changed. Meanwhile, confidence among Chicano Catholic activists grew. As it grew, Chicanos found the courage to openly question these contradictions.[87]

Chicano Catholics in San Diego, most of whom were low income, organized and drew up a list of demands that was presented to the local bishop and endorsed by the local priests' senate. The demands included the following: (1) the establishment of a special office with the authority to make sure Chicano needs were being met; (2) the appointment of a native Mexican American priest who would serve as head administrator of the special department; (3) greater respect for the Spanish language; and (4) the immediate establishment of Chicano Studies in Catholic schools.[88] By making these demands, Chicanos were implicitly arguing that they lacked standing in the church. The effort was therefore two-sided: On the one hand, it was an attempt to claim greater cultural ownership of their church; on the other hand, it was an attempt to pressure the church hierarchy to meet their material and social needs.

Soon changes began to be made by the hierarchy, but this did not satisfy everyone. At a weekend conference sponsored by the church in 1969, Chicano activist college students who seemed to think that change was not coming quickly enough and that the church was not using all its power, seized the compound. They drew up a list of their own demands and were eventually arrested. At this time CPLR was formed. They were not separatists. They were radical reformers who remained unconvinced that the Catholic hierarchy was committed to the Chicano cause and remained suspicious that the hierarchy was loyal to the growers.[89]

On Christmas Eve, 1969, CPLR led demonstrations outside St. Basil's Catholic Church in Los Angeles. Demonstrators clashed with police as Cardinal Archbishop McIntyre held Mass inside. As Burns writes, "The clash dramatically symbolized the growing tension between young Chicanos and the Catholic Church. One protester voiced a common perception among the protesters, 'Any fool could see that the Catholic Church has done nothing for our people.'"[90]

Like CPLR, the vast majority of PADRES founders were aware that the Catholic Church was "simply not responding"[91] to the pressing justice needs of Mexican American Catholics. They were also aware that the church was neglecting the spiritual dimension of its membership because of its lack of respect for Mexican American culture. But it was not CPLR or the activist Mexican American lay Catholics who brought this neglect to the attention of PADRES founders. Instead, it developed through direct involvement in various Mexican American communities and through direct contact with the church bureaucracy during the 1960s. It developed through what Father Romero calls "living the life"[92] of an activist priest. In other words, they became aware of the injustices because they experienced them directly. The laity's criticism of the church was not insignificant, however. Some founding members welcomed it for affirming their perceptions.

The following comments by PADRES founders make clear their awareness of the church's neglect of the Mexican American community.

Lack of response? Yes, I would say it was perceived by a lot of people, like Católicos por la Raza and a lot of us [Mexican American priests] were feeling that. The church is rich, it's not using its resources for the Chicano. Well, yes and no. The money was spent on schools, and it benefited. But in another sense, kind of the political and the economic and in an explicit way the church wasn't interested in political and economic empowerment at least on the high level. On our level we heard the cry of the poor, *el grito* "Chicano power!" and identified with it. We felt and knew that something was wrong. From our own experiences, yes, the resources of the church were not being adequately or proportionately used for the needs of the people, especially the people who are growing in number. We need to serve them pastorally and also socioeconomically. (Fr. Juan Romero)

The best-kept secrets of the Catholic Church are the social justice doctrines. The church is so far ahead on this. Even before the black movement and the farmworker movement. Remember when the people came from Ireland and settled in the Northeast? They brought their priests with them. They said you have a right to organize. The Chicano people began to say, "We're citizens, why should we be treated this way?" When you have college students like José Angel Gutiérrez and others who were beginning to be conscious of their situation and standing up and fighting for their rights, then you saw the farmworkers, you began to see people at the local level becoming conscious that they were being discriminated against. And why didn't the church help? I saw the church. It was just teaching. All the social teachings, I don't know how many documents we have on social justice and peace. But no putting it into practice at the local level. They were teaching, but when it came down to commitment, public commitment, it was very, very different. The church was concerned about their sacraments. Not their souls. The soul is not just spirit. It's body that needs clothing and food and health care and good schooling. The church was focusing only on the spiritual and neglecting the material. And I found it to be a naive spirituality. I could never, never see evangelization without the complete human being who has a body. You want to be baptized, well what about after? You go to school barefoot. There should be some decency in your life. I couldn't separate the spiritual from the material. . . . And I was angry because I wanted to move the church this way. (Fr. Roberto Peña)

I saw what was happening with César Chávez and the church kind of dragged its feet. And I took it upon myself, if I was ever in a position, I would not, on my watch, have that said of me. . . . Realizing that St. Philip's [in San Antonio] should never have existed. It's a little triangle. It should never have existed because they're the same people as St. Henry's. Same geographical area. They were created at the time when the Germans at St. Henry's didn't want the Mexicans around so they created that church. (Fr. Henry Casso)

Social issues were not part of the structure of the church. They are outside the church. I felt you had to be accountable. So we had to bring social justice issues inside the church, and that was our job, PADRES. Bring our values inside the church, to the hierarchy, to the Council of Bishops, to the highest levels of power in the church. (Fr. Ralph Ruiz)

I was very involved in getting the church to look at the social situations in our diocese [Santa Fe]. In fact, and this is what we found, that one of the greatest discriminators is the church itself at the time. We began to ask for changes. We felt we needed to give a new direction to the church, not just sacramental. (Fr. Ramón Aragón)

The church, or rather the institution, to put it more correctly, the institution was not responding to the needs of the people who were giving the most. Because they were not only giving of their money but also of their time. They would be in parish committees and councils and come clean the church and clean the yard. (Fr. Roberto Flores)

Father Ruiz recalled seeing injustice articulated in dual treatment:

There was this priest in my parish, hard as hell, who used to beat little kids, hard, with a belt. One time he couldn't find a belt so he hit with an electrical wire. He controlled the whole neighborhood, the whole parish. If somebody would come up in the area of leadership, from the pulpit, he would denigrate them. I saw that. That was the way it was. He could never do that in an Anglo congregation. Never.[93]

Perceived Need for Protection

The church also showed its true colors when it punished activist priests who openly challenged the dominant centers of power in society. During the mid- to late 1960s, many of these priests met resistance from conservative bishops and their functionaries within the church. And it was common for bishops to punish activist priests by forced relocation or other disciplinary means. Examples abound. For instance, in 1966 Frs. William Killian and Sherrill Smith, two distinguished activist priests in the San Antonio diocese, were punished by Archbishop Lucey after they defied an order to stop their involvement in the farmworkers' movement in South Texas. After they were arrested by police and then released, the archbishop exiled them to a monastery for a week.[94] During this period, priests (activists or not) in the San Antonio diocese functioned in an atmosphere of fear.[95]

It is not unreasonable to speculate that many activist or would-be activist priests feared church reprisals or at least felt insecure. In fact, several PADRES founders believed they needed protection from anti-activist bishops. Significantly, one of these men was Father Ruiz, who became the main force behind the first PADRES meeting and one of the most vocal initial agitators. He recalled: "One of the main reasons why we organized was to protect ourselves, Chicano priests, from the bishops. . . . Look at the experiences of others. We needed protection because we were getting involved with the movement and we were challenging the status quo and the bishops were getting pressure from the wealthy to remove us, to send us to the sticks."[96]

PAIN, FRUSTRATION, AND ANGER

So it came down to this: after spending years in the seminary, PADRES founders found themselves treated like second-class priests by a church that treated their ethnic kin like second-class Catholics. PADRES founders were caught in a web of injustice. Quite understandably they were filled with deep pain. One of the earliest and most passionate expressions of this pain came in the form of heartfelt testimonies by PADRES founders at one of the first PADRES meetings. One of the PADRES founders, who chose not to be identified, recalled:

They all seemed so similar. They had to struggle with church authorities like conservative pastors who didn't understand or who didn't care about taking care of Mexican Americans. It was very hard for a Chicano priest to become a pastor at that time, and there were very few. There was great frustration and pain of having to go through that. Many of them were really put down as they tried to get involved. I could understand it. I had some very good priests who supported me, but there were others who wondered what I was doing. They thought activism was not priestly work. So I can understand if some of these guys didn't have anyone else backing them up. I remember that meeting: They were really hurt.[97]

This experience is perhaps articulated best by Father Reyes:

You go in very idealistically with the romantic idea of the role of the priests and then being hit, someone just slamming you against a hard wall, and having the cultural shock of realizing that the church, the more you analyze it and critique it, it's not your church. Culturally and linguistically, every which way. The religious sentiment of the people, the devotion of the people, their religious expression, *curanderismo* and all these kinds of things, they were just criticized. And then on the religious side of it, I didn't sense any knowledge of it or any appreciation of who we were as religious entities in the church. And, of course, then beyond that you have the more social dimension of it, educational and economic and all the things that were going on, and then the church was not there and not responding. It's the realization of, you trust that your mother is going to be there supportive and looking after you and being affirming, but you are virtually all alone. And it's that sense of loneliness and sense of rejection even.[98]

In time, the pain of church injustices turned to frustration and anger.

I was very discouraged from working and working and every bit that you'd do to see progress would be squashed. You organize and push and then with one "no" from the pastor it would die and it would take months and months to get the groups together and get the thing going again. So much discouragement and pain. . . . We were so angry of how we were being kept down, how we were not allowed to grow, how you were to remain quiet and submissive to mother church. Don't try to figure out what it is you want or how you were going to get it because mother church knows best. Huh, mother church didn't know best. (Fr. Roberto Flores)

Thinking back, I think a lot about the anguish, a lot about the frustration and the anger, and just everything that went with that. I think when we talked about *derechos* [rights] in PADRES we were also talking about *derechos* in relationship to the church. I think particularly how Chicano priests and religious were being treated was the cause of great anger. It was like Patricio [Bishop Patrick Flores] said, when they step on your in-grown toenail, it hurts and they need to get off. And I think it was that kind of oppression that brought up a lot of this. And of course there was a lot of negative reaction to us and that aggravated the situation. (Fr. Lonnie Reyes)

The church, then and now, is the most powerful institution in the lives of the Mexican Americans. So it was only natural that we turned to her, the mother church. Here was an institution that we trusted, even though it continuously kept us down, like second-class citizens. This made many of us very angry. The Chicano priests were saying to the church leadership, "Stop mesmerizing us with your doctrine of submission. We are human beings. We will no longer allow you to take our people to the slaughter-house like sheep." (Fr. Ralph Ruiz)

I think what really brought us together was the frustration that we were experiencing. And then nobody really wanted to know about us. They [the church hierarchy] didn't know about the Hispanics and they didn't care. We were still Mexicans, Greasers. (Fr. Albert Gallegos)

I was very angry. For me, it's a paradox if you say in the church to love your neighbor. I took it to mean speak out for your neighbor. And the church didn't say anything. And I saw the blacks going forward and using their own church. I was angry with the church. Why didn't the church come out? There was the bracero movement. And I saw injustices there. I was in the Texas Valley. You heard about the *colonias?* Well, back then we didn't have good water. And I was working with these people. . . . This was the time, you talk about being angry and why we were angry, in 1967 look at the conditions that our people were living in. Without good water and hepatitis so I tried to bring good water to the ranches. I was here at St. Alfonso. The church was poor, and the bishop was living in a palace. I couldn't understand that. And St. Alfonso with its broken windows. A poor place. I was angry because it was inconsistent for me to say love your neighbor and then treating them this way. I was angry. But not an anger that would bring about violence. I believe in nonviolence; but I wanted us to speak for ourselves. I didn't want others speaking for us. And a lot of Chicano priests felt that way. (Fr. Roberto Peña)

Church injustices were not the only cause of these priests' anger. As Sandoval writes candidly, "[T]here was great anger among [Mexican American priests] when they realized that they had been unwitting accomplices in the neglect of their people by the institutional Church. As a consequence, some gave up their vocations and returned to the laity. Others opted to confront and demand that the Church fulfill its responsibility for [Mexican American Catholics]."[99]

INSPIRATION

"I am Chicano"

In the course of direct, day-to-day contact with their people, PADRES founders rediscovered their culture, reversing the cultural whitewashing that the seminary system had practiced. In fact, many took advantage of this cultural reimmersion and relearned Spanish. And it was during this time that they were influenced by the emergence of Chicano consciousness. One of the founders explained, "You couldn't be involved and not be influenced."[100]

During the turbulent 1960s, in response to generations of cultural, ethnic, and class oppression, some people of Mexican descent, particularly those among the poor and working class, redefined the pejorative term "Chicano" to form a new action-oriented political class.[101] This new class began to redefine the economic, racial, cultural, and political position of the people. They used the term "Chicano" to denote the person and group and the term "Chicanismo" to denote the associated beliefs, identity, and political practice.

As a set of beliefs based on the working-class experience, Chicanismo emphasizes dignity, self-worth, uniqueness, and cultural pride.[102] It embodies an ancient truth — "that man is never closer to his true self as when he is close to his community."[103] It defines the self-determination of the Mexican American community as the essence of the Chicano commitment.[104] And it encourages social and political action and in practice often translates into ethnic populism and in some cases separatism.[105] As an identity, Chicanismo emphasizes the nonwhite indigenous past and the working-class history of the Mexican American people.[106]

As a conscious choice, identifying oneself as Chicano was an overtly political and controversial act. Mirandé writes that a Mexican American who self-identified as Chicano was analogous to an African American who self-identified as black.[107] In Texas, it was especially dangerous because the word was popularly associated with communism. Several authors have noted important distinctions between those who identify as Chicanos and those who identify as Mexican Americans. Both Rubén Salazar and Nathan Murillo found that Chicanos appear to be Mexican Americans who have nonwhite images of themselves and are concerned more with group advancement and less with individual advancement.[108] Armando Gutiérrez and Herbert Hirsh, in their study of militancy, found that Chicanos show greater political awareness and readiness to engage in militant forms of political action.[109] Philip E. Lampe found that Chicanos express greater ethnocentrism, greater acceptance of blacks, and greater rejection of whites.[110]

Despite criticism from many who viewed "Chicano" as a pejorative term, the first wave of PADRES priests publicly identified themselves as Chicano and adopted Chicanismo. In doing so, they embraced a politically activist stance and publicly accentuated their differences. Typically, they rejected the violence and exclusion that some promoted, but they identified strongly with the ideas of self-determination, group solidarity, the fight against cultural whitewashing, and embracing their indigenous roots. In addition, they identified with Chicanismo's emphasis on activism and allegiance with the poor and working class. In these ways, Chicanismo enhanced the ethnic ties they naturally shared with Mexican American lay Catholics.

The Black Civil Rights Movement

During the 1960s, when the black civil rights movement was in full swing, the numerous displays of insurgency across the nation by aggrieved African Americans, in particular mass marches and sit-ins, had a profound impact on those who would form PADRES. These dramatic events, which seemed to occur daily and which received a great deal of media attention, increased the sense of urgency that these priests were already feeling. Father Flores sums up the feeling that most had: "Seeing the blacks moving so fast and so furious, and here we were the larger number and being left behind and not being paid attention to. There was a lot of anger. I think that was the biggest motivational impetus that we had."[111]

A few PADRES founders had direct experience with African American insurgency. For instance, Father Gallegos, who was ordained in 1964, spent the mid-1960s ministering to Mexican American communities in Chicago. By the late 1960s he was teaching sociology at Malcolm X College and was chair of the Department of Student Affairs. There, he gained insight into the black civil rights movement and on several occasions participated in marches and demonstrations. Some of these marches were led by Dr. Martin Luther King Jr. "King, we always respected him. We walked many times with him in Chicago on the south side," Father Gallegos recalled. He added: "[W]hen they [the police] saw a white priest [at the marches], they wouldn't do anything." This apparent protection was due to then-Mayor Richard Daley's relationship with the Catholic Church, Fr. Gallegos suggests. "Daley, he used to go to daily mass. And I knew him very well. See, I was the chaplain at the Presbyterian hospital and his wife was there a couple of times so I was her chaplain. And every time we had a public event he would always come over and shake my hand if he saw me. . . . Mayor Daley, I think it's important to note that he helped PADRES a lot. Anything we did in Chicago. He was for us and he helped us a lot."[112]

But it was the peripheral but vocal and militant Black Power movement that had the greatest impact in terms of igniting the flames of righteous activism among PADRES founders. As Father Juan Romero explained, "PADRES emerged on the coattails of the Black Power movement."[113] The Black Power movement was radical in its refusal to accept the term "Negro," which was associated with their long history of oppression and slavery, and to instead adopt with pride the term "black" to demonstrate their resistance to white mainstream thought. This was captured in the popular 1960s slogan, "Black is beautiful." Father Ruiz, who was in San Antonio at the time, said that the Black Power movement led him and his fellow Mexican American priests to think about brown power:

> Mississippi is far from here. But there is the media and that's important. We heard it. We saw on television, at least I did, with much concern and consternation, how they were burning their own homes. . . . [I]t scared me. They were saying "Black is beautiful, black is beautiful, rah rah rah." We began to ask ourselves, if black is beautiful, why not brown? We saw what was happening. We needed to liberate ourselves because we were in no different condition than they were. We were in denial. But we were not blacks, but what the heck; we were eating out of the same dish. We were victimized in the South here, in Texas, in San Antonio.[114]

Role Models

PADRES founders were inspired by activist role models. For some, this inspiration came early in life. Fr. Roberto Flores, for instance, recalled:

> My mom was an activist and my grandmother before that. She was always involved in the community. Always taking care of how things were done in the community. Very involved politically. My mother, the same way. She had been a precinct judge. My brothers and sisters have always been precinct chairs, involved in the Democratic Party, movers and shakers. So even though we were poor, we were always involved in what was going on in the city [Corpus Cristi, Texas].[115]

Father Edmundo Rodríguez said, "My mother took clothing to the migrant camps near El Paso. She, being from a poor farming family, knew the plight of these trapped people very intimately. I learned from her that one should do whatever one can, even if all the problems are not solved."[116] Father Rodríguez also credits the Jesuits Harold Rahm of El Paso and Carmelo Tranchese of San Antonio who actively worked among the Mexican American poor when he was a boy.

As a young man, Fr. Roberto Peña was especially inspired by Eleanor Roosevelt:

I saw Eleanor Roosevelt being a delegate for the United Nations and coming over here to San Antonio and she helped the Jesuits with the unions at the pecan factory. I saw Mrs. Roosevelt helping the priests get that housing project that's close to Our Lady of Guadalupe. All of that excited me. And I said, well why not the priesthood? Why not? This is what Christ did. I had the dreams about changing the world. Changing how the church related to us. I had a dream that Christ didn't want us to live in the conditions we were living. That Christ really meant what he said, "Love one another as I have loved you." When I was being ordained I remember saying, "God, if someone doesn't kill me because of my faith I'll never be saved; I'll be a martyr." That's how I saw the priesthood. For the good of the people.[117]

During the 1960s, older white activist priests inspired many PADRES founders. Father Romero of the Los Angeles diocese says Fr. Bill Dubay, who among other things publicly denounced Cardinal Archbishop McIntyre of Los Angeles, was very radical and inspiring:

I was ordained in '64. There was a young priest who I called the first bad boy priest. Since the mid-sixties guys have left the active ministry and been very vociferous about what they're saying and doing, but Bill Dubay, with a flair, had a public press conference in Santa Barbara to denounce the cardinal for gross malfeasance of office. He was taking him on because he was very old-fashioned in terms of his policies in terms of race relations and economic issues and a variety of things. Bill, that year, was kind of on the outs and suspended, as a matter of fact. But I saw him at an NAACP banquet and he gave the invocation and he told me very prophetically, "Go to Delano." This was barely '64 so I hadn't been really tuned in with César and what was going on but it was an introduction and I did follow it up.[118]

Father Ruiz was especially encouraged by the infamous Berrigan brothers, two priests who made national headlines when they broke into the Selective Service office in Baltimore and destroyed draft records in protest against the Vietnam War.[119] To Father Ruiz, who was also opposed to the war, they were heroes and prophets; and more important, they were priests who had the courage to fight publicly for justice despite the risks.[120]

In 1966, at a meeting in San Jose, California, César Chávez spoke to a large gathering of priests. Father Romero was in the audience:

> César was talking to us and bawling us out as priests. He was making a point that the workers were Catholics—Filipinos and Mexicanos. The ranchers, the majority, were Catholic. And who is helping us organize? The Protestant church. "Where is my Catholic church? Where are my priests?" So he was kind of egging us on, using that strategy. "Where are you guys?" And it was a wonderful meeting. It challenged me. It provoked me. It agitated me.[121]

All founders held Chávez in the highest regard and were encouraged by him. The same can be said of Dr. Martin Luther King, Jr. Father Ruiz:

> King, he preached all the time against injustices. Then he began to march. And when he had thousands of people behind him—that's outrageous in a prophetic way. That's what prophets do.[122]

THINKING TOGETHER

The Mexican American priests were largely isolated from each other throughout the early and mid-1960s. Despite this, by the late 1960s something remarkable occurred. They started to talk to each other. Five in Texas, two in Arizona, three in California—all talking about their experiences, feelings, and ideas in informal settings, free from the gaze of the bishops and their cronies.

Beginning in 1968 in San Antonio, at the initiative and coordination of thirty-two-year-old Father Ruiz, about five diocesan and religious Mexican American priests who worked in the city began to meet informally. The meetings began as social gatherings. They laughed and joked and spoke Spanish freely and affirmed their culture. They had managed to carve out a space in which they could be themselves and forget about their frustrations for a while.

But in time these meetings turned into serious discussion sessions. The priests, most of whom were in their early thirties, discussed two main themes. The first dealt with the many social problems of the Mexican Americans who lived on San Antonio's westside: hunger, malnutrition, unemployment, underschooling, and lack of political power.[123]

According to Father Ruiz, the group was asking, "Why are our people the last when it comes to education, the last when it comes to economics, to politics? Why? Why have we no leaders at the grassroots?"[124] The second dealt with the Catholic Church's relations with Mexican Americans.[125] They called into question the church's lack of commitment to social justice for Mexican Americans. Father Ruiz recalled:

> We were saying that we were living in a church where the priests had no vote. The bishops had the power. We're just like little kids. Also, Why didn't we have more Latinos in the seminaries? Why were there so few Chicano priests? Why didn't we have any Latino bishops in this country? We had no voice beyond the parish. Why are our people the last when it comes to being treated in a holistic way, both spiritually and corporally? We baptize our people, but what happens afterwards? Baptism is not enough. Should children go to school barefooted and hungry? We should not separate the spiritual from the corporeal needs.[126]

Then they began to analyze the structure of the church and other social institutions. Father Edmundo Rodríguez recalled:

> We did an institutional analysis of the main social institutions: the economic, the political, the educational, the religious, the media, the family, etc. We looked at who might benefit and who are hurt by the various policies by which these institutions are governed and how the institutions form systems and how systems interrelate with each other forming powerful cultures. We saw how institutions serve basic human needs, but by this very fact, they can hold the consumers hostage.[127]

Meanwhile, completely separate from the San Antonio meetings, similar developments were occurring in Arizona. On the mission trails throughout the Southwest, Alberto Carrillo and Vincent Soriano, two Redemptorist priests in their late twenties, had come to know several Mexican American priests from New Mexico, Arizona, and California. In Tulare, California, near Fresno, Father Carrillo mused with Fr. David Durán of the Fresno diocese about the need for a new religious order that would do for Mexican Americans what the Redemptorists had done for the German immigrants: serve their religious needs and help them in their transition. Father Durán, who would later become the first chaplain of the United Farm Workers, was thinking about the same thing. In fact, Durán had already talked about it with priests in the Bay Area, including Franciscan fathers Anthony Soto and Reynaldo Flores, who shared the same vision.[128] But as Father Carrillo recalled:

> We just didn't have the resources for a separate order, so we thought, no we have got to get a coalition of people and stay within our own orders. So when we were doing the missions in the San Joaquin Valley we met a few Mexicano priests and they were saying the same thing and we were saying the same thing. We were all saying we gotta get an organization. So the little group of California guys and ourselves who were from Tucson—we said to Father Soriano, who was from Texas, you go to Texas and talk this thing up. So he goes to San Antonio to talk up the idea and he finds out it's already started over there. This idea. This concept. We were separate but thinking the same things. We were in Arizona, and they were in Texas.[129]

Clearly, in the years before PADRES was formed, many things were happening in the lives of the Mexican American priests who would found the organization. They were victims of church discrimination. They were directly involved in the social struggles of the Mexican American poor and working class. They were frustrated because the church was negligent. They were filled with pain, frustration, anger, and urgency. They were coming into their own as activist priests and Chicanos. They were being inspired by leaders, activists, and movements throughout the country. And they were working together to make sense of this reality within the context of Vatican II. These were the main elements that comprised the spirit of the times. And it was this very spirit that led Father Ralph Ruiz to call the first meeting of concerned priests that would soon become the PADRES movement.

FOUR

PADRES

In the Beginning

†

L ate in summer 1969 in San Antonio, a frustrated but undaunted thirty-three-year-old Fr. Ralph Ruiz surveyed the scene: Mexican American Catholics were poor, oppressed by society, and abused and neglected by the church. His heart and mind could no longer bear it, so he decided to do something. As he recalled, "I said, 'Hell, I'm going to try because my people need it. They are the ones who are suffering. If not, this shit will continue.' "[1] He thought the only solution was organized resistance.

Acting on his own initiative, he decided to call a Texas-wide meeting of concerned priests who he hoped felt the same way. From a church directory, he collected the addresses of all the Spanish-surnamed and white priests working among Mexican Americans. "I wrote a letter to them and said on this day we're having a meeting."[2] He then notified San Antonio Archbishop Furey that the meeting would take place. "We never kept anything from the bishops. We wanted it to be on the up and up. It wasn't like we were asking for their permission but just keeping them informed."[3]

On October 7 through 9, 1969, between twenty-five and fifty Chicano priests gathered at LaSalle Catholic High School on San Antonio's westside, which recently had been closed (reportedly due to financial hard times).[4] But it turned out to be more than a Texas-wide meeting. Somehow the word had gotten out, and to the surprise of the San Antonio priests, most participants came from outside Texas: New Mexico, Arizona, Colorado, California, Illinois, Wisconsin, Washington, and the District of Columbia.[5] Several were in their early to mid-thirties.[6] Among the participants were a few Mexican American Protestant ministers. At least one white priest attended.

The Chicano priests shared stories and quickly realized that the problems they and their people faced at the hands of the church were widespread. Father Gallegos, who was stationed in Chicago, recalled: "First we talked about what was happening with the Latinos in our own districts. It was bad."[7] They also talked about the fact that the U.S. Catholic population was more than 25 percent Latino, predominantly Mexican American, yet there were no, nor had there ever been, Mexican American bishops. A great deal of anger was expressed—as well as the feeling that something needed to be done or the problems would continue. According to Father Ruiz, the mood was one of readiness: "The vast majority were eager to move on."[8] Like Father Ruiz, the vast majority felt the best course was organized resistance.

At this most crucial moment, despite seemingly insurmountable odds, these Chicano priests were filled with hope that they could change the church in significant ways for the benefit of their people. For some, this hope arose from the unexpectedly high turnout at the meeting. As Fr. Edmundo Rodríguez explained:

> I think what always gives you hope in that type of situation is the fact that you have people interested and willing to do it with you. I was very surprised at the LaSalle meeting. We wanted to have a statewide meeting so we sent out a few invitations to guys in Houston and Laredo and other places. And people came from Denver, Phoenix, they came from far away. And we said, "What are you guys doing here?" Because all of a sudden you had this interest coming form everywhere and you figure if you have that kind of interest then something's gonna happen. You don't know exactly what and you don't know how, but you figure there's something working here. There's some power here that we're not even aware of.[9]

For others, it was the spirit of Vatican II. Fr. Manuel Martínez credited the vision they had of what the church should be doing for Mexican American Catholics: "The hope we had came from our vision of a new church for our people."[10] Father Casso credited inspirational national leaders: "I think the hope came from creative individuals with voices in the arenas where decisions were made on a national level."[11] Fr. Roberto Flores pointed to faith: "We had faith in the church. We really had faith. And strong faith in the people—that the people really wanted to be a part of the church. And faith and hope in each other—that what we wanted to do was right and just and had to be done."[12]

The gathering needed a name. Wasting no time, several Chicano priests sat down and busied themselves with the task of creating an acronym that would encapsulate the group's vision. Father Roberto Flores, a Franciscan stationed in San Antonio, recalled: "Several of us—Frs. Ralph Ruiz, Edmundo Rodríguez, Henry Casso, and myself—sat for hours looking for the right combination for the acronym. I know that it was an inspiration to us. Fr. Ralph Ruiz and I finally put it together for approval by the others."[13] This acronym was PADRES: Padres Asociados para Derechos Religiosos, Educativos y Sociales.

Participants took part in several sessions that were characterized as "fiery."[14] They worked together and developed thoughtful, hard-hitting criticisms of the Catholic Church as well as resolutions and recommendations. Provisional officers were elected: chairman, Father Ruiz; first vice chairman, Father Gallegos; second vice chairman, Fr. Rodríguez.

The decision was made to hold a national congress in February. The group planned to "contact and invite other Mexican-American priests, Puerto Ricans, Cubans and others involved in the Hispanic problem throughout the country."[15] There, the organization's bylaws would be adopted and permanent officers elected. Fathers Soriano and Carrillo successfully lobbied for the national meeting to be held in Tucson, because they felt neutral territory was necessary. Father Soriano said, "The Texans think that they're the only Mexicans in the world and the guys in the Bay Area are probably way ahead of everybody and the L.A. diocese we'll just ignore."[16] This negative attitude toward the Los Angeles diocese, under the leadership of Cardinal James McIntyre, was due to its reputation for anti-Mexican American sentiment and fear among priests.

The group crafted a press release and held a press conference on October 9. Four Chicano priests—Fathers Rodríguez, Ruiz, Gallegos, and Casso—sat at a long table facing several reporters. Father Casso served as press secretary.[17] Reportedly, at this time Father Casso was helping to establish the Mexican-American Legal Defense and Educational Fund in Los Angeles.[18] According to Father Ruiz, Casso was invited to San Antonio to take part in the LaSalle meeting for strategic reasons: he was charismatic and effective at bringing attention to an issue.[19]

The group publicly accused the church of discrimination against Mexican American Catholics and of "forgetting the Mexican Americans" as they struggled for social justice.[20] Father Casso, who had been director of the Bishops' Committee for the Spanish Speaking, then asserted that the Bishops' Committee "had done very little[;] . . . as a matter of fact, it [was] getting in the way."[21] Then, announcing that PADRES represented a united front on behalf of Spanish-speaking Catholics,[22] he read the press release, which included the following statement:

> One of the reasons we have come together is that we are aware of the great social revolution taking place in the Mexican-American community. No meeting in the past two years dealing with the Mexican-American community has taken place wherein the Church has not been taken to task for seeming lack of concern and commitment to the great quest for human rights of the Mexican-American in this country. Because of this we as Mexican-Americans and Spanish-speaking priests in the United States must make our own personal assessment as to our own role and involvement, as well as fulfill our responsibility in translating and transmitting the cry of our people to the decision makers in the Catholic Church in America.[23]

Father Casso emphasized that the group considered this a "movement" and a "historical event" that "would produce a giant step to the future of the Church."[24] He stated: "[I]t is the first time in the history of the Catholic Church in America that Mexican-American priests and other concerned priests have ever met on their own initiative to form a national organization."[25]

That same day, as provisional chair of PADRES, Father Ruiz sent a lengthy, thoughtful letter to San Antonio Archbishop Furey that explained the group's intentions. He wrote, "We are deeply concerned in seeking to analyze the reasons for this growing dissatisfaction with the Church."[26] Pointing out the lack of specialized ministry attuned to the culture and social condition of "our people," he then wrote candidly about the seminary system:

> We realize that one of the solutions would be a greater number of Mexican-American priests. We are all well aware of the often-quoted phrase: "If only more Mexican-Americans would give themselves to the priesthood." We emphatically reject as a myth that the Mexican-American has not given himself in sufficient numbers to the priestly ministry in the Church. All of us present at this meeting experienced during our seminary days the anxieties of many of our contemporaries who were forced out of the seminary in one way or another. Some of us also experienced the systematic rejection of Mexican-American applicants to the seminaries. We don't want to judge the motives of those who forced or kept them out, but we do know the fact: that they were forced out or kept out. Hence if we do not today have a sufficient number of them it is not because

sufficient numbers of Mexican-Americans have not tried, but because our formation in one way or another forced them or kept them out of the system.[27]

On October 10, 1969, the local press reported that "a national association of Mexican-American priests has been founded in San Antonio" with the intent of "translating the cry of our people to the decision-makers of the Catholic Church in America."[28]

A few days later the newly formed PADRES began its campaign by attempting to make its voice heard within the power structures of the church. The group asked for the opportunity to address the U.S. hierarchy at the National Conference of Catholic Bishops in Washington, D.C.

> We have drawn up a number of resolutions indicating the areas which we feel require immediate attention. These resolutions are directed to specific issues regarding the stance of the Church towards our people and our people's stance toward the official Church. Many of our resolutions concern the need for structural changes within the Church which can best be effected by American bishops working with priests and people. We, therefore, ask that representatives from our organization be allowed to address the assembled bishops at the National Conference in November. In short, we ask for a place on the agenda.[29]

In November, PADRES sent letters to all U.S. bishops. The group was trying to "articulate the aspirations of our people and to convey the emotional overtones of our peoples' stance toward the structural Church." But they did much more than that. They fully articulated their criticisms of church structures and presented a pro-Raza agenda. They began by thoughtfully and diplomatically defining themselves as "spokesmen for the Mexican-American and the Spanish-speaking Catholics of the United States" because of their shared "language, culture, social mores and religious values of our people." At the same time, they pointed out, they were "members of the Church structure as it exists in the United States." "Many of us," they continued, "have experienced the problems which generally affect our community, either directly and personally or through familial ties."[30] Then they took their gloves off.

> We feel that the Church in the United States has largely abandoned its own poor, allowing them to become isolated. It is almost as though we had removed the poor from our presence because they embarrass us.

Therefore we ask the Bishops, who are anointed to serve all of God's people, to mobilize the resources of the entire Church on behalf of the poor, especially its own. . . . If the Church does not become vital and relevant to our people, they, especially the young, will by-pass the Church as an obsolete, un-renewable structure. You will hear the same thing from our Catholic laymen. We only tell you what is already becoming a fact. . . . If the more fortunate members of the Church in the United States refuse to hear the anguished cry of the poor and fail to respond in proportion, how can they call themselves "Christian," when Christ's foremost criterion for gaining entrance into the Kingdom, is what one does for the poor, the forgotten, the down and out, "the least of my brethren."[31]

A fact sheet was attached to the letter outlining the various ways in which the church was neglecting the Mexican American community. PADRES' use of facts to bolster their arguments was a common tactic, and that they felt the need to use facts in their defense is an indictment of the forces that they were up against. Among these facts were the following:

- There are twelve million Mexican Americans and other Spanish-speaking people in the United States.

- One of every four Catholics in the United States is of Latino origins.

- Sixty-five percent of the Latino population of the United States is 18 years of age or younger [and] . . . this group finds that the Church is not relevant to its needs.

- There are no native-born Spanish-surnamed bishops in the United States.

- In Texas, the Mecca of the Mexican American, there are only twenty-nine Mexican American diocesan priests in ten dioceses. A situation which repeats itself throughout the United States is exemplified by the fact that in the Archdiocese of San Antonio[,] where over 51 percent of the population is Mexican American[, . . .] there are only 8 diocesan Mexican American priests and of those 8 only one is a pastor.

- In San Antonio alone it has been verified that over 100,000 Mexican Americans are suffering from hunger and malnutrition.

- The Mexican American population has the lowest level of formal education attainment of any ethnic group in the United States. Nearly 40 percent of the Mexican Americans in the United States had, according to the 1960 census, received less than four years of formal education and therefore were considered functionally illiterate.

- In 1960 five times more Mexican American males were laborers (32 percent) than were Anglo males (6 percent).

- Slightly more than half of the Spanish-surnamed population of the United States has an annual income below $3,000. The incidence of poverty increases as one moves from urban to rural residences. In El Paso's Metropolitan Area where the Mexican American makes up 37 percent of the total household, 85 percent of the substandard and 71 percent of the overcrowded houses are inhabited by Mexican Americans. These conditions are typical of other Texas cities with large Mexican American populations. The cities with the highest incidence of poverty in the United States are in Texas, where Mexican Americans are concentrated, namely San Antonio, Laredo, El Paso.

- Forty-five percent of eligible Mexican Americans are called up by the draft to serve in the Armed Forces, whereas only 19 percent of eligible Anglos are called up. Mexican Americans make up 12 percent of the population of the southwestern states, yet 25 percent of the casualties in Vietnam are Mexican Americans.[32]

The letter contained seven resolutions (actually, they were demands). The first resolution, which dealt with the most pressing item on PADRES' agenda, demanded U.S-born Mexican American bishops.

Whereas, Mexican-Americans are members of the oldest and one of the largest and most forgotten segments of Catholicism in the United States; and in view of the social, economic and educational strides which the Mexican-Americans are making, in many cases independently of the Church; be it resolved that Episcopal appointments be made from the ranks of the indigenous Spanish-speaking clergy in areas where there is a heavy concentration of Spanish-speaking people.[33]

This resolution was followed by an acknowledgment of the fact that there were few Mexican American priests. They nevertheless defended their call for Mexican American bishops by arguing that the situation was so critical that the church should look among the small pool of Mexican American priests that existed. In addition, they stated what they felt was the reason for the lack of Mexican American priests:

> Lack of vocations was a problem we discussed at some length in San Antonio. After exchanging experiences, we felt compelled to issue an emphatic denial that not enough young men from our communities have had the generosity to respond to the priestly calling. Rather, it was our feeling that young men of promise have often failed the training because seminary programs have often failed to take into account the special needs of these students as members of minorities.[34]

PADRES demanded that the seminary system begin to account for the special cultural needs of Mexican American boys who wanted to become priests.[35]

The second resolution addressed discrimination at the parish level. The group demanded that native Spanish-speaking priests be appointed immediately as pastors in large Spanish-speaking communities. The third through fifth resolutions reflected PADRES' strong allegiance to the poor and working class. "Something must be done," they wrote, "so that poor parishes do not continue to be isolated and left to rot."[36] They called on the church to consider subsidizing "low-income parishes, many of which serve Spanish-speaking people . . . from a national Catholic source in order to help these parishes provide for the most basic needs of their people."[37] Further, they called on the church to recognize as valuable and place "high priority . . . on Inner City projects which involve priests and religious more deeply with the day to day economic, social and religious life of the people."[38] They also called on the church to give serious "attention to the question of educating children from low-income areas and to the support of these educational efforts, and that Catholic schools develop programs of bilingual education in areas that encompass a large Spanish-speaking population."[39]

The sixth resolution addressed the question of cultural relevance and church liturgy. It demanded that a Mexican American unit of the National Liturgical Commission be formed to adapt the liturgy to the Mexican American culture in the United States. The seventh called for the church to use its power to help the farmworker movement:

> Be it resolved, we support the cause of César Chávez and the California grape pickers and call upon the Bishops to use all their powers of influence

to bring both sides to the negotiating table again, with the condition that if the growers continue to refuse to negotiate as reasonable men, the Bishops will throw their full weight behind the only sanction available to the farm workers, the boycott of California table grapes.[40]

ESTABLISHING FORMAL CHANNELS

In December PADRES attempted to establish permanent channels of communication with the U.S. Catholic hierarchy. Following protocol, they began communicating with the regular Liaison Committee of the National Conference of Catholic Bishops (NCCB) chaired by Archbishop McDonough. But PADRES found the bishops on the committee ignorant of and unconcerned about the struggles of their people.[41] The organization therefore pushed for the establishment of a permanent liaison committee for PADRES at the NCCB so that PADRES could deal directly with the hierarchy. But the NCCB argued that such an arrangement would set the precedent of establishing a committee for every nationality or minority group. This, according to Cardinal John Francis Dearden, would lead to an endless multiplication of committees and emasculate the regular Liaison Committee.[42] The NCCB encouraged PADRES to communicate with the regular Liaison Committee. Many PADRES members perceived the bishops' stance as inconsistent: the NCCB had formed a special liaison committee to deal with the National Office for Black Catholics (NOBC). The NOBC was established to assist the black Catholic community, which at the time constituted less than 2 percent of the U.S. Catholic population. The NCCB general secretary, Bishop Joseph Bernardin, acknowledged, albeit with some condescension, this inconsistency: "I realize, of course, that the establishment of an ad hoc committee to assist the black Catholic community with the establishment of the National Office for Black Catholics probably gave PADRES the idea."[43]

After more agitation from PADRES, the NCCB agreed to set up an informal liaison committee made up of five bishops suggested by PADRES. These were Bishops Francis J. Furey of San Antonio, Timothy Manning of Los Angeles, Francis J. Green of Tucson, Humberto S. Medeiros of Brownsville, and Charles A. Buswell of Pueblo. The committee was ratified before the end of the month, much to the relief of Bishop Bernardin, who privately hoped that meeting with the committee "would help calm the group."[44]

STANDOFF IN TUCSON:
TOWARD EXCLUSIVE MEMBERSHIP

The First PADRES National Congress took place February 2 through 6, 1970, in Tucson at the Pioneer Hotel and was attended by between two hundred and four hundred people from twenty-three cities and sixteen states.[45] The congress had already begun when Father Janacek, who was known to be sympathetic to the cause of Mexican Americans,[46] and Father Patrick Flores of the Houston-Galveston archdiocese arrived. They had driven together from Texas.[47] Father Janacek recalled walking into an auditorium filled with priests, nuns, and laypeople, the vast majority of whom were white. Then he saw Father Gallegos standing in the front of the crowd wearing cowboy boots and a cowboy hat and exclaiming in a loud, urgent voice: "¡Es tiempo que nos agarramos los huevos y marchamos!" (It's time we get some balls and march!)[48]

The founders originally planned to create an organization composed of priests, both whites and Mexican Americans, who were committed to the advancement of Mexican Americans. Their intention was not to create an exclusively Chicano priests' organization, but this is what happened as a result of a standoff between Chicano priests and an uninvited contingent from northern California composed primarily of white laity, white priests, and white nuns. This contingent, which far outnumbered the Chicano priests, wanted PADRES to have an open membership policy that included laity. They wanted to substitute "People" for "Priests" in the name of the organization. Some Chicano priests, especially those from Texas, feared that if successful, the contingent would sabotage the organization and kill PADRES as a voice for the Mexican American poor and working class. After three tense days of heated debates and infighting,[49] there was a dramatic climax, which Father Ruiz recalled:

> I saw people who couldn't be trusted. So that night I met with Edmundo [Father Rodríguez] and we wrote a draft constitution for PADRES. Then we impounded the name PADRES as an acronym and registered it at the post office and made it official so that they couldn't take it away. Priests. PADRES. Not PUEBLOS. And we put all the records in the bank, in a strong box. But nobody knew, not even the people who met with me, what was going to happen the following day at 2:30. The following morning we were supposed to have a vote whether to have PADRES or PUEBLOS and to change the whole nature of PADRES at 2:30 in the afternoon. So at the first planning session in the morning I told this to no one because I didn't want anyone else to be blamed for it. At that session

Fr. Ralph Ruiz addresses the assembly at the PADRES First National Congress, February 2–6, 1970, at the Pioneer Hotel in Tucson, Arizona. Photo courtesy of Fr. Ralph Ruiz.

I got up and said, "Folks there are some of you who are here who were not invited, and there were more of those people than the ones who were invited. The intent was to have PADRES members come. PADRES, not pueblos. Some of you want pueblos and to change the whole nature of the organization. Those of you who want to form an organization of Pueblos Asociados are welcome to stay in this hall. Those that want Padres Asociados and are for having this organization for Chicano priests will follow me to the room next door." And I walked. I didn't look back. I walked into the next room, and it was full. They were standing around the walls. Chicano and Anglo priests. And I said, "This is only for Chicano priests. Anglo priests can be associate members. They have to attend meetings and pay dues. They have a voice but no vote. This is the way it is. You don't like it, you can go to the next room." And one Anglo priest spoke up and said, "It's about time you Chicanos take the bull by the horns and become self-energized. Don't depend on us anymore. Learn on your own. I for one am happy to be an associate member." "Yeah, me too, me too." So we voted and said okay.[50]

Chicano priests walk out of the PADRES First National Congress,
February 2–6, 1970, at the Pioneer Hotel in Tucson, Arizona.
Photo courtesy of Fr. Ralph Ruiz.

This Anglo priest was Father Janacek. He suggested that widespread paternalism toward Mexican Americans by foreign-born priests may have influenced the move toward exclusivity:

> I remember when we would bring missionaries in from Mexico for missions as I was a young priest in Edna, Texas. It was really something else. The Spanish missionary tended to be totally paternalistic and his approach to the Mexican-Americans during the mission itself, while he was preaching the mission. It was obvious. It was really a paternalistic approach to the whole thing. And that was there so much so that at the very first convention the idea cropped up, who's going to be voting members. . . . I surely was in favor. I walked out with them. . . . And it wasn't like they wouldn't listen to others but that they would develop a ministry that would come from the Mexican-American community and because they also knew that there was also a spirituality in the Mexican American community that simply needed to be picked up on and developed.[51]

Fr. Edmundo Rodríguez (standing) addresses priests after they walked out and reassembled at the PADRES First National Congress. Also shown: Fr. Albert Gallegos (sitting to Fr. Rodríguez's immediate right); Fr. Henry Casso (sitting to Fr. Rodríguez's immediate left). Photo courtesy of Fr. Ralph Ruiz.

Father Janacek said that he actually took the time to explain the importance of this move to a Spanish priest who felt rejected and did not understand. He recalled hearing this Spanish priest, a seminary professor, say, "How could they do this to us?"[52]

There were other white priests who worked among Mexican Americans who, like Father Janacek, were supportive of a Chicano-controlled PADRES. But some were personally hurt by the move. Some even found it highly offensive and accused the fledgling organization of reverse discrimination. This caused tension between some Chicano and white priests.[53]

Some Chicano priests also felt a certain personal tension from white exclusion. Fr. Vicente López, a Carmelite priest, recalled:

> In 1968 I was newly ordained and I came as a member of the Latin American committee of the Archdiocese of Chicago. And I came with . . . a priest, deacons and laity who were involved in Hispanic ministry and they

Some of the original PADRES founders at the PADRES First National
Congress. Sitting in the front row, left to right, Frs. Manuel Martínez, Albert
Gallegos, Ralph Ruiz. Standing, second row, far right, Fr. Patrick Flores.
Photo courtesy of Fr. Ralph Ruiz.

thought PADRES was going to be a call for all people who are involved
in Hispanic ministry . . . to be part of it as members. And I remember one
of the difficulties for me was with Dominic. Dominic was in charge of the
office for Hispanic ministry in Joliette, Illinois. . . . Seferino Ochoa, a dea-
con, was director of the office. . . . When the conflict occurred they were
excluded. . . . I was not working with Hispanics directly, I was teaching
languages at Mt. Carmel High School. They who were involved in Hispanic ministry were being excluded from membership. I, just because I
was a Mexican-American priest, was accepted. And that really created a
tension in my life. . . . I worked de facto with a variety of men, women,
lay, religious, Latino and non-Latino and really more non-Latino in the
Midwest. But I walked out with them because I felt that was where I belonged. I could identify with Father Ricardo from Tucson who was there.
With Father Carrillo who was in Tucson. So I went out trying to figure
out perhaps even my own identity and my own ministerial call, since I
was teaching at a prep school for boys in Chicago and not really serving
the Spanish speaking.[54]

Soon after the Tucson congress, Father López left the prep school and began a long career of service to Latino immigrants that continues to the present day in South Central Los Angeles.

Some laypersons criticized PADRES, calling them clericalists. One lay group, the Confederación de la Raza Unida of San Jose, California, denounced PADRES for inadequately representing their interests.[55]

Frs. Alberto Carrillo and Edmundo Rodríguez offered their rationales for Chicano exclusivity.

Carrillo: "We needed to be a Chicano organization because we were going to ask for Chicano bishops. Now if we had taken non-Chicano priests, let's say our first director of PADRES is a neat Irishman, and then he goes over to the bishops asking for a Chicano bishop and [the bishops] say hey you [Chicanos priests] can't even control your own group. So it had to be. And I don't want to denigrate. We had many, many non-Chicano priests who at that time did a hell of a lot more in the apostolate for Mexicanos than a lot of Mexicanos did, so there was a lot of good ones, but we needed to have our own identity and that's why we started it.[56]

Rodríguez: "The question really was if we were to really have any influence in the church, who would the bishops listen to? Would they listen to a group of laypeople, priests, and religious? Or would they listen to a very focused group of priests who would bring certain issues to them. And who would people like the people who were opposing César Chávez's movement in California listen to? So it seemed to us that it should be a very focused group, which is what resulted.[57]

Another PADRES founder said:

We became very effective in influencing the bishops precisely because we were all priests, and the bishops were going to listen to a priest more than laymen at the time. Later on a bishop commented to me: "Every time you guys showed up, God, not again." But he said, "You always had pastoral issues in mind, you were always concerned about the people. But you guys were a pain in the ass."[58]

Despite the membership and voting restrictions, which effectively killed the possibility for costly battles between Chicano priests and white priests for power within the organization, PADRES welcomed collaboration with white priests as well as Protestant and Methodist ministers, laypersons, and nuns. Still, the issue of who could be full voting members of PADRES plagued the organization throughout its life.[59]

At the end of the First National Congress, the daring Chicano priests who founded PADRES crafted a press release that left no doubt as to their ideology and urgent resolve.

> The Mexican-American is on the move. Its youth is on the streets and marching out of the schools throughout the country. The poor in the *barrios* are pushing for human rights. They are demanding better housing, expecting better health care, clamoring for human dignity for themselves and their children. The farm workers with the grape boycott are continuing in their quest for equal opportunity. The choice of the Mexican-American clergymen was, and is—are we going to stand with our people or let the procession of people pass us by? It was this decision that caused us to organize PADRES. So determined were we to be with our people and on the other hand be united among ourselves that we Mexican-American priests saw it as imperative to walk out of a plenary session. For once, we Mexican-American priests felt we had to stand for what we are and what we want to be as Mexican-American priests![60]

Before the congress adjourned, permanent officers were elected: national chairman, Fr. Ralph Ruiz; first vice chairman, Fr. Edmundo Rodríguez; second vice chairman, Fr. David Durán; national secretary, Fr. Albert Gallegos; national press secretary, Fr. Henry Casso.[61]

With the membership issue settled for the time being, PADRES became "a support system for Chicano priests who often felt isolated and tended toward burn-out during the hard days of the *movimiento* [and a] national network of fraternal support developed and . . . nourished by the individual meetings, as well as national conferences and retreats."[62] At meetings and training seminars, when one member shared stories about his experiences in the trenches or expressed leftist views, the others encouraged and validated him. PADRES's monthly newsletter also helped. It gave positive coverage, as well as crucial ideological support, to the courageous things they did.

The bringing together of Chicano priests in a spirit of solidarity and support, and occasional humor was, according to Fr. Juan Romero, "very important to us."[63] Fr. Lonnie Reyes added:

> I think that in a way we felt as priests there wasn't a support system for us, there wasn't a way of affirmation or anything like that. Like here in Austin I kind of felt isolated being virtually the only Chicano, except for Uresti, but he never really associated too much with the Mexicano element and in terms of fighting and in terms of doing the things that really

needed to be done. We really didn't feel there was anyone to communicate with or talk about things. It was pretty much an Anglo type of experience. And I remember that's why I always liked to go to San Antonio, to just kind of meet with these guys, just kind of talk and share with people who could understand.[64]

Father Gallegos explained:

We knew that we had a lot of people behind us, other PADRES priests. We knew that if we needed help that other PADRES priests would jump in and help. And that became apparent as we gathered priests from all over the nation. And we had names, I had names and so did the other guys. We all had names of people and they were ready to help us.[65]

Fr. Héctor Madrigal, who went to his first PADRES meeting in 1987, had this to say about his first impression: "Here were priests that just really loved the church and who were very in touch with who they were and they just responded to a need. . . . The most significant thing I can remember is just seeing so many Latino priests and there was a real sense of pride, a real sense of, 'I'm not alone,' like I felt in the seminary. I got a lot out of seeing and being around them."[66]

PADRES also functioned as a homogeneous environment in which there was no cultural misunderstanding and as a space in which Chicano priests could feel good about being Chicanos. Members who shared their thoughts on Chicanismo encouraged and were encouraged by the others. They even encouraged each other to speak Spanish correctly. Fr. Juan Romero recalled:

One time Bishop Patrick Flores—he's perfectly bilingual—bawled us out as PADRES for not speaking Spanish or chopping it up and speaking it so poorly. And that was physically true. Even though our hearts were in it, there's a process of assimilation—and especially through the educational system and not using and practicing the language—that we became and do become deculturalized. And that was part of our seminary and college experience, so we had to reenter. And not only reenter, but reenter and create the new culture that we are becoming. . . . PADRES as an organization was the main thing that helped.[67]

This supportive environment had such an impact on Father Romero that soon after becoming executive director in 1972, he "Chicanoized" his name: "I went through a name change from John Romero, which I had been called all my school life, to my baptismal name, Juan Romero, and I keep [it] to this day. It was a reidentification, in solidarity."[68] He made the change public in a PADRES newsletter.

Others also Chicanoized their names. There was a tacit movement among PADRES members to reject the names by which the church officially recognized them. This can be seen in a comparison of the *Official Catholic Directory* and the *PADRES Directory*. So, for instance, in the 1969 edition of the *Official Catholic Directory*, Father Soriano is listed as Fr. Vincent Soriano, but in the 1970–1971 *PADRES Directory*, it is listed as Fr. Vicente José Soriano. Fr. Ralph Ruiz became Fr. Rafael Ruiz; Fr. Albert Carrillo became Fr. Alberto Carrillo; Fr. Patrick Flores became Fr. Patricio Flores; and Fr. Robert Peña became Fr. Roberto Peña. According to Father Ruiz, "PADRES members began using their Spanish names instead of their English names because they were influenced by the Chicanismo at the time."[69]

PADRES was not shy about publicly expressing its Chicanismo. For example, numerous letters to bishops as well as monthly newsletters emphasized ties with the poor and working class, cultural affirmation, self-determination, self-identification with the word *Chicano,* and the need to teach Chicano history in seminaries.[70] To show allegiance with the farmworker movement, in 1970 PADRES made buttons with the UFW eagle, a crucifix, and the PADRES logo.[71] The buttons were made by Father Durán, who was working closely with the farmworker movement in California. They were to be distributed at the PADRES Second National Congress, scheduled for August 31, 1970, in Delano, where the farmworkers were struggling mightily. Scheduling the congress in Delano was a deliberate solidarity gesture, but because of a massive farmworker strike in August, the congress was postponed and the buttons apparently never distributed. As an overt expression of their heritage, many PADRES members occasionally wore Mexican-style ponchos when they celebrated Mass.[72] Verta Taylor and Nancy Whittier call such observable practices ways in which activist identities are enacted.[73]

In the resolutions following a national meeting in 1971, PADRES defined the "ideal Chicano" as one who is "on his way to better things economically and socially [for his people while] not allowing himself to be swallowed by a value system that demeans his character, negates his background and destroys his Hispanic and Indian heritage." The organization was opposed to people who behaved like "tyrants, those whose only concern is to see how much money, power and prestige they can accumulate without much regard for other human values." The resolutions conclude with the following pledge to the Chicano movement: "Only through conscious effort will PADRES have a significant impact on the Chicano movement. The charge that we are latecomers should not disturb us. If the movement started without us, let it not continue without the special flavoring which we as Chicano Christians can give to it."[74]

Evidently, this ideal Chicano felt free to openly criticize white America. In a PADRES newsletter dated October 1970, the group wrote that "the fact that whites as a group have not been faced in recent times with conditions requiring revolutionary tactics is why many in the white community are not in sympathy with black and brown demands." The group added that "it would certainly do the white community well to develop a culture that includes more than shooting Indians and making money."

For some, calling oneself "Chicano" was natural and automatic. One PADRES founder explained:

Going into it, I had no problem with the label "Chicano," and I considered myself a Chicano. It is a very activist label, and I identified with it. I had no problem with it. That's what I considered myself first and foremost. I considered myself a Chicano from the vision of an American of Mexican descent who becomes aware of his culture. Well, I was always aware. My father was very good at never letting me forget my roots—my indigenous Mexican heritage.[75]

For others, it was a longer, soul-searching process. Father Romero said:

First of all, in my own upbringing, the word *Chicano* was not used too much. But it wasn't the time and place. And when I was in the seminary Chicano wasn't in. But around the late 1960s it resonated. During the Chicano power stuff, yes, it connected with me. But I remember at my first PADRES meeting we were talking about Chicano so much and I wasn't really sure if I qualified as Chicano. Now, the word in New Mexico, where I was raised and where my family is from, was negative and people didn't like it at all. PADRES members did and those who identified with PADRES. But my parents didn't. They were much more "Spanish," and if you talk to people from New Mexico they emphasize the Spanish blood. I have some of that in me and I affirm it. But the *mestizaje* [mixed blood] is there. Anyway, that meeting helped me realize and affirm within me a certain identification with the word *Chicano*. It was a process. And it's a process for anybody who enters it. Like, what am I and who am I? PADRES was the thing that helped us realize, "Yo soy Joaquín," I am Chicano. And we all identified with the symbol "Chicano Power!" Not as a bad thing. As something positive. I felt good about saying it, and I could say it.[76]

PADRES founders strongly identified as both activist priests and Chicanos and experienced no conflict between the two identities. As Fr. Roberto Flores recalled, "For us it was possible to be a Chicano and to be a priest and to be as radical as you possibly could."[77] But there were a few who at first did not identify themselves as activist priests or as Chicanos or who had conflicts with these identities. In time, with the help of the nurturing environment that PADRES provided, they overcame these concerns. The experience of Fr. Ramón Aragón of the Santa Fe diocese is illustrative:

> PADRES woke me up and I began to see and I began to identify myself as a Hispano, as a Mexicano. Before that, no, I couldn't identify with that, no. To say "Chicano" was very, very radical. We were Spanish, that's what we were taught, not Mexicano. And all of a sudden I said, "Hey, I'm not Spanish, I'm a mestizo," so Chicano became a real identity for me. But I had a hard time trying to deal with it at the beginning. . . . Yes, there was [conflict in being a priest and being Chicano]. For me there was a little tension. Because I was a priest I was supposed to be a certain way and act this way and be legitimate in this way. And then I began to see that being Chicano didn't deter me from being a priest. I was a Chicano priest. And that's what I learned from PADRES. I really did. And that's what PADRES taught me. And that's what the organization was originally, Chicano priests.[78]

Most of the approximately two hundred Mexican American priests in the United States in 1970 became PADRES members, but some did not. The latter's reasons are not known with certainty, because no interviews with these priests have been conducted. However, many PADRES founders think that the reasons stem from disagreements over the exclusionary membership policy and an unwillingness to play the role of an activist out of fear that it would hurt their chances for advancement. But the biggest reason seemed to be conflicts over the dominant activist-Chicano-priest identity. Father Romero explained:

> Once the identity question was resolved in our guts, and that was done for anybody who really identified with PADRES, identified with us as a Chicano priests' group which had a certain activist bent. But we were interested in the totality—as integrated people and priests. That would

take us into the political and socioeconomic realms. Those who felt tension about two worlds or felt uncomfortable simply didn't belong. They didn't apply for membership, and they were not active in the organization. I'll name some names. One was Pete García who was a priest here in the diocese of Los Angeles, also born in New Mexico. He used to wear French cuffs all the time and was very careful not to ever be labeled a Chicano priest. He wasn't comfortable with that. He never became a member, although I made a special point to invite him to that first meeting that Bishop [Patrick] Flores was going to be at, but he didn't come. Anytime we had a meeting to discuss the initial things about the organization, he never came. He worked on the diocesan level as the first executive director of the Office for the Spanish-Speaking. Authorities wanted to pick somebody "safe," and that was Pete García. He didn't run around with PADRES. Another safe person was Manny Moreno, whom I love. He came to some of the initial meetings. But he was based in Tucson and that was where they didn't want activist guys. They wanted safer men.[79]

Fr. Roberto Flores suggests that the Mexican American priests who were not involved in PADRES were those who assigned a "conservative" meaning to their priesthood. These were the ones who believed that "being in position as ordained priest meant you were there for sacramental reasons and nothing more; not to get involved with the community. It meant being a part of the hierarchy and reaching a status that was beyond any race, color, creed."[80]

THE ARTICULATION
OF INSTITUTIONAL DISCRIMINATION

A PADRES newsletter dated October 1970 sharply criticized a Labor Day statement made by the United States Catholic Conference (USCC). It argued that the rhetoric "seeks to placate the backlash of the white community towards the black and brown movements for equality and justice." And "the recommendations worsen the situation since they are along the same lines which recently have caused so much disenchantment with the whole concept of the War on Poverty program." PADRES also argued that "if the Labor Day Statement reflects the thinking of the USCC as to the solution of the problem of white backlash, one could only wish that Ralph Nader would give a conference there." By making these public criticisms, PADRES not only took aim at the church, it also overtly displayed its class allegiance.

In spring 1971 PADRES' public criticism of the church turned to angry condemnation. In an article in the *National Catholic Reporter,* Fr. Aragón, PADRES director of the Santa Fe diocese, wrote: "Chicano people are the poorest single minority within the Church, but often the Church has ignored the needs of our people. They are often taken for granted and treated like children who don't know what's good for them. This has got to stop. We need more Chicano priests working with Chicano people and we need more Church programs to help our people overcome their poverty." The article detailed how on Sundays in the Albuquerque diocese, where Mexican Americans were the overwhelming majority, Father Patricio López held Mass in a community center for some two hundred Mexican Americans because they did not feel welcome in the parish church. "Father López thinks that the Church is failing to relate to his people and practices cultural discrimination against their heritage. . . . He feels this almost smacks of racism."[81]

In a PADRES newsletter dated March 1971, an excerpt of a letter sent to PADRES headquarters and addressed to Fr. Ralph Ruiz by Fr. Alexander Guara of Racine, Wisconsin, was published. Father Guara talked about the problems in the Northeast:

> The prejudice that we find in the Northern Church is frustrating to the point of rebellion. Unless the Irish-Germanic Hierarchy changes its attitude in relationship to the Spanish-speaking, I can see no other result but an exodus of the people from the structure. A thousand examples could be given to bolster the above thesis, but I am sure you know most of them through your own experiences. I am sick of hypocritical Christians, narrow-minded clerics and asinine bishops. I find a greater Christian response to the needs of the poor from the established Protestant churches, such as Lutherans and Methodists. My frustration and that of the people who know the situation has reached the boiling point. My only hope for the future is in revolution, albeit peaceful. I also have some hope in PADRES.

In a PADRES newsletter dated April 1971, Father Ruiz commented on an "extensive Census Bureau survey" that ranked Latino-Americans "at the bottom of almost every statistical measure":

> Fr. Ralph Ruiz, National Chairman of PADRES, criticized both government and Church efforts aimed at helping Hispanics. He said that the "only people who can reverse this form of slavery are the Hispanic-Americans themselves."

At the PADRES National Congress in Los Angeles in October 1971, reactionary condemnation took the form of logical social theory as Fr. Alberto Carrillo articulated the essential reasons for PADRES's condemnation of the white-dominated U.S. Catholic Church. As Father Carrillo explained, "They [PADRES leadership] said try to tell them what we mean by institutional discrimination. Well, there were five bishops there, a cardinal, all foreign-born Irish, sitting in the back. They crashed our organization and I said to myself, hey, they're on our turf. [The bishops used to tell us] don't worry fathers, we'll take care of you. Well goddammit we've been waiting 150 years and you've taken care of us, all right. . . . So I let it out."[82]

Reading an essay he had written, Father Carrillo argued not that the church was guilty of overt racism but that it was guilty of systematic institutional discrimination encoded in the very structure of the church, which had the same effect. At one point, he said:

> We do not feel that it is the discrimination of hatred, of a KKK, of an overt nature that is dangerous. It is recognizable and consequently easy to fight. However, the discrimination the Chicano feels is the systematic, the inadvertent, one that is not based on hatred or malice, but one that is based on a system, a systematic discrimination. . . . It is important [to recognize this] because the Church has discriminated in this [latter] way against our people.[83]

This discrimination, Father Carrillo argued, was based on four principles. First, the majority culture assumes that minorities are incapable of policy making so they freeze them out of the policy-making process. Thus the majority culture determines the policies that affect the minority and also the qualifications of who might make policy.

> In the United States eighty-one percent of the Hierarchy is either Irish or Germanic decent who come from different value systems. They make the policy for our people. People who do not know the problems cannot be expected to find their solutions. Bishops who do not know the educational problems of the Chicano cannot be expected to put bilingual education into his schools.[84]

Second, the majority culture assumes that the problems are the fault of the minority.

> How many times have you been asked, Why don't the Mexicans give more money? Why are they so lazy? Why don't they have the initiative to

go to college? Why are there no more Mexican priests? When only one percent of our kids get to college, how can they possibly survive the academic and cultural shock of a seminary? How can people be blamed for being poor? How can people be blamed for being deprived of education? How can a person be blamed for not wanting to become Irish and prefer to celebrate Guadalupe rather than St. Patrick's Day? Our people are not in the mainstream of Catholicism in this country because the Church has not been relevant to them, they have not been given the dignity of being accepted for what they are, what they wish to be, why God made them . . . so it is not a Chicano problem, it is an Anglo problem the same way it is with education, etc.[85]

Third, the majority culture assumes that no problem exists until it affects them.

Let us be honest even though it is painful. What would the official Church attitude be if the grape pickers had been Irish? You know it and I know it. What would the official attitude of the Church be if 60% of the Catholic kids dropped out of school because they were Catholic? What if all the problems that Chicanos faced were faced by Anglo Catholics? . . . Drugs were not a problem as long as they were confined to the barrios and ghettos, but now that the drugs are hurting the middle-class youth, we have a drug problem.[86]

Then Father Carrillo recalled:

I pointed to the bishops. "You're telling me the Irish Church, love it or leave it." I said, "What would your stance be if Gaelic were the language that was being torn up? You expect us to lie on our backs and not fight for our language just because you guys caved in to the British?"[87]

Fourth, the solution has to be brought about by the majority culture.

The Church has assumed with the rest of American society that we are a melting pot. Ecclesiastically we are an Irish melting pot. In general, cultural differences in religious expression have not been allowed because it was assumed they did not exist. A "good" Catholic was one who accepted the Irish ecclesiastical value system. Yet there is a vast cultural difference in expressing religious sentiments and practices. Vatican II spelled this out quite clearly. The Chicano has a different view and different insights into the interpretation of law, liturgy, moral theology, which have been suppressed. And when one's values are suppressed, a person has two choices: cultural suicide, or rejection of the institution. Both

74

phenomena are normal for the Spanish speaking person in the United States towards his church. In conclusion, the Chicano finds himself with all the disadvantages of being in a foreign mission but none of the advantages. Ecclesiastically the Chicano again suffers an inadvertent but real bloodless persecution in this country.[88]

Fr. Carrillo then proceeded to make several recommendations and underscored them by arguing that they "are not luxuries but necessities for the religious survival of our people." He warned that "patience and time in this case are vices and real obstacles to the message of Christ and must be treated so."[89]

Father Carrillo's analysis sent the church a definitive message.[90] The church was now faced with a group of Chicano priests possessing not only the will to challenge them but also the intellectual and moral ammunition with which to buttress their challenges. In addition, the church was told that it was being held to the same standards that secular institutions were being held to by civil rights groups.

PADRES VERSUS THE U.S. CATHOLIC CHURCH

To get a clear understanding of PADRES' dissidence, it helps to imagine the church as two arenas: the institutional church and the theological church. The institutional church includes the seminary system, rules and regulations, iconography, and organizational and decision-making processes. The theological church includes official church teachings, those fundamental truths and dogmas that constitute basic Catholic beliefs. These beliefs must be accepted without challenge. There are, however, beliefs that are open to debate and disagreement, such as birth control, the ordination of women, and the teachings of various theologians. Fr. Juan Romero explained:

> Let me make a distinction. Behavioral dissent is going against the policies and procedures of the establishment. I'll talk about theological dissent. I remember a footnote in dogma [seminary textbook in Latin, *On Dogmatic Theology* by Hervé] that talked about dissent and the Ordinary Magisterium. For instance, when we say that Jesus Christ is true God and true man, that He has the fullness of the human and divine natures—that is faith explicitly defined . . . If anyone denies that, then they really can't be considered a Catholic. Mormons, Jehovah's Witness, Seventh-Day Adventists do not believe it like mainline Christians and Catholics believe it. Other teachings might have a much less stringent theological note, like

the common teachings of theologians. The point is that some things are clearly defined and there is sometimes room for theological objections about nondefined teachings.[91]

PADRES dissented from aspects of the institutional church that they believed resulted in oppressive and unjust effects. Therefore, they had to be challenged. There were, however, aspects of the institutional church, such as protocol, that they did not challenge, because doing so would be counterproductive.

PADRES did not dissent from the theological church in terms of going against official dogma. In fact, they were very faithful to church dogma. But they did reinterpret certain aspects of theology—namely, the way it was applied—to fit the needs of people they were trying to help. As Father Carrillo explained:

> We all dissented [from the institutional church]. We all had the spirit of dissent. But we never dissented—never, never did we dissent from theology. We never criticized the dogma of the church, nor were we ever against it. We just wanted to apply it to how would be the Christian way to do so. We reinterpreted theology for the times, for the needs. As I told the Irish, what would your theology be if the grape pickers were Irish?[92]

This progressive reinterpretation and application of theology centered on the principles that one must respond to human need and that the church should be the church of the poor. These principles served as the theological foundation on which PADRES pushed for change.

In sum, PADRES did not view the entire U.S. Catholic Church as illegitimate, only some of its practices, and these they relentlessly challenged. PADRES was therefore reformist in its overall mission while remaining faithful to the dogma on which the church is based.

PADRES GOALS

As San Antonio Archbishop Patrick Flores recalled, the original thrust of PADRES "was . . . to become a voice in the Church and to speak to the bishops for the needs of Mexican Americans and to do more about it."[93] Father Ruiz added, "We wanted the bishops to open up the church, we wanted them to understand us culturally, and to support us and to help us obtain the goals and objectives that we set."[94] Father Roberto Peña said: "We were trying to get the church to pay attention to the plight of our people, who were mostly Catholic. We also saw that we wanted power within the church. We didn't have bishops. We needed Mexican-American bishops. Because we wanted to stay within the church and fight within the church so we could change the church to serve our people."[95] Fr. Vicente López said: "It was priests called to engage in the very empowerment, politicization, and mobilization of the Mexican American people in the United States."[96] And Fr. Alberto Carrillo recalled: "We were all heavily involved in the Chicano movement, and the purpose of PADRES was to bring the Chicano movement to the church."[97]

To achieve these goals, PADRES laid out an ambitious agenda that reflected the group's sophistication. Publicly disclosed in a PADRES newsletter, the group sought to (1) mobilize the manpower and resources of the Roman Catholic Church and other private institutions toward the solution of problems of poverty, education, economic development, employment, health care, and housing that afflict Mexican Americans; (2) obtain funds from charitable foundations and government agencies to support remedial schooling projects, adult education programs, instructional programs on nutrition and health care, cultural and recreational programs, summer camps, and other poverty-oriented programs that because of lack of funding and personnel cannot be properly undertaken at the present time; (3) recruit and help to train teachers and other personnel to work among the Mexican American poor; (4) develop small teams of clergy to minister to religious needs on the grassroots level; (5) bring together existing Mexican American organizations to solve common problems; (6) establish awareness programs to promote better understanding by all of the movements of the Mexican American community.[98]

While PADRES had many items on its agenda, their efforts focused on two strategic fronts: changing attitudes within the church and developing leadership among Mexican Americans both inside and outside the church. In doing so, PADRES functioned as the nonsecular arm of the Chicano movement.

MIXED INTERNAL SUPPORT

Support for PADRES members from bishops and white priests varied. Some PADRES received active support. Fr. Edmundo Rodríguez, a Jesuit, said: "I was never exiled for my activism. In fact, my superiors were very supportive of my work."[99] According to Fr. Roberto Peña, of the

Oblates of Mary Immaculate order, "Some of our white brother priests, Americanos, who worked with our people, supported us in our efforts from the very beginning. They were important factors in our movement."[100] Fr. Ramón Aragón: "I think for us one of the biggest hopes was that we began to see that some of the bishops were starting to listen. Very, very slowly but they were beginning to listen. At least they were acknowledging PADRES as legitimate."[101] Fr. Juan Romero writes that "Archbishop James Peter Davis gave immediate and strong support to his priests' proposal to form a chapter of PADRES in New Mexico."[102] After a meeting at the NCCB in November 1969, one influential bishop wrote a letter to PADRES: "For your information, I appealed from the floor of the meeting for the implementation of the most urgent resolutions that you have adopted. I noticed all around me a very favorable reaction."[103] Such bishops functioned as strategically positioned allies.

PADRES even received token but legitimizing recognition from Pope Paul VI. In 1975 several PADRES members, including Bishop Gil Chávez, Archbishop Sánchez, Fr. Vicente López of Joliet, and PADRES executive director Fr. Juan Romero, had a twenty-minute private visit with the pope in Rome.[104] Father Romero wrote about the meeting in a PADRES newsletter: "Pope Paul is very well informed on the Hispanic scene in the U.S., and knew of the work of PADRES which he called 'prophetic.'"[105] Archbishop Sanchez presented the pope with a PADRES button, and His Holiness exclaimed, "'Yo conozco a PADRES, and I am one with you in Spirit.'"[106] Since 1970 PADRES had been communicating with Rome about its activities and about the many changes it desired.[107] From 1972 to 1976 the PADRES newsletter was sent to Msgr. Justin Rigali, who was at the Vatican to advise the pope on matters pertaining to the United States.[108]

Still, many white priests and bishops opposed PADRES and made their views known to its members. Many PADRES were called rabble-rousers, troublemakers, radicals, and communists. As Father Roberto Flores recalled, "They would try to minimize the work that we did so we would look stupid to the people. And I saw that here in San Antonio at one of the local parishes. It was unbelievable. And all our resolutions and petitions were constantly put down by the bishops and by conservative white priests."[109] And Father Aragón reported, "We got a lot of flack from the Anglo clergy. Opposition. They said it was divisive."[110] Father Carrillo added:

> There were a lot of foreign-born Irish. They were the most oppressive. Same thing with the Spaniards. They were like the foreign-born Irish,

most of the Spaniards were a pain in the *nalgas*. But the American Irish, they were with us all the way. So basically it was the old Europeans versus the Americanos. . . . We wanted to tell the bishops, hey our people are hurting. Back us on the issues of the farmworkers and bilingual education, getting Chicano candidates, helping the poor, making sure we get sacraments and we're not turned away because we don't speak Irish. . . . I remember very clearly at one national congress of bishops. And the little white auxiliary bishop from San Diego, little white-haired guy, and we're talking about getting scholarships and education for Chicanos. Hey, let Notre Dame and the Catholic schools and Catholic universities lead in this. And this guy stands up, this little Irish guy, he says, "Fathers, Fathers, but if you educate these people they'll lose their simple faith." Father Soriano berated him severely. "How can you be so ignorant?" etc. This was the kind of crap we were getting. We pointed out to this stupid little bastard, "What right do you have to interpret with your Irish mentality and preclude the right for these children to have an education and to be whatever they could be?" They were violating their rights! You know, civil rights is theology, and you can't separate the two.[111]

In the beginning, Father Gallegos said,

[n]obody really wanted to know about us. They didn't know about the Hispanics, and they didn't care. Our bishops wouldn't listen to us, they wouldn't help us. They just didn't want anything to do with us. Some bishops were not supportive. There were a couple of them that were really bad. Bishop Green, in Tucson, in the beginning, he didn't like us. He was terrible. We had a meeting over there and he says, "Where are all the qualified Mexican Americans? I don't see any." And Ramón Aragón told him right to his face, "What about you, bishop? How come you're qualified?" And that changed his whole attitude. He became very supportive. Chicago was bad. Cardinal Cody was there at the time, and he wasn't about to give us anything. But in time he realized that PADRES was an organization that was trying to help the Hispanics. And you got to give him credit because he didn't try to stifle us.[112]

FICKLE FUREY

Archbishop Furey of San Antonio was a significant player in the early years of the PADRES movement for several reasons. He was bishop to Fathers Ruiz and Casso and sat on several influential bishops' committees. Also, San Antonio was the city in which PADRES located its national headquarters and the Mexican-American Cultural Center, which will be discussed later. Publicly, Archbishop Furey was cordial and diplomatic. Yet several people believe that he may have covertly agitated against PADRES. The following excerpts are suggestive. In a letter to Bishop Bernardin, general secretary of the USCC, Furey writes, "The contention that the Church has done little or nothing for the Mexican-Americans is grossly exaggerated."[113] In a letter to Bishop Luigi Raimondi, the apostolic delegate, he writes:

> The two "principals" from San Antonio were Father Ralph Ruiz and Father Henry Casso. Neither has much ability. Both have a great capacity to make noise and to call attention to themselves. "*Vox et praeterea nihil*" [They're all talk]. It is difficult to say just what success the new organization will have. I doubt that any of their representatives will be permitted to address the U.S. Bishops Conference later this month in Washington. I don't believe that the group is speaking for the average Mexican-American.[114]

In another letter, this one written in 1974 and addressed to USCC Associate General Secretary Monticello, Furey strongly agitated against putting PADRES in the *Official Catholic Directory,* which undoubtedly would have increased the group's legitimacy.[115]

THE PONCHO AFFAIR

PADRES held its Second National Congress in Los Angeles on October 11–13, 1971, at the Holiday Inn in Lincoln Heights. As a courtesy, PADRES invited Los Angeles Archbishop Timothy Manning to address PADRES on October 11 and to be principal celebrant of a Mass scheduled for October 13.[116] Despite being fearful of PADRES and nervous about attending the gathering, Archbishop Manning managed to make a showing.[117] In his address, Archbishop Manning tried to develop a parallel between the Irish immigrants of the potato famine and the plight of Mexican Americans. This greatly offended many PADRES members.[118] Two days later, another offense occurred. On arriving for the Mass, which was being held in the California Room, the archbishop's secretary, Msgr. Clem Connolly, saw several PADRES priests wearing ponchos over their priestly attire. Monsignor Connolly immediately began to insist that they remove their ponchos or not concelebrate. According to Father Romero, Connolly was probably acting under the orders of Archbishop Manning.[119] A poncho-clad Father Carrillo, who had been confirmed by Manning, and several others were deeply offended and angrily walked upstairs where they conducted a separate Mass.[120] Father Romero, who at the time was a diocesan priest in Los Angeles under Manning, recalled:

> Cardinal Manning comes, a lot of guys were dressed in their ponchos to celebrate Mass and making a fashion statement of Chicanismo. The Irish-born Cardinal Manning seemed fearful and nervous as a cat to be with PADRES. It is recognition and respect for all of us as an organization to have the cardinal archbishop celebrate Mass with us. But the Irish-born secretary of Manning, Connolly, probably at the direction of Cardinal Manning, asked the guys to take off their vestments. That's not becoming of Mass and such. Some of the guys got mad and took them off and didn't even celebrate Mass. It was a very un-unifying moment, lack of solidarity. I didn't have one of those ponchos so I didn't feel offended. I concelebrated. He was my bishop.[121]

THE AUSTIN SHOWDOWN

The Austin Showdown, as I like to call it, dramatically illustrates the struggles many Chicano priests (and many white activist priests) faced when trying to help Mexican Americans struggle for justice. In addition, it illustrates how PADRES sometimes functioned as protection for Chicano priests.

During the late 1960s, the Catholic church in Waco, which is in the Austin diocese, concerned itself with the spiritual needs of Mexican Americans but was not involved in social justice issues—economic, judicial, political, educational. In fact, the Waco church suppressed Chicano activism. This was reflected in the church's removal of newly ordained Fr. Lonnie Reyes of the Austin diocese soon after he became actively involved in Chicano struggles in Waco. This was met by resistance by local activist Chicano groups. Demonstrations led by Chicana/o laypersons against the bishop of Austin were held, and tensions rose. This process revealed the deep contradiction between the Mexican American laity's need for justice and the class loyalties of the church. While the majority of church members were Mexican American, the majority of church funds came from wealthy whites.[122]

Father Reyes was placed in the city of Austin in 1970. There, at Santa Julia Church, Pastor Joe Znotas and Fr. Dan Villanueva were heavily involved in Chicano movements such as the strike against Economy Furniture and the federal suit against the Austin school district, which was an effort by Chicano parents to achieve desegregation.[123] Father Reyes said:

> In Austin I was with Fr. Joe Znotas at Santa Julia, and I was the general minister for Mexican American ministry in the diocese and the only Chicano, so I used to travel around the diocese and visit different places and Mexican Americans and all of that. And I encountered some resistance by some pastors who didn't want to see Chicano activism because it would divide the people and create a lot of problems and there wasn't really any problems in our community as far as they were concerned. So I went through a lot of that, and after about a year, and because of the activities of Father Joe, the old bishop was getting reports of a lot of social activism.[124]

In late June 1971 Father Znotas was informed by Bishop Louis Joseph Reicher that he was being transferred to San Saba, Texas. The feeling was that he was being removed because, in his activism, he had "stepped on some big Gringo toes."[125] Chicana/o laity and several priests tried unsuccessfully to pressure the bishop not to remove Znotas. Meanwhile, the bishop tried to put Father Reyes in a parish as an associate priest, which would have taken him away from the contact he enjoyed with Mexican Americans. Then, Father Villanueva, who was an associate priest at Cristo Rey Church and in line to become pastor, was passed up for promotion and was instead named assistant to a new pastor. This new pastor was one of Villanueva's seminary classmates. As Father Reyes recalled, "All of those kinds of things combined and then the whole thing just exploded. Something needed to be done."[126]

On June 29 Father Reyes informed PADRES headquarters in San Antonio about the situation. Immediately, Father Ruiz traveled to Austin and stormed into Archbishop Reicher's office unannounced. Father Ruiz told the bishop he knew about property the bishop owned in Florida. He then told the bishop there was a rumor that he had been using church money to accumulate private property and other wealth. Father Ruiz threatened to hold a press conference and expose the rumor. Even if the rumor were eventually proven false, Father Ruiz argued, it would undoubtedly cause a devastating scandal. Subsequently, the bishop backed off from his plans to relocate Fathers Znotas and Reyes.

Shortly after, in a PADRES memo, Father Rodríguez and Bishop Flores stated that the "incident with Father Znotas is by no means isolated."[127] While it is not known whether Father Rodríguez or Bishop Flores knew of Ruiz's tactics, the memo concluded, "Congratulations are in order to Ralph for his statesmanship."[128]

Another story, albeit less dramatic, illustrates PADRES' struggles. In 1972 Fr. Rubén García in the Northwest was angry and frustrated because of the discrimination he faced at the hands of the church while trying to minister to Spanish-speaking Catholics. Father Romero, acting as executive director of PADRES, used Pope Paul's *Motum Proprio* (On the Care of Migrants) as ammunition in García's defense. In a letter to Bishop Trinan of Idaho, Father Romero reminded the bishop that the "language and customs of migrants are to be respected" and that "there should be . . . specially appointed chaplains to serve well the needs of the migrant people by persons who are prepared to do so."[129] Therefore, Romero argued,

> in accordance with this very pastoral and strong Apostolic Letter and Instruction, I request these things on behalf of my brother Fr. Rubén García. That he be given the freedom and flexibility to minister to any Spanish speaking migrants in the diocese or to any Spanish speaking resident of the diocese, especially if the person is monolingual.[130]

FIVE

PADRES INSURGENCY

†

PADRES used several pressure tactics to gain influence in the church. Directly engaging the bishops at the NCCB and at the archdiocesan level through formal meetings was common. During the early years, according to Father Rodríguez, PADRES used labor union tactics: "Ask for more than you hope to get, negotiate back down, but hopefully get what you wanted in the first place. There was also a kind of good cop, bad cop approach, though after a while most of the sessions became bad cop, bad cop."[1] In time, several PADRES members attended the Industrial Areas Foundation (IAF), a Saul Alinsky training institute based in Chicago, and the group began to use its tactics to confront various bishops. As Father Romero recalled, during a meeting with several bishops, including Bishop Quinn, who was president of the NCCB, and Bishop Cummins, who was president of the California Catholic Conference, "[t]here was a lot of tension and hard negotiations, but it was a very civil meeting with some of the strategies you saw at the COPS [an IAF-modeled community action group in San Antonio] meeting. We knew how to do that, and we were doing it with these bishops."[2] Also, as we have seen, to support their position, PADRES used statistics, papal decrees, Vatican II documents, and a leftist interpretation of Scripture.

In the early years, the style of PADRES movement activity was typically angry and confrontational. This was seen as necessary because initially the hierarchy did not take the organization seriously. Confrontation was an easy tactic for the many PADRES leaders who by this time already possessed the confrontational spirit of the sixties. But some members were reluctant to use this approach. Father Roberto Flores recalled: "There were some among us, 'Come on, guys, let's not be so foolish as to yell and scream at them [the bishops].' But then, boom, we'd get a slap in the face. And then we'd say, 'See, look what happened. We were nice and kind. Now we have to get tough.' And they'd say, 'Yes, yes, now we have to be forceful.'"[3]

Gradually, the more radical leaders left and were replaced by more moderate leaders. Father Romero refers to these distinct groups as the "shock troops" and the "institutional guys." In the years that followed, PADRES kept up the pressure, but the angry confrontations lessened in intensity and the tone became more diplomatic. Archbishop Patrick Flores stated: "Thank God that that was the case, but we were ready to do the other because we were not going to give up on this. We had to bring them [bishops] into discussions, questions and answers."[4]

As another pressure tactic, PADRES was willing to make threats. On several occasions, PADRES leaders threatened to call a press conference and expose the corrupt activities of certain bishops, as the aforementioned Austin showdown illustrated. This kind of threat was far from an empty one, since PADRES had both the ability and the willingness to call a press conference and make substantive charges, as they boldly demonstrated on several occasions.

According to Father Carrillo, at one point during the early days, PADRES threatened the NCCB with an employment discrimination lawsuit. Using techniques learned from affirmative action battles in the community, Father Carrillo determined the number of bishops and pastors with German, Irish, Italian, and Polish surnames and then compared these numbers with the ethnic lay population.

> They were bringing in pastors from Ireland. They were bringing in bishops who were foreign-born Irish, we called them the FBIs. So we said, hey, we're going to sue you. We're going to take this case to the EEOC and say you're bringing in foreign workers and displacing and not giving opportunities to the local workers. We would never have done it, of course, but we threatened. . . . We used civil rights tactics, we used boycotts, we used demonstrations. We threatened the Spaniards in particular. The way they were getting into the country, they just go to Mexico and go to a tombstone and get a name and use that guy's name, because they were not allowed to enter Mexico. So we threatened to blow their cover in Mexico if they didn't treat Mexicans with dignity here. It was strange.[5]

PADRES perhaps caused the greatest fear as a result of the controversy over the idea of a separatist National Chicano Church. In 1971, at the PADRES National Congress in Los Angeles, when Father Carrillo read his infamous paper on institutional discrimination in the church, he suggested possible solutions. Directing his arguments at the NCCB, he pointed out that the church makes provisions for the care of its migrant members: "The entire document 'On the Care of Migrants' by Pope Paul insists on Episcopal vicars, personal parishes, special concern for youth in colleges, and all necessary innovative means to end cultural shock, economic atrocity, educational abortion within society and the Church."[6] He then called for the naming of a Mexican American bishop who would take care of Mexican Americans everywhere and then finished the speech by declaring: "You don't want to take care of us or you don't know how to take care of us or you won't let us take care of our own people and we're damn tired of begging you Irishmen for the privilege of working for our people. Okay, what's the solution? The solution is we get a National Chicano Church directly under the propagation of the faith in Rome."[7]

PADRES was not serious about forming a national Chicano church mainly because it was impractical, but when the idea caused an uproar among many white clergy and bishops, PADRES seized the moment. Father Romero recalled:

We didn't say separatist, but that's the way it was understood and perceived, but that's not what we were advocating. We were asking for a Personal Prelature along the lines of the Military Ordinariate and we were basing ourselves squarely on the 1969 *Motu Proprio* of Pope Paul VI, *Pastoralis Migratorum* (On the Care of Migrants), which was at that time a recent document. Proposing the National Chicano Church was done, I would say, almost deliberately to provoke a reaction, and that it did. I mean, it got press in the *L.A. Times*.[8]

And Father Roberto Flores added:

That was our manipulation, a scare tactic. But it came from them, not from us. There was such a tremendous fear among the Anglos [priests and bishops] and they presented that to us and we said, okay, let's play on that fear and tell them we want a Chicano Church. And all of a sudden it grew and people began to believe it. Yeah, we do need it. And they thought, my God, these many people want a Chicano church, separate and with its own bishop? They thought we were manipulative. And I'm sure we used manipulative ways but only because we were aware of the truth of our position.[9]

Father Carrillo suggested that the call for the National Chicano Church sent the U.S. Catholic hierarchy an ultimatum: "I think it brought home a message: include us in the mainstream or let us divide off; integrate or segregate for self-determination. This was the continual question of the sixties. And perhaps it created fear or worry about what we, PADRES, were going to do next."[10]

As a means of making an indirect threat, PADRES took advantage of the fact that the church was weary of the loss of its Mexican American members as a result of Protestant proselytizing.[11] PADRES stressed this point during meetings with bishops in the hope of gaining valuable bargaining leverage.

PADRES also created the appearance of being larger than it really was. Using its media savvy, PADRES held press conferences and disseminated monthly newsletters to a sizable list of people. These newsletters, which often contained angry, militant language, highlighted the struggles of PADRES priests throughout the country and functioned as a vehicle through which to spread their dissident views. Mailings were sent to as many as two thousand people during the mid-1970s and included key members of the U.S. Catholic hierarchy. Also, by 1974 PADRES had established eleven national regional groups.

Though we do not know what the hierarchy was thinking at the time, PADRES founders believe the direct and indirect threats generated a considerable amount of fear within the church. According to Father Flores, "They got scared. We scared the living pants off of them. The whole Church. The whole Anglo Church."[12] This fear may have increased PADRES's leverage, thus making the granting of concessions a more attractive option.

MAJOR BATTLES

PADRES fought many battles inside and outside the church. Some of the most significant ones occurred within the first few years. These include the fight for the first Mexican American bishops, the development of the Mobile Team Ministry, and the establishment of the Mexican-American Cultural Center. These meticulously planned battles show how PADRES was both aggressive and visionary. It should be noted that PADRES priests engaged in these and other efforts in addition to their required priestly work.

The Struggle for Mexican American Bishops

At the outset, PADRES' goal of securing the first Mexican American bishop in U.S. Catholic history was given the highest priority. This was not a self-serving move by PADRES but one that was genuinely altruistic. As Father Ruiz stated, "The goal of PADRES was not to see Chicano priests organizing to grow themselves into power as bishops, but to serve our people better."[13] One of the reasons that PADRES believed it was so important to have Mexican American bishops was because it saw a need for greater understanding of the Mexican American people among the white hierarchy. As Ralph Ruiz argued in a letter to Archbishop Furey:

> Just as our people have the need and want priests who can feel with them in a total way, who can experience what they experience, who can identify with them in a completely natural way, so do we as priests, along with our people, want bishops who can also hear us from the inside and from the point of view of our cultural identity.[14]

In addition, there was a common desire to open the decision-making process to Mexican Americans and to infuse the church with more progressive values. For example, Fr. Carrillo said:

> We need Chicano bishops because the bottom line is this, if you have no policy making ability in your organization you're zilch. We were 25 percent of the Catholic population and we did not have one bishop so we had no say, absolutely no say in the policy making of the church.[15]

And Father Ruiz said:

> We felt that unless we got into the system, through the Episcopal door, we were going to remain third-rate citizens within the Catholic Church, and therefore in society at large. It was embarrassing that at that time when the Catholic population was 25 percent Latino, we did not have one Latino bishop. We had to bring social justice issues inside the church. That was the purpose for PADRES. Also, we needed to bring our values inside the church to the hierarchy, to the Council of Bishops, to the highest levels of power within the church. This is why when Patrick Flores became bishop, so many of us became hopeful and full of joy. It was not a total triumph, but it was a beginning.[16]

Father Carrillo explained that the selection of bishops favored the foreign born and amounted to de facto exclusion of Mexican Americans:

> I saw this in Tucson. They would have a foreign-born Irish bishop, he would bring a young nice Irishman from Ireland then within two or three years make him the chancellor and then groom the guy to be the bishop. And we couldn't crack that thing. The old boy's thing.[17]

At the First National Congress in Tucson, a committee was assembled and assigned the task of composing a list of names of Mexican American priests as possible Episcopal candidates. Father Janacek recalled telling Fr. Patrick Flores, "You know we're going to be sending in a list to the apostolic delegate and we surely don't want you to pull some kind of humility stunt and say 'No, I'm not worthy,' but to accept it. It's a responsibility that you have; to accept this for the good of the Mexican American community."[18]

PADRES sent the list to Rome, to the apostolic delegate, the chair of the committee for the nomination of Episcopal candidates, the president of the NCCB, various Mexican American organizations, and the bishops of the nominees.[19] Father Carrillo writes, "Some bishops were irate over this. Others were displeased but low-key about it. And others sent in helpful suggestions on how to pursue the matter in a more astute way."[20] Others responded condescendingly, doubting the qualifications of Mexican American priests. As Father Ruiz remembered, "An auxiliary bishop to Archbishop Furey of San Antonio told me, 'You want bishops? You Chicanos don't have Episcopal timber. You guys are lucky you became priests.' That's a bishop talking."[21] Father Roberto Flores remembered being chastised by several bishops. On one occasion, he was told bluntly, " 'How dare you ask for your own bishops. You don't have a right to ask for a bishop.' "[22] These attitudes pointed to the many uphill battles that lay ahead. Frustrated but undaunted, on many occasions PADRES responded with the same boldness. As Father Casso recalled, "Cardinal Manning. We encountered each other in the hallway and I introduced myself and he said to me, 'What do you guys want?' And I looked him straight in the eyes and said, 'We want your job.' "[23]

Soon after Tucson, a fiery battle with a committee of bishops occurred at the NCCB in Washington, D.C. Father Carrillo recalled that event:

> This to me was the epitome of PADRES. Here we have Ralph Ruiz, . . . the Luna boys, . . . the Gallegos boys, Rodríguez, Henry Casso, Soriano, and

I were there. We all came in from our different flights. We came in from Tucson. Some came in from Texas. Some guys came from California. And here we were meeting at one of the Gallegos brothers' apartment, who was an ex-priest at the time. And naturally we brought a couple of bottles of tequila from Tucson and put it in the middle of the table, but nobody touched it for a long time. And for eight hours we role-played. And so we say, priority one, we got to crack the Hispano bishops. We gotta get one. At least one. And we talked about it. Well, should we go on a fast? Should we ask people to go on a fast? Would we do this or do that? And our conclusion was, why should people or even ourselves weaken ourselves physically and everything else and sacrifice for something that they should be doing? And so what we did, to be very honest with you, we had eight or nine guys, we role-played every possibility. Plan one, we go in there like good Christian gentlemen and we ask the bishops and give them the statistics and we say hey this is what's needed. You know it and we know it. Do it. Plan number two was that if they didn't listen, then we go into anger. Good cop, bad cop. And before we got down to it, we took a couple of swigs of tequila and this lasted all night, we role-played this over and over for eight hours. Because we knew we had just thirty minutes and they are going to start saying, "Oh, you're doing such a great job," and all of that stuff [using up our time] and so we were preparing for that. So it came down to this: we said how many of you guys can survive outside the priesthood? Six raised their hands. How many can't? Three. Okay, you guys be quiet. You guys be quiet, you be the good cops. And when we show anger you say bishops we're sorry we apologize, these men really mean what they are saying, however we disagree with their tactics blah blah blah.[24]

The PADRES group was scheduled to meet with a committee of about five bishops. PADRES arrived at the room first and found it arranged hierarchically, with an elevated platform for the bishops and a few chairs below. Father Carrillo continued:

We looked around and said screw this. We changed the room. We took the platform down and took their tables down and made a big circle. So they were going to sit on our level or we were going to sit on their level. It wasn't going to be *patrón*. So they were over there in their general convention and then they were going to come to the committee room. We were not allowed to address the whole convention. So they come in and we start talking about all the needs and all the stuff and all the neglect, the neglect for the Mexican people. Extreme neglect either from prejudice, ignorance, or just insensitivity or just the fact that these guys didn't know how to deal with it and if you don't know how we'll teach you. Or if you don't want to learn let us do it. But get off our back, you know, let us do it. And we're talking and talking and talking and I'll never forget him, Archbishop Medeiros from Brownsville, Portuguese, who later became cardinal archbishop of Boston, but he's sitting there literally tears streaming down his eyes. "Bishops, bishops, please listen to these men. They are angry, and they know of which they speak." And he went on begging them. Bishop Quinn, the auxiliary of San Diego, was the guy who kept pushing us and pushing us. So, talking with an Irish brogue, he tells us that we don't need bilingual education, and he's speaking with an Irish brogue, that what we need is to learn English and he knows the people. Then when we came down to the point of bishops, he says, "I don't know if a Mexican bishop will be acceptable to the people in my diocese." And one of them said, "Well, they have to be qualified." And as soon as they said that, Ralph goes, "Plan B." I stand up and go, "You stupid sons of bitches." And we practiced this, role-playing this, to make sure we could cuss right. Soriano gets up and says, "You stupid shits, and our people told us that it was a waste of time to talk to you people. You just don't give a shit blah blah blah. And we'll meet you. If we don't ever see you again I'll see you, I'll be standing in front of the judgment seat of Jesus Christ and when you turned us down you turned down the people, the poor blah blah blah." And so six of us get up and say the hell with you guys and then we stomp out. Three people stay. "Well, we're sorry, we apologize blah blah blah."[25]

Soon after, Fr. Patrick Flores made a presentation to a group of bishops from four states in San Antonio on behalf of PADRES and argued for a Mexican American bishop. He recalled:

I was a priest in Houston at the time. But they said that only three of us could come and then they said that I would be the only one that would be allowed to speak. [I told them that] we really felt that Hispanics were being overlooked in two ways, that they are not getting the services that they need and I showed all kinds of examples of that. And then, that they're not being allowed to serve. I said we're talking about the Mexican Americans, we're talking about the priests, the sisters, the brothers, and laypeople in the community, and we gave all kinds of examples. And then I said, for example, don't you find it embarrassing that if somebody were to ask you of the three hundred bishops in the United States, how many are Hispanic and Mexicans and so on? And you'll have to say none. And we've been here over two hundred years but not one Hispanic bishop. And Bishop Furey, he was kinda acting as a devil's advocate. He said, "But you know why we don't have Hispanic bishops? Because none of them qualify. They're not good enough to be bishops." I said, "Do you think you qualify to be bishop here in this diocese? You don't speak Spanish. And the diocese is predominantly Hispanic." I said, "I've met other bishops in predominantly Hispanic parishes and they don't speak Spanish. Do they qualify?" And then I said, "You know, bishops all over, they all make mistakes." I said, "We're not going to qualify if you don't give us a chance." And the bishop even asked me, "Do you think you could even be a bishop?" I said, "If you give me a chance, but I'm not looking for an opportunity for myself but for some other Hispanic." Well, he asked me all kinds of questions and shortly after he submitted my name to be a bishop. He didn't tell me then, but when I was called I was in Houston, the Holy Father wanted me to be an auxiliary bishop in San Antonio. I said, "In San Antonio?" Well, the bishop didn't seem like he really wanted a Hispanic. He talked to me and said, "The day that you made the presentation to us you convinced me that you needed to come to San Antonio." And then he said, "When I retire you take over."[26]

Contrary to Bishop Flores's claim that San Antonio Archbishop Furey was playing devil's advocate, Sandoval, who interviewed Furey, presents evidence that suggests Furey may have actually believed in the inferiority of Mexican American priests. In late 1969 Furey nominated Father Flores for the bishopric. When asked to nominate two more priests, he wrote Flores's name two more times. "If I had three Mexican-Americans who were equally qualified, I would write them all down," he said.[27]

PADRES member Fr. Patrick Flores became the first Mexican American and Latino-American bishop in the history of the Catholic Church on May 5, 1970, in San Antonio. At the Mass celebrating Father Flores' ordination, PADRES associate member Father Janacek read the homily in Spanish. César Chávez presented one of the readings, as did Texas Chicano activists José Angel Gutiérrez and Ramsey Muñiz. At one point in the ordination ceremony Bishop Flores was flanked on either side by PADRES founding members Frs. Ralph Ruiz and Henry Casso. Martin McMurtrey writes, "As auxiliary bishop he was living proof that PADRES and its protests had had some impact on the Catholic Church."[28] Father Janacek recalled:

Fr. Ralph Ruiz (left) and César Chávez (right). Taken in San Antonio, Texas, on May 5, 1970, at the episcopal ordination of Fr. Patrick Flores. Photo courtesy of Fr. Ralph Ruiz.

Later on in 1970 when Patrick Flores was actually called to Washington to the apostolic delegate, Raimundi, the apostolic delegate, said to him, "Father Flores, you know this is not because PADRES has put pressure on us that this is happening. It's the Holy Spirit that is guiding." Patrick, in his neat, humble way, God bless him, simply said, "Well, I know that the Holy Spirit works, but I also know that for centuries there have been the naming of bishops by kings. You know, they have the right of nomination to the episcopacy and Rome accepts them of course." And so it was dropped there. But the pressure did work. It did work.[29]

THE AGITATION CONTINUED

The appointment of Bishop Flores was a significant victory for PADRES. It filled many with hope and served as moral fuel with which to continue their agitation. Then, PADRES members Fr. Gil Chávez of San Diego and Fr. Robert Sánchez of Santa Fe were ordained in 1973 and 1974, respectively. PADRES' historic effort to bring about the ordination of the first Mexican American bishop began the process of organized struggled against what Cadena calls "142 years of Episcopal discrimination."[30] It is important to note that PADRES was not alone. Las Hermanas and Mexican American laity were also working toward this goal. But PADRES perhaps spoke with the highest authority because they, like the bishops they confronted, were priests.

In the spring of 1971, PADRES lobbied intensely for a Mexican American bishop for the diocese of Brownsville, Texas, which according to PADRES records was 85 percent Mexican American. But instead Father John J. Fitzpatrick, a native of Canada who had been serving as auxiliary bishop in the Archdiocese of Miami, was appointed. PADRES issued an angry press release that was carried by the national media, including the *New York Times*.[31] Father Ruiz recalled, "When they appointed Bishop Fitzpatrick to the diocese of Brownsville, I raised all kinds of hell. And the media asked me, are you against the Irish? I said, I'm not against the Irish. I'm for Mexican Americans being appointed bishops. And if any diocese needs one it's Brownsville where [about] 90 percent of the Catholic population are Mexican American."[32]

In 1972, PADRES and Las Hermanas confronted the hierarchy with the argument that "the number of native Spanish speaking bishops in the United States should be increased so that the proportion of Spanish speaking in the hierarchy is similar to the proportion of Spanish speaking in the total Catholic population."[33] Subsequently, a committee of bishops was formed to respond to this conclusion. According to Father Romero, the committee "interpreted this recommendation as asking for a mathematical formula or quota of Hispanic . . . bishops for the church in the United States. Their report further implied that there were too few qualified as potential candidate for Episcopal ministry to have a proportion of Hispanic . . . bishops. In a formal reply, PADRES admitted that there were many facets to the question but affirmed that something could be done if there were enough will."[34]

PADRES argued that a double standard existed in the church. In a PADRES newsletter, the group publicly proclaimed, "When the church makes a decision to create a native clergy and hierarchy, it does so."[35]

This was followed by a detailed listing of indigenous bishops in Africa and Asia. Indigenous bishops in Africa numbered 2, 60, 101, and 133 in the years 1945, 1963, 1969, and 1971, respectively. In Asia, in these same years, the number of indigenous bishops was 20, 92, 122, and 128, respectively.[36] PADRES sometimes argued that black Episcopal candidates were treated differently than Latino-Americans. To remedy the situation, PADRES suggested: "Hispanic religious order priests should be seriously considered as candidates for the episcopacy. Most Hispanic priests are members of a religious order and thus traditionally serve in Spanish-speaking areas more than diocesan priests. The black bishops are religious order men, yet not one Hispanic bishop is from an order."[37]

Controversy erupted in 1978 in the newly created diocese of San Bernadino–Riverside in southern California, an area densely populated by Mexicans and Mexican Americans. Years of agitation from Mexican American laity, clergy, and nuns reached a head when the first archbishop of the new diocese was Fr. Philip Straling and not one of the then-three auxiliary Latino bishops of southern California, Chávez of San Diego and Arzube and Moreno of Los Angeles. Father Straling was a native of San Bernadino–Riverside and spoke Spanish well, but the same was true of Chávez. According to Father Romero, "Not only Mexican American activists but also many of the general Mexican community took it as a rejection. It seemed to be a value judgment that none of these Hispanic bishops were qualified and moreover no other qualified Hispanic priest could be found for the position."[38] The decision created a storm of angry protest from PADRES, Las Hermanas, and Mexican American laity that became known as the San Bernadino Affair.

On at least one occasion, PADRES was encouraged to stop its agitation. In 1977 the PADRES board met with Apostolic Delegate Archbishop Jadot in Washington, D.C. Father Carrillo argues that "the very fact of getting the meeting with the nuncio was a recognition of PADRES."[39] At the meeting, PADRES raised questions about the process by which bishops were selected, to which Archbishop Jadot testily replied, "Hot potatoes burn."[40] Undaunted, PADRES emphasized the need for more Mexican American bishops, to which Jadot sternly warned, "Rome knows about you and Rome does not respond to pressure. . . . Ten years is like a hundred. If you push Rome too far, she will close her doors and one day could be like a hundred."[41] "Nevertheless, PADRES members felt a kind of sympathy from the archbishop and even encouragement."[42]

DID PADRES HAVE A SIGNIFICANT IMPACT?

It is impossible to fully ascertain PADRES's role in the election of the first Mexican American bishops, for doing so would require us to know what the hierarchy was thinking—information that is not available. It is plausible that the church capitulated because key members of the hierarchy were fearful that PADRES would have separated or publicly rebelled, encouraging Mexican American laypersons to do the same, which would have harmed the church's legitimacy in an already volatile social climate. It is also plausible that the hierarchy, with some persuasion, acknowledged the demographic reality that the U.S. Catholic Church was becoming increasingly Latino and therefore could no longer justify its discriminatory practices.

Nevertheless, one fact remains clear. The election of the first Mexican American bishops came during a time when both PADRES and Las Hermanas, the first nationally organized attempts by Chicana/o Catholic leadership to articulate a Latino-specific agenda, were aggressively agitating for Mexican American bishops.[43] Medina writes that PADRES was instrumental.[44] Among PADRES founders, it is generally believed that the presence of native-born Mexican American or Latino bishops is due in large part to PADRES's agitation, and many proudly acknowledge this. According to Father Rodríguez:

> The PADRES organization had a powerful impact on the Catholic Church in the United States. By the time of the 1975 national convention in San Antonio, Texas, five Hispanic bishops were in attendance: Bishops Juan Arzube of Los Angeles, Gilbert Chávez of San Bernadino, Patrick Flores of San Antonio, and Roberto Sánchez of Santa Fe. Other priests who would later become bishops were also present: Raymond Peña of Corpus Christi and Ricardo Ramírez . . . [a native of Texas but stationed in Tehuacán, Puebla, Mexico]. PADRES was the organization leading the fight to have the Catholic Church open its hierarchical doors to Hispanics.[45]

Fr. Juan Romero writes, "Success in helping to promote native Hispanic priests to the episcopacy was almost immediate."[46] And in Father Gallegos's view, "Getting whatever number of bishops that we've had, I think that's an accomplishment because at the time we didn't even have one. Just the pressure that we put on them."[47] Father Casso said, "You can quote me. I look back at what PADRES accomplished and those [Latino bishops] are a major accomplishment."[48]

WERE MISTAKES MADE?

As Moisés Sandoval has argued, "The assumption of PADRES and Las Hermanas had been that a Hispanic, by virtue of his ethnicity, would naturally take up the struggles of his people. It turned out to be an overly-optimistic estimate."[49] Father Romero agreed: "It was the intention of PADRES to eventually have its best people in Episcopal positions in order to effectively advance the Latino agenda. However, it didn't work out that way."[50] While PADRES generally applauded the appointments of the first three Mexican American bishops, Flores, Chávez, and Sánchez, many believe that the hierarchy deliberately crushed the movement for fair Episcopal representation by subsequently appointing conservative Latinos. According to Father Romero, "Initially it was very important for us to have Mexican American bishops. But the Episcopal candidates that were accepted later on were co-opted and very conservative."[51] Timothy Matovina writes that these conservative Latino bishops "overshadowed PADRES' leadership and replaced their activist vision with a more patient and compromising approach."[52] According to Father Romero, these bishops were put off by PADRES' aggressiveness and its tradition of agitating and challenging the hierarchy for the good of their people.[53]

In 1981 PADRES became "polarized" and "estranged" from these Latino bishops when it pushed to have Bishop Flores returned to San Antonio from El Paso.[54] According to Father Romero, these bishops "wanted PADRES to become more respectable and sophisticated."[55] Ironically, it seems, the very people PADRES helped to elevate into power had turned against it.

In addition to their conservatism, many of the Latino bishops were foreign born. Between 1970 and fall 1988 twenty Latino bishops were ordained, but half were immigrants. Two were from Cuba, two from Mexico, two from Spain, two from Puerto Rico, one from Ecuador, and one from Venezuela.[56] Sandoval writes, "None, immigrant or native, showed the commitment to the poor that Flores did."[57] And Fr. Vicente López is famous for saying, "They beat us at our own game."[58]

Some have questioned PADRES' emphasis on Mexican American bishops. Father Ruiz feels PADRES should have put more emphasis on lay leadership schools: "Our own Hispanic bishops did us a favor. They helped us realize that bishops are helpless and even useless because they have to follow so much protocol. [E]ffective leadership will . . . come from the laity . . . not the hierarchy."[59] Father Reyes agreed:

I've been ambiguous about that because at the same time you need the leadership of the bishop but you gain so much more experience in a parochial setting working directly with the people. .... I think it kind of tempered some of the idealistic notions that if you have Hispanic leadership you're going to have a really good Hispanic church.[60]

Father López told me:

> On May 5 Pat Flores is made auxiliary bishop of San Antonio, and from that moment on there is a naming of Hispanic bishops and archbishops across the country. Unfortunately, the institutional change is token. .... [W]e don't have significant numbers of Mexican American priests, we don't have seminaries committed to the forming of Mexican American priests or Spanish-speaking bilingual priests to the degree that the population warrants. So it just went so far. Maybe it was co-opted.[61]

Mobile Team Ministry

The Mobile Team Ministry (MTM) was a program that PADRES began to develop soon after its founding. The MTM sought to develop lay leadership among the Mexican American poor and working class, which was one of PADRES's constant battle cries and an area of historical neglect on the part of the church. As Father Ruiz said: "You don't get leadership from the clouds. They have to be trained."[62] The main thrust of the MTM was for priests to play an active role in enabling the poor. "In the name of enabling, too long had the parish priest failed to take a clear stand in vital community problems affecting his parishioners. By failing to take a position, he has relayed an attitude of acceptance of the injustices extended to the poor by our system."[63] Father Romero said:

> In Tucson in 1970 in February it was clear that we wanted something to reach out to our people and not just give them pious sermons. That wasn't enough. We needed *concientización*, something of a politicization, an internal affirmation of one's own dignity, as a basis, so that we can *en conjunto* [together] do something to change an oppressive situation. So the vision was pretty clear but still mixed up too much with "War on Poverty" and government dependency.[64]

According to Fr. Edmundo Rodríguez, the concept of the MTM was influenced by the Ecumenical Institute of Chicago, the Jocist Cell Movement, which was popular in Europe during World War II, and training programs set up by the Conference of Latin American Bishops, CELAM.[65] "Then," Father Romero recalled, "the vision became purified when we . . . saw the rightness of Paulo Freire's insistence on the need for changing from the inside."[66] In addition, the MTM was shaped by the experiences of many members of PADRES and Las Hermanas over years of social activism.

The MTM involved the strategic location of a three-member team well versed in the theology of liberation that could facilitate the process of *concientización*. According to Father Rodríguez, this process refers to the

> formation of the critical conscience in a man, especially the oppressed man, begins with his ability to objectify his situation and become aware of his ability to be an agent of change in that situation. It is not enough that a man sees problems, but rather that he sees causes and most especially the root causes of the problems he experiences. He must be able to see his own lack of freedom and to recognize his oppressors, whether these be circumstances, persons, or institutions. He must then discern the means within his grasp to effect liberation (no man is freed by another, but only by his own self in concert with others) and to change what can be changed in his particular situation. Thus, a man must be brought through a process of issue discernment: he must become aware of the problems. He must also be brought through a process of self-awareness and empowerment through group consensus and group action.[67]

Father Romero explained how the MTM worked:

> We would either proactively search out networks and church-based groups in these areas, or we would be invited in and we would come and do workshops on the weekends or during the week, depending on the crowd. Usually about thirty people to fifty people would come. We used a lot of heavy group dynamics that challenged their group thinking and their actions. They learned how to do some critical thinking. Most of the issue discernment workshops were it was in the Southwest because of connections, but I also went to places in Chicago, Detroit, New York.[68]

According to Father Rodríguez, who has a well-deserved reputation for intellectual depth and is widely credited with being the architect of the MTM, the MTM is based on the idea that God is known in the act of the fulfillment of the moral imperative of justice.

> The mission of the church is to carry this vision of the new humanity in Christ from age to age. Her ministers must therefore be the agents

whereby this vision is woven into the fabric of the society of their own time and place. Their forms of service must contribute to the radical restructuring of unjust societies and the preservation and development of just ones. Ministry is service to the community in its efforts toward liberation, toward complete adult growth in Christ. The desired point of liberation is reached only when men are truly free to exercise choice over the options placed before them by the rich variety of creation itself. This means that men must be free internally and disposed to accept the responsibility of such freedom, while societal structures are such that they foster rather than hinder such freedom. Efforts to create a just society must therefore be a service of liberation.[69]

Father Romero explained further:

The idea was this: just as there have been certain religious orders that developed in the history of the church to meet certain specific needs, PADRES is not going to be a religious order, but to at least mobilize itself and collectively use its energy and resources to do something such as in prior times was done by mission bands of religious orders in a culturally appropriate way in places where people are not being taught and to teach. Even though we were not calling it liberation theology yet, but some kind of workshop in which people would be able to define their experience, to think about it and move ahead to the next phase.[70]

In 1971 the MTM was funded by a $100,000 grant from the Campaign for Human Development. According to Father Romero, "This was the first and only time we got money from the Campaign for Human Development. This is when Patrick Flores was a young bishop, and the PADRES organization was using *movimiento* tactics to mau-mau the bishops. We used heavy guilt trips on them by saying if you don't up and do something about it, all our Mexicans are going to become Protestant and that's the bottom line. We usually got some kind of reaction."[71]

The Mexican-American Cultural Center

The Mexican-American Cultural Center (MACC) developed out of what PADRES saw as the need for a pastoral approach that took into account the culture and the oppressive social conditions of the Mexican American people. This idea was first articulated in the resolutions of the LaSalle Provisional Congress in 1969. In February 1971, at a PADRES retreat in Santa Fe, there was some movement toward implementation.

During a brainstorming session, Father Elizondo promoted the idea of setting up a national seminary for Mexican Americans. But when it became clear that this was impractical, the discussion turned to a special training center. It was resolved to go ahead with establishing a national center for Mexican American socioreligious studies emphasizing systematic theology, biblical sciences, liturgy, music, sociology, psychology, anthropology, community development, economics, and linguistics. In addition, lay leadership training and a unique Mexican American theology would be cornerstones. PADRES was clear from the start that it wanted MACC to be based on the principle of Chicano self-determination. As stated in the resolutions: "The center should be entirely 'Raza controlled' in distinction to current 'Mexican American Studies' as established in many universities. That its philosophy should dovetail with that of the Chicano Movement and it should be used as a place where an exchange of experience and knowledge can take place."[72]

Father Elizondo, who studied at the East Asian Pastoral Institute in Manila in 1968, was given the task of developing the center. He presented a proposal arguing that, among 25 percent of U.S. Latino Catholics, 18.7 percent are Mexican American, and that based on immigration trends, this figure would steadily grow. Furthermore, this group had specific needs and problems that were not being met by their church. MACC, he argued, was an organic attempt at a partial solution to the church's shortcomings. He went into detail:

> Discrimination has up to now been an accepted way of life for great numbers of Mexican-Americans. . . . The Church too is today recognizing that in reality, she had for the most part given only token ministry to the Mexican American communities. . . . The honest recognition of the beauty and uniqueness of the Chicano culture and of the problem of various forms of devastating discrimination is the first step towards effective Christian ministry. . . . The Church as *Mater et Magistra* must help the Chicano in his painful process of self-discovery, of liberation from the many interior and exterior forces which oppress him. . . . In our pluralistic society, the Church cannot fall into heresy of saying: "If he is going to live in America, let him become an American." The Chicano, as Chicano, is an American! The Church in the U.S. will not minister effectively to the Chicano by simply bringing catachetical and liturgical materials from Mexico, Spain or Latin America. Nor will she minister effectively by trying to reach them with WASP oriented materials. These materials might be excellent for the groups they were prepared for but they are not the answer to the real pastoral problem. Neither will the problem be solved by

bringing Spanish-speaking clergy and religious into the U.S. from Spanish-speaking countries, nor will it be solved by sending North Americans to study in the great centers of pastoral formation of Latin America. It is the responsibility of the entire U.S. Church—bishops, clergy and laity—to face the problem seriously and to begin tackling it from the grass-roots. . . . Thus the need for a serious center of research, formation of leaders and production of materials.[73]

The need for cultural respect within the white-dominated U.S. Catholic Church is best articulated by Father Romero, who argued that the church was not serving Mexican Americans pastorally:

> There must be cultural expression. . . . It's a legitimate request to hear the Word in Spanish, in one's own language. It's not they who have to learn English. The pastoral agent needs to learn Spanish if they're going to serve in Spanish-speaking territories. MACC is a pastoral center. We were interested in Quinceanera, Masses in Spanish, liturgy[,] . . . the cultural dimension and expressions in our Catholic Church. We learned how to do that by establishing MACC.[74]

Father Carrillo said that in the seminary students "got no training on the pastoral or psychological issues, no training on how to deal with Mexicanos, so PADRES, with MACC, was very involved with that."[75]

After the Santa Fe retreat, Father Elizondo and members of Las Hermanas acted quickly to establish connections with some of the world's leading theologians and educators, such as Gustavo Gutiérrez of Peru and Paolo Freire of Brazil. Gutiérrez would later conduct many courses at MACC. Ideas were developed further at a three-week symposium proposed and sponsored by PADRES before MACC existed. It was held from May 24 to June 11, 1971, at Assumption Seminary in San Antonio. Two weeks of the symposium were conducted by the Instituto de Pastoral en Latino América (IPLA) and CELAM personnel, among whom was the theologian Edgar Beltrán, the anthropologist Alfonso Gortaire, and the sociologist Manuel Velásquez.[76] The main themes were Mexican American culture and liberation theology. The third week covered government programs for community development.[77]

Though the idea of MACC was born at the PADRES's Santa Fe retreat, it became a collaborative effort of PADRES and Las Hermanas. In August 1972 nine PADRES members completed the IPLA's five-month course. Six PADRES completed the IPLA course in January 1972. Many more eventually received training there.[78] In early 1972 the first

Hermanas team—Sisters María de Jesús Ybarra, Gregoria Ortega, and Carmelita Espinoza—studied at IPLA.[79] For many, these experiences encouraged a greater commitment and helped to attach a certain theology to the activism in which they had been engaged for several years. Father Romero said: "My recollection was this was really important because it gave me intellectual categories for experiences I had had."[80]

In 1972, with Father Elizondo at the helm, PADRES and Las Hermanas opened the Mexican-American Cultural Center in San Antonio. Soon after short courses, lasting from two to four weeks, began to be offered. The courses focused on cultural awareness and Chicano studies. Most of the students were Chicana/o and white priests and nuns, but laypeople, both Chicano/a and white, also attended. In time, Spanish-language courses were offered. In addition, both PADRES and Las Hermanas members taught leadership training in Mexican American communities.

Among the whites who took courses at MACC was the CEO of United Parcel Service. Leonard Anguiano, a layman and MACC vice president for twenty-four years, recalled:

Mr. James McLaughlin, the president of United Parcel Service, who was a very good Catholic, his sister was a nun—we started getting funding from him and we started training the international vice presidents of UPS to make them aware of the culture because they started expanding in the Southwest and they were hiring Hispanics and a lot of them didn't understand why when an aunt or a grandmother dies they want to take leave to go to the funeral. Even when McLaughlin died . . . only five or six people . . . came to the funeral, and that to us is unthinkable.[81]

In addition, Anguiano said that MACC trained Latino diocesan directors from throughout the United States, helped to set up Latino diocesan offices, and began a prison ministry among Latinos.

The establishment of MACC was an occasion for optimism. In a letter to Father Elizondo, Father Romero wrote, "The efforts of MACC to meet the need and supply the demand will be one of the most significant events of authentic renewal of Christian worship in the American Church since the Vatican Council."[82]

MACC TAKES OVER MTM

MACC's lay leadership component got off to a strong start with the establishment of the Leadership Institute under the direction of Anguiano, and it was through this program that the PADRES' MTM concept found fuller expression. PADRES began conducting MTMs in 1972, and by year's end more than four hundred people had participated in the Southwest and in other parts of the United States. For instance, in that year MTMs were conducted in Ft. Worth, Texas, with 42 participants; Phoenix, Arizona, with 25 participants; Denver, Colorado, with 45 participants; Pueblo, Colorado, with 40 participants; and Houston, Texas, with 35 participants.[83] Throughout the 1970s participants numbered in the thousands.

PADRES began collaborating with members of the Leadership Institute, and in time PADRES was replaced by the institute as the main means of implementing the MTM. The Leadership Institute's methods were identical to those of the Mobile Team Ministry concept, which emphasized *concientización* and the philosophy of Freire. According to Father Romero, "When the Campaign for Human Development monies ran out, MACC was able to absorb it and continue [its work]."[84] Father Rodríguez recalled, "This was more manageable because Leonard Anguiano . . . set up schedules, etc., and the rest of us were part-timers who had other full-time jobs."[85]

In the early years the Leadership Institute organized twenty-five to thirty workshops per year. Team leaders included Anguiano, Sister Lucie Mario Barron of Las Hermanas, and Frs. Juan Romero and Edmundo Rodríguez of PADRES. The team, as Father Rodríguez recalled, traveled to "various towns where the Hispanic was disenfranchised politically and economically and used a process of community analysis and reflection to help the community understand their situation and to become motivated to organize and take action. The process was fairly successful."[86] Among the cities that the team visited were Crystal City, Texas; Chicago; Union City, California; Tucson; New York; Los Angeles; San Francisco; and New Orleans. In New York, the team worked with impoverished Puerto Ricans. Father Rodríguez said that "eventually the alumni of the leadership workshops were invited to come to MACC in San Antonio for further learning and for networking with those in other places."[87]

IN THE BEGINNING:
A CENTER FOR PROGRESSIVE THOUGHT

True to the spirit on which it was founded, MACC developed the reputation of being a center of progressive activity in the early 1970s. A progressive curriculum was established that emphasized *concientización,* social justice teachings of the church, and critical sociopolitical analysis of U.S. society. Many lectures and workshops were given by visiting scholars from Europe and Latin America. The following are but a few of them: Dutch scholar John Linskens, Jacques Audinet of the Institut Catholique in Paris, Chicano historian Rudolfo Acuña, Paulo Freire, Benjamin Bravo, José Marins, Gustavo Gutiérrez of Peru, and Casiano Floristan of Spain. Sandoval writes, "Their talks, workshops and courses helped to build MACC's reputation and attracted thousands of students to its halls for the best in ministry formation to Hispanics."[88]

Under Anguiano's management, MACC maintained ties with progressive Chicano artists and held numerous art exhibits. As Anguiano recalled: "I was the one who did it because the other ones were not too fond of having these bearded, radical guys around."[89] This relationship is best evidenced by the Chicano Literary Conference held at MACC in 1975 and attended by dozens of Chicano poets and artists. With a grant from the Texas Commission for the Arts, an anthology titled *El Quetzal Emplumenze* was published that showcased the work of those in attendance. In addition, Anguiano said that MACC was visited on occasion by Tomás Rivera, who read poetry.

During Fr. Roberto Peña's tenure as PADRES national president, 1975–1979, MACC opened its doors to several Chicano activist groups, among them the Texas Farm Workers and the San Antonio chapter of the national Chicano organization, Centro de Acción Social Autónomo/Hermandad General de Trabajadores (CASA/HGT; Center for Autonomous Action/General Brotherhood of Workers). Antonio C. Cabral, former head of CASA/HGT of San Antonio, recalled:

Fathers Peña and Anguiano were very instrumental in opening the doors of MACC to progressive groups that were organizing the community. CASA/HGT was an independent progressive Chicano organization. It had a national formation based in Los Angeles and its central purpose was to elevate the political conscious and ideology of Chicanos and Mexicanos in the U.S. We formed a group here in San Antonio of CASA/HGT and we needed a centralized location to meet and hold discussions. Back then, our offices were at the Rubén Salazar Cultural Center that was located in an area difficult for people without cars to reach. We were given access to the classrooms that were at that time located across the street from the main MACC building. We had access anytime we needed them but we used those classrooms primarily for our Saturday morning sessions with community activists and other community people to talk about what we wanted as Chicanos and as workers. We discussed short- and long-term goals as well as tactics and strategies needed to reach those goals. We also discussed Chicano/Mexicano history and the history of U.S.

working-class movements. Our Saturday meetings would start at 10:00 A.M. and we tried to use various Paulo Freire techniques, which were popular back then, including having alternate persons chair the sessions. Our central goal was to facilitate the ideological development of community activists through such group discussions and also study groups but we also included community people that showed an interest.[90]

Cabral added that laypeople, not priests, organized and led the Saturday sessions.

According to Cabral, CASA/HGT sometimes sponsored speakers who were well known and respected organizers on both sides of the U.S.-Mexico border. "In the late 1970s CASA/HGT brought in Valentín Campa and Heberto Castillo from Mexico. Both are still respected figures in the history of Mexico's workers' movements. Campa was one of the leaders of the famous railroad workers' strike in the early 1900s. Both men are still well known and revered in Mexico for their sacrifices on behalf of the working class."[91]

Other speakers CASA/HGT invited were Burt Corona, Reyes Tijerina, and members of Corky Gonzales's Crusade for Justice. Cabral said: "We also brought the controversial Mexican Bishop Méndez Arceo once. He was already loved by many and hated by some in Mexico who called him the 'Red Bishop' because of his work in the poorest parishes. He was considered a radical priest and he suffered political persecution that included being accused of supporting the guerilla struggles common in Mexico then. In fact, his only crime was practicing the teachings of Christ and a strong believer and practitioner of the theology of liberation."[92] Cabral recalled Bishop Méndez Arceo as a "very gentle and Christ-like person."[93]

CASA/HGT was allowed to use MACC's telephones and copying equipment to make leaflets and brochures: "If it hadn't been for MACC, a lot of community organizing projects could not have been carried out. Peña and Anguiano were progressive enough to recognize that their facilities, such as the auditorium, should be utilized by the broader community and they didn't limit their use only for MACC's internal religious agenda."[94]

AT THE END: CONSERVATISM

Soon after Father Peña left his post as executive director of PADRES, MACC closed its doors to CASA/HGT and, according to Cabral, to all community activities that were not traditional religious events. As the 1970s progressed, because of the constant need for funding and the changing ideological climate within the church, it became harder for MACC to maintain its commitment to liberating the poor. A conservative turn and purge of progressives was inevitable.

The constant need for funding made servicing a predominantly white clientele more viable. Thus, offering training to white ministers who intended to work among Latinos became the focus.

The Vatican's growing hostility toward liberation theology created a conservative climate that made MACC's radical focus more risky. This caused tension between progressive PADRES and Las Hermanas who defended MACC's original goals and those who saw survival as the highest priority.[95]

Progressive feminist Hermanas, who enjoyed a considerable role at MACC in the early 1970s, were hit especially hard. During the late 1970s, tensions between these aggressive feminists and the conservatives grew. Many Las Hermanas members became alienated and frustrated. By 1980 Las Hermanas' representation on MACC's board of directors was effectively silenced. In 1983 several Hermanas taught courses, and Hermana Yolanda Tarango was hired as director of MACC's pastoral program. Tarango was terminated in 1985 for reasons that are unclear. It is believed her termination was due to her success in developing a progressive curriculum.[96]

MACC began as an attempt by PADRES and Las Hermanas to counteract anti-Raza cultural oppression in the church and to contribute to the material liberation of poor and working-class Mexican Americans. Initially, it made great strides. In time, however, MACC became an ideological microcosm of the larger society.

OTHER BATTLES

PADRES waged a number of other noteworthy battles, often in collaboration with Las Hermanas, in the pursuit of social change. These battles were fought to gain representation within the USCC, establish the National Hispanic Secretariat, organize the national Encuentros, organize the grassroots, and reform the seminaries. PADRES also supported a variety of progressive issues, including the struggle of the farmworkers. The group also fought to make the church aware of the needs of their people.

Cracking the USCC

At the outset PADRES endeavored to gain representation at the highest decision-making levels. This meant infiltrating the USCC—a difficult and frustrating task for the impatient leaders of PADRES. In mid-January 1970 PADRES was given a verbal promise by Joseph McSweeny, first director of the newly formed Campaign for Human Development, that a Mexican American would be given a staff position at the USCC. According to Father Ruiz, it was important to have Mexican American representation on the USCC because none existed. In addition, while it was known that one Mexican American could not radically change the USCC, it was a start and would have meant a symbolic victory for PADRES. Fr. Joe López, then the PADRES field director, was to be the first; he was to be appointed to the board of the Department of the Campaign for Human Development.

As of March 2, 1970, $5,000 of the $39,400 promised by the USCC had been received by PADRES and the organization was on schedule to receive the rest of the monies. At this time, $15,000 had been approved for disbursement and $15,000 was set for an April 1 disbursement and the remaining $4,400 on June 1. Father Ruiz and his staff had been busy making arrangements for Father López's departure for weeks when, according to Father Ruiz, a priest friend who worked at the USCC informed him that the position had already been filled. Father Ruiz called the USCC, which confirmed this news.

On March 11 a furious Father Ruiz sent a letter to McSweeny, with copies to USCC General Secretary Bishop Bernardin:

> The National Office of PADRES seriously resents the duplicity with which you have been dealing with our staff. . . . We realize now that you had no intentions to hire him for this position but merely used double talk to further deceive us. . . . We realize that you are nothing more than a shield and a buffer for Bishop Bernardin and Fr. Rausch and not capable of decisions or executing your promises. . . . Because of this lamentable weakness in your character, the National Office of PADRES will make this information known to all its members that you are not to be trusted. The participants in the Campaign for Human Development will further share this information and be assured that you may consider this a formal declaration of war.[97]

Bishop Bernardin responded defensively to Ruiz in a letter dated March 16:

I take strong exception to the accusations you make against Mr. Mc-Sweeny. To accuse him of duplicity and irresponsibility is totally un-just. . . . I do have confidence in Mr. McSweeny's competence and in-tegrity. It is true that the question of whether or not to hire Father Joe López was one that was discussed by those responsible for the Cam-paign: Mr. McSweeny, Bishop Mugavero, Bishop Dempey, Father Rausch and myself. We are committed to two criteria in determining the com-position of the staff, (a) that the persons hired have the special expertise needed for the particular job in question, (b) that, within the context of "a," there be as much of an ethnic mix as possible. We are NOT com-mitted, however, to hiring anyone who is representative of a particular organization.[98]

Bishop Bernardin went on to say in no uncertain terms that the forth-coming monies that PADRES expected from the USCC and any future monies were in jeopardy if Father Ruiz did not retract his letter. Fa-ther Ruiz fired back a response to Bishop Bernardin in a letter dated March 21:

Is it the case that we cannot express our feeling of frustration over an issue which we feel is an extremely important one and with which we have been struggling for over a year? And that is, that of having a Chicano priest on the USCC staff. There is absolutely no doubt that as long as there is no Chicano priest on the USCC staff, the Chicano community will continue to be marginal in the concerns of the National instrument of the Catholic Church. We say priest rather than simply a Chicano because we must face the reality of clerical governance in the Church. . . . What is distressing us now is that either you do not agree with us on the importance of having a Chicano priest on the staff of the USCC or simply that you do not wish to do anything about it. . . . In closing, I wish to stress again that the real issue is our original request and not the subsequent recriminations which have passed back and forth through the mail. Would you please address yourself again to this issue?[99]

But Father Ruiz wasn't finished. He wrote another letter to Bishop Ber-nardin but this time without notifying the PADRES executive commit-tee or carbon copying the Bishop's Committee. The letter was hand-delivered by Fr. Joe López and Lutheran pastor Jack O'Donnell in Washington, D.C. Father Ruiz recalled what he said:

Up to this point, you and I know that we have talked and kept the abuses of the church against Chicanos behind closed doors. You wrote me a letter saying that if I did not retract what I said, you will find it difficult to fund PADRES. If we don't get funded within the next two weeks, the following will happen: We will converge in Kansas City. We will call the press, television and radio. We will march from Kansas to Washington, D.C., and tell the world how this Catholic Church has historically treated and how it currently treats the Mexican American.[100]

Three days after Father López and Reverend O'Donnell left for Washington, D.C., Father Ruiz received a telephone call from a USCC staff person who was also a friend of his. Father Ruiz recalled the conversation as follows:

"Ralph, what the hell happened?" I asked. "What are you talking about?" He said, "López and O'Donnell just left Bernardin's office. A while later, Bernardin was taken to the hospital." I said, "They went to deliver my letter." He said, "Yeah, I bet." Two days later I received a letter from Bernardin. In essence, it said, "Dear Ralph. I know many times we act in anger and say things we don't mean. Call Archbishop Furey who is the chairman of the committee dealing with PADRES. All you will need to do is write a one-page proposal on how the money will be used, and he will release the money." Within days PADRES was funded.[101]

Father Ruiz explained his rationale:

You have to understand the temperament of the times. I was at the end of my rope. If I had retracted what I said about McSweeney because of money, I might as well have hung up my gloves, because this is how they, the hierarchy, control people. I knew I wasn't going to be able to get anyone to Kansas City to march all the way to D.C. How could I get all kinds of people to converge in Kansas City within ten days? How were we going to walk all the way to D.C.? But Joe Bernardin didn't know that for sure. Do you know what Joe knew? He knew that almost every night the blacks in Washington, D.C., were burning down the city. Their cry was, "Burn, baby, burn." And they were not kidding. I wasn't kidding either. I might not have succeeded, but I would have tried to make that march to D.C. I knew people at CBS whom I could call to help cover the event, and they had a tremendous sense of justice. Those were terrible times, . . . times of social upheaval and revolutions which are unfortunately the last options to bring about necessary change.[102]

The National Hispanic Secretariat

At the First National Encuentro, participants drew up a list of seventy-eight demands and addressed them to the USCC. Some demands were considered too radical and not taken seriously, for example, the ordination of women and that Base Christian Communities become a national priority of the church. One demand that enjoyed success was the creation of the National Secretariat for Hispanic Affairs housed at the USCC in Washington, D.C.

The secretariat was created when the Division of the Spanish-speaking, which had been moved to Washington from San Antonio in 1971, was elevated to secretariat status in 1974. PADRES, Las Hermanas, and Pablo Sedillo (then head of the Division of the Spanish-speaking), agitated successfully for its creation.[103] According to Sandoval, this agitation included at least one rather remarkable measure. In early 1974, "Sedillo was presented with a plan that would have made the Division a desk in another department."[104] This was a fate that Sedillo refused to accept. "For a time, there was talk of bringing ten to fifteen thousand Hispanos to march upon the USCC."[105] In the end, the agitators got their wish, and the division was elevated to the position of National Secretariat, with Sedillo as its first director. Father Romero explained, "The change in status from a 'division' to a 'secretariat' came by way of discernment, decision, and political action. That made a big difference for Pablo Sedillo by giving him immediate access to the general secretary of the USCC. The lines of communication were now much more direct. It's a status thing and an access thing, and it translated to more power from the inside."[106]

PADRES was also successful at creating offices for Latino affairs at the diocesan level. As Bishop Flores reported, "We were suggesting the bishops do two things. That they would establish an office in their diocese for Hispanic Affairs. Secondly, especially on the frontier states, that we would have an office for immigration, and it was to help those who were here undocumented get their documents and so on and so forth because we would see the injustice that would be committed against them. Then, thank goodness, practically every diocese from Brownsville all the way to San Diego in California [had one]."[107]

PADRES spawned other organizations. One was the Association of Hispanic Seminarians. After going to his first and only PADRES meeting in 1987 when he was a seminarian in Chicago, Fr. Héctor Madrigal decided to organize Mexican American seminarians in the Midwest: "Hearing about what PADRES had done really motivated us to start something over there. We were struggling there and were feeling a bit abandoned by, in a sense, the church, because there was so much going on that was so different from our experience in the Southwest or from wherever we came from. And we also felt very isolated because there wasn't a lot of Hispanics in that area."[108]

National Encuentros

PADRES, Las Hermanas, and many laypeople began the Encuentros Nacional Hispano de Pastoral, which were national conferences intended to confront the church hierarchy and promote a national Latino Catholic agenda. Father Romero explained, "In IAF terms it would be recognition and respect. There are Mexican Americans and Latinos on the national level, there are many, and we need to take care of them pastorally. So it was not so much like what Católicos Por La Raza were doing with the negative speech of denunciation. Now we wanted to announce! If the church was being correctly denounced by prophetic voices within the church, we wanted to counterbalance that by announcing the way we are going to go, where are we going to go, and how, to develop plans and strategies and not just complain."[109] The Encuentros were inspired by Fr. Edgar Beltran, a former staff member of the Conference of Latin American Bishops who at the time was on the staff of the Division for the Spanish Speaking at the USCC. According to Father Romero, "Beltran had been the main pedagogue for the May 1971 San Antonio symposium on *teología de liberación y pedagogía de concientización* held for PADRES members and some Protestant clergy."[110]

The First National Encuentro took place in June 1972 at Trinity College in Washington, D.C. It was attended by about two hundred fifty people, among whom were Latino Catholics from various subgroups— Mexican Americans, Puerto Ricans, and Cubans. Only a handful of bishops attended. According to Sandoval, one of these bishops was "the imposing Cardinal John Krol, who tried to convince the audience that everyone was equal in the Church. The participants, however, would have none of it. Bishop Patrick Flores, elevated to the episcopacy barely two years before, charged that the Church had been silent while his people had been robbed of their lands, forced to live in conditions of semi-slavery . . . and deprived of their way of religious expression."[111] PADRES member Fr. Vicente López recalled Bishop Flores's keynote address:

> By that time we were accustomed to being frank and open about our Church, even if it meant being critical. Bishop Flores talked about an

older teenage girl he knew who had tried to commit suicide. He went to visit her, and upon seeing her, he told her that her mother was crying outside the hospital room. "I don't want to see her, ever," the young girl said. "Why?" asked Bishop Flores. "Because when I was fourteen and fifteen my stepfather tried to abuse and rape me. Then I went to my mother who told me that I was the one who must have been teasing him. Finally when I could no longer resist his advances *él hizo lo que quiso conmigo* [he did what he wanted with me], my life became worth little. I went to the streets and became what I have become. Now at eighteen I have determined that life is not worth living." Then Bishop Flores explained, "That is the relationship of the Hispanic people with the Catholic Church. We have appealed to the church, and have been abused, and the church has remained silent."[112]

In his own way, Bishop Flores was restating the arguments that Católicos por la Raza and many PADRES priests had been making: the church had been and was still a colonial functionary of the dominant white society.[113] Overall, the highly confrontational first Encuentro reflected the mood of the times. It spawned several smaller-scale regional and diocesan Encuentros in the years that followed.[114]

The Second National Encuentro was held in 1977, the third in 1985. Both were much less confrontational than the first and had more significance in terms of institutional influence. The second emphasized grassroots views on the church and called for the church to recognize lay leadership. The third was attended by 1,200 delegates from 130 dioceses, and each delegation was led by a bishop. Places were reserved for farmworkers and other marginal groups. Together they approved a national pastoral plan for Hispanic ministry. Father Janacek saw the plan as "a forceful vindication of the original thrust of PADRES."[115] Subsequently, some dioceses developed their own pastoral plans for Hispanic ministry.

A significant change occurred between the first and third Encuentros: at the former, most of those in attendance were white; at the latter, Latinos were the dominant presence. Father Janacek is quoted as follows: "We were the ones working in Hispanic Ministry. In those days, they used to put, what few there were, Hispanic priests into Anglo parishes. But after the *Tercer Encuentro,* it was a whole different ball game. Hispanic leadership had emerged, in no small part due to the prophetic efforts of PADRES."[116]

Father Rodríguez recalled: "[The First National Encuentro] was our [Mexican American Catholics] first real coming together with Puerto

Ricans and other Latinos to look at a more nationalized agenda. I remember that that first Encuentro between us southwesterners and the easterners was somewhat tense because nobody knew quite what to expect."[117] The result was many disparate groups vying with each other. But, according to Sandoval, in the long run the Encuentros taught different Latino groups how to work together, and this may have been their most significant achievement. Latino Catholics "emerged from the Third National *Encuentro* with more mutual understanding and unity."[118] Throughout the process, lay leadership was identified and developed, and they in turn returned to their dioceses to play important roles. In addition, the process made bishops more aware of the need to serve the Latino community.

Grassroots Activism

While not all Mexican-American PADRES priests were hard-core Chicano activists, a committed group was, and they distinguished themselves in battles both inside and outside the church, in city trenches throughout the Southwest and in places like Chicago, Kansas City, and Boise, to name a few. Although PADRES was a national organization that in principle sought to fight for all Latino Catholics in the United States, its efforts at the grassroots level seem to have been concentrated primarily in the predominantly Mexican American Southwest. For instance, in the early 1970s PADRES Fr. Peter E. García was leading an eight-hundred-member neighborhood organization in a fight against proposed development that called for the relocation of 235 parish families, of which 90 percent were Mexican American. The organization pressured the city of Denver to provide housing for these people. In 1971 Father García, a native of Denver, ran for a city council seat. His platform included affordable housing for low-income and disadvantaged people. PADRES became involved with Chicano students in East Los Angeles during the formation of MEChA and also in organizing teachers in the fight for bilingual education. PADRES member Fr. Luis Caramillo was working with the Brown Berets in Albuquerque. As Fr. Alberto Carrillo stated, "Here we're talking about the civil rights movement within the church in PADRES because outside of PADRES we were dealing with the city council, we were dealing with the state legislature, we were dealing with the *politicos,* we were dealing with the police, we were dealing with everybody. Every institution. But within the church, my God, how can you be a priest, a Catholic, and how can you be that when you are going to limit somebody's rights?"[119]

In addition to developing lay leadership with the MTM, PADRES endeavored to unite Mexican American activist groups on the state level. They succeeded in certain locations such as Albuquerque, New Mexico. Father Aragón recalled, "One of the first things we did was organize the Federación de la Raza, a coalition of all the Mexican American organizations. We formed them into one group to put pressure. We were the first group that ever brought suit against the Albuquerque public schools for discrimination in the early seventies. Then we pressured KGGM [a local TV station] because of hiring practices and because they had no Hispanic programs and we made an impact on them."[120] Father Aragón added that New Mexico was a hotbed of PADRES activities.

PADRES' grassroots work is illustrated by Citizens Organized for Public Service, or COPS, a nationally known community-based group formed in the early 1970s on San Antonio's impoverished Mexican American west side. A similar group, called United Neighbors Organization (UNO), was formed in East Los Angeles. Both are styled after the organizing philosophy of Alinsky's IAF. Both are extensions of the MTM in terms of their emphasis on the need for the development of lay leadership among the poor and working class by using the process of *concientización.*

IAF organizer Ernie Cortez is widely credited with starting COPS. Cortez was undoubtedly an important presence, but he took advantage of a context that was favorable for organizing. For several reasons, PADRES contributed significantly to this context. First, the local church hierarchy was very supportive, due in no small part to PADRES' agitation. Second, the MTM workshops had developed local leaders. Father Rodríguez explained, "I would say that it wasn't the same people that had taken our workshops that became strong in COPS, but there was at least a new understanding in the area, especially in the west and south sides of San Antonio, a kind of new understanding of the church in the sense that it made sense for churches to be involved in social, political action, so there wasn't a lot of resistance to it. . . . [T]he ground had been plowed quite a bit by those of us who had been accused of being communists and other horrible things."[121]

Third, several PADRES took IAF training in Chicago soon after the group's formation. Two of them, Frs. Edmundo Rodríguez and Albert Benavidez of San Antonio, became key organizers of COPS, and Fr. Juan Romero became a lead organizer of UNO. Most significantly, Fr. Rodríguez, a founder of PADRES, was also a founder of COPS.

Fourth, a few years before COPS was established PADRES organized the church-based network called the Six-Parish Coalition on the west side. The coalition promoted community-based social activism. As Father Rodríguez recalled:

> I believe we formed the Six-Parish Coalition beginning in 1971. . . . It was at the Ecumenical Institute's workshop that our staff decided to move full force into doing something about the housing in our section of town. When I was pastor of Our Lady of Guadalupe in San Antonio, six pastors of adjacent parishes got together to see how we might work together in our section of the diocese and the city. Gradually, we brought in the parish leaders and met once a month to exchange information and do some planning. These were probably the poorest parishes in the diocese. The Six-Parish Coalition became the backbone of COPS and together we worked to get better streets, sewerage, housing, etc. We even started a school for undocumented children when the State of Texas decided that such children were not eligible to attend public schools. I was chairman of the Sponsoring Committee for COPS. Some of the lay leaders of COPS were from the various coalition parishes. Our biggest accomplishment was rebuilding blocks and blocks of dilapidated housing by pressuring the city to use community development funds for that purpose. The Coalition was also involved in the revision of the City Charter so that the city of San Antonio went from a council which was elected at large, so that only people with money could get on the council, to elections by districts. Thus it was that the poorer sides of town got represented on the council. Our Coalition was asked by another group of pastors to help them form another coalition just to the north of us. We tried, but there wasn't any one pastor willing to throw himself into the hard task of organizing it. Thus we ended up being the only Coalition of Parishes.[122]

Father Romero said:

> PADRES had a direct relation in the formation of COPS and UNO in terms of the need for organizing base and broad-based community organizing, and it became one of the explicit themes of one of our congresses in Kansas in '77 or '78. Just like the Encuentro movement, PADRES was a ferment. The members planted seeds, the agitators, the movers. They possessed the intellectual kind of thinking power to say this is where we need to go and here are some of the things we need to do to get there. The IAF was the next logical step for us after the Mobile Team Ministry. In other words, we were trying to develop critical consciousness with the ragtag Mobile Team, but then it became easier to do on a broader base utilizing professional organizers. We had to keep thinking that we

were utilizing them, not they utilizing us. The second IAF organization after COPS was UNO. Ernie Cortez went to East L.A. and this happened around the time I was returning from PADRES back to East L.A. There was great euphoria, a lot of heady atmosphere. Some of the stuff that was happening with PADRES was happening on the parish level—a good parish staff, a good Parish Council, a good sense of team, the beginnings of UNO. I was very involved with UNO. In fact, shortly after coming back to the parish, I was sent to San Antonio for a national training of IAF which took place at MACC that year. That was my first very formal experience with IAF. I was familiar with IAF and COPS just by following some of the actions and by going to some of the local actions. UNO was formed that year in 1976. I was sent as a delegate from the parish from the beginning stages of UNO. The explicit thing was to identify and train organic leadership, always identifying new talent and mentoring them. In Paulo Freire's terms, we were continuously and consciously trying to help people learn to think critically and strategically. Issue discernment is the main thing that IAF pushes. In PADRES, we did the workshops with the Mobile Team Ministry. The Issue Discernment workshop was a similar kind of thing. We were trying to build critical consciousness, and IAF does it in a different way and on a much broader level, all together as we are moving in the process.[123]

Former PADRES national vice president, Fr. Luis Olivares, now deceased, was also active in UNO. He was a powerful force in the early days and had a key leadership role in a variety of other struggles, including the campaign to lower insurance rates in the state of California.

While Mexican Americans in the Southwest were first on PADRES' agenda, they were not the only ones it tried to help. As Father Rodríguez explained, "PADRES started in San Antonio, branched out to Colorado, Arizona, New Mexico, and California, so, of course, the immediate and pressing needs we experienced were those of the Mexican American but also the Mexican immigrant. Early on we hooked up with the farmworkers in California, many of whom were Mexican nationals and Filipinos as well as Mexican Americans."[124] PADRES then moved east and north and became aware of the needs of the Puerto Ricans, the Dominicans, and the Cubans. PADRES did indeed become aware of the needs of Latino Catholics in the Northeast. This was due in large part to the activism of a young priest, Anthony Stevens-Arroyo, a Puerto Rican American of the congregation of the Passion order from New York, now resigned, who became national vice president of PADRES. At one point during the 1970s, Father Stevens-Arroyo invited Chicano

PADRES members from the Southwest to New York to see the situation themselves. Many were shocked at the poverty they saw.[125]

The situation of Latino Catholics in New York was not much different from that of Mexican Americans in the Southwest in terms of church neglect and the lack of native-born Latino priests. In November 1974 PADRES reported in its official newsletter that the New York archdiocese was over 55 percent Latino, mostly Puerto Rican; but of the more than two thousand priests working there, less than five were Puerto Rican.[126] A year earlier, eight hundred New York priests met with the cardinal to determine pastoral priorities. They touched on ninety-five points, but not one concerned the Latinos of New York.[127]

Yet while PADRES was in favor of helping Latino Catholics in the Northeast, according to Father Stevens-Arroyo, it accomplished very little in this regard. He suggests that this was in part a result of the group's heavy commitments in the Southwest and its refusal to give up this regional base, lack of manpower, and the inability to form a working partnership with the Northeast's Asociación Sacerdotes Hispanos (ASH), a support group for Hispanic priests, many of whom were foreign, that formed in about 1972.[128] The members of ASH declined PADRES's invitation for affiliation because they feared PADRES would "swallow them up."[129] Nevertheless, Stevens-Arroyo became one of the group's most active members, according to Father Rodríguez, and was involved in grassroots leadership training among Puerto Rican Catholics. He has since distinguished himself as a scholar and a prolific writer.

Seminary Reform

For PADRES, the small number of native-born Mexican American priests and the large number of Mexican American Catholics, coupled with their own seminary experiences, were harsh reminders of the racism and discrimination that existed within the seminary system. As mentioned, many PADRES members believed that the ideal solution lay in the establishment of a separate seminary and religious order geared to meeting the special social and spiritual needs of Mexican Americans. At a separate seminary, cultural denigration would be replaced with cultural respect, and white theology would be replaced with a new, more organic theology. As Fr. Ramón Aragón argued:

> It is the only way we can work ourselves out of this thing. . . . We have to develop a native Chicano liturgy. Right now we're using everybody else's

liturgy but our own. A mariachi Mass [a Mass that showcases mariachi music] is not enough. We have to develop new forms of worship that fit our people. . . . We are tired of being dependent on everybody else. We want to create the theology of La Raza. We want our own experts in scripture, theology and liturgy. The Chicano has great insights into the faith but his contribution is being lost to the Church. The only way this can be changed is through our own seminary.[130]

Despite having historic precedent on their side and the moral will, the ideas of a separate seminary and religious order never got off the ground. The reasons were practical: it was financially infeasible; and it was believed that the hierarchy would never support such a venture. This, however, did not stop PADRES from openly criticizing the seminary system and making recommendations. At the PADRES National Congress in October 1971 PADRES resolved that "seminaries throughout the United States, especially those training priests who will be serving in centers of significant Mexican-American population, implement specific programs to insure that the future clergy become aware of and respectful toward the Chicano culture."[131] PADRES recommended that the following be made available to seminarians: Spanish-language classes, Mexican culture and history classes and Chicano studies courses, field education programs in barrios, opportunities to live and work in Mexican American parishes, opportunities to live and work in Mexico, and opportunities to develop Chicano-oriented liturgies. In addition, the college and theology departments of the seminary should have a chair of Mexican American Studies.

In the early 1970s PADRES made a creative proposal to the Bishops of the United States to develop a bilingual and bicultural seminary pilot program at the Corpus Christi, Texas, Minor Seminary. The goal would be to give Mexican American students "an adequate college preparatory program. This is necessary because inadequate secondary education methods now being used in 'gringo-oriented' schools are adversely affecting the Mexican-American. This fact is attested to by the high rate of push-outs from among such schools. A bilingual and bicultural seminary with a properly qualified faculty, infused with the Chicano mentality, would help bridge the educational and cultural gaps in our bicultural areas."[132] In the proposal for this pilot program, PADRES urged "that the following be implemented immediately."[133]

At the First National Hispanic Encuentro in June 1972, proposals for cultural and Spanish-language training were put forward, but they were rejected by the bishops as too radical. By 1992 Spanish-language training had become a requirement in many dioceses with considerable Latino populations. Other reforms would eventually find expression in the Mexican-American Cultural Center.

Progressive Issues

Throughout the years, PADRES priests played supportive roles in Chicano student movement activity and agitated for such reforms as bilingual education. PADRES agitated for Spanish-language Masses in parishes with sizable Latino populations and was critical of parishes that offered Spanish-language Masses at inconvenient times or in church basements. PADRES has also been credited with promoting mariachi Masses and with popularizing the traditional Mexican serape. Several PADRES testified at civil rights hearings throughout the country. In New Mexico, they took part in the meetings of the Federal Alliance of Land Grants. The Alliance, led by Reyes López Tijerina, was trying to recover lands illegally taken from Latinos.[134] PADRES became a strong advocate for the rights of Latino immigrants, especially in the early 1980s, and for prison reform and bilingual education. It endorsed the struggle for women's rights and the National Organization for Women (NOW) in 1974, which was a significant move considering that the president of NOW was excommunicated at about this time. PADRES also encouraged the NCCB to support human rights in Chile that same year. PADRES pushed the church to be more involved in dealing with the government. In November 1972 five members of PADRES, including Bishop Flores, and two national representatives of Las Hermanas met with a twelve-member liaison committee of the NCCB in Washington. The group requested that the NCCB hire a spokesman before the government to represent church concerns in regard to its Latino-American membership.[135] During the 1980s, PADRES was active in the opposition to America's terrorist war against Nicaragua and other Central American countries. The group also helped many Central American refugees in cities such as Los Angeles.

PADRES brought a certain moral dimension to Chicano activism. As Father Carrillo explained, "We needed an organization that would speak to issues from a religious and moral point of view. We could say we need bilingual education because it's immoral to teach a kid in a language he doesn't know. And we could give the whole weight of the church if you will, or if not the church, at least Christian doctrine. It's immoral to have the people that feed you, to treat them like they've been treated. I mean, that's just rented slavery and that's immoral. So we could deal with the moral issues."[136]

PADRES played a small role in the Chicano Moratorium in Los Angeles. A day after the killing of journalist Rubén Salazar, Father Casso, who was living in Los Angeles and working for MALDEF, convinced newly appointed Bishop Patrick Flores to console Salazar's widow. Bishop Flores was in town for the second PADRES national congress in Delano, which was canceled because of the Salinas lettuce strike where seven thousand UFW workers walked off the fields. Fathers Casso and Romero and Bishop Flores arrived at the Bagues Mortuary on Brooklyn Avenue, and there Bishop Flores consoled Mrs. Salazar. Bishop Flores and Father Casso sang "De Colores," the Cursillo, and the UFW song, all of which was captured by a local television crew. That night, Bishop Flores met with about thirty members of the community to try to heal the fear and anger that lingered throughout East L.A. Present at this meeting and at the Moratorium were several Chicana nuns who would soon after help form Las Hermanas. These included Sisters Clarita Trujillo and Theresa Basso.[137]

A few hours later the group came to a consensus that a press conference would be called, and Bishop Flores agreed to lend his name to convoke the conference. Father Romero writes, "It truly was a gutsy thing to do, especially considering that only three months previous he had been named an auxiliary bishop."[138] At Salesian High School a group of PADRES priests and students worked through the night to prepare for the press conference, set for ten o'clock the next morning. Father Romero remembers Bishop Flores at the typewriter and wearing a white T-shirt.[139] Chicano student activists called the City News Service and other media to invite them to the press conference. A press release was collectively written with guidance from Father Casso. Father Romero was named spokesman and translated the press release into Spanish. The priests identified themselves as participants in the Moratorium and as members of the local chapter of PADRES. They denounced the violence and the deaths and demanded a thorough congressional investigation of the circumstances surrounding the death of Rubén Salazar. It was the first time they had gathered or spoken as a group. Much of their statement was televised, but visual or spoken reference to Bishop Flores was censored. Father Romero speculated that this may have been the work of "local ecclesiastical influence in order to deprive the statement of any semblance of official approval."[140]

The Farmworkers

Throughout its existence, PADRES supported César Chávez and the farmworkers. Early on, PADRES pressured the NCCB to support the farmworkers' struggle. For instance, according to Father Romero, PADRES advocated for a Personal Prelature for migrant farmworkers throughout the United States. That is, no matter where migrant farmworkers would be, they would be served by the same bishop in the country.[141] Many PADRES priests were directly involved with the farmworker movement, and several enjoyed close personal ties with Chávez. On August 3, 1973, Father Romero, then executive director of PADRES, was jailed for thirteen days for his involvement in pro-farmworker demonstrations. He was among forty-five priests and nuns who were arrested and imprisoned after alleged illegal assembly and failure to disperse while joining in the picket line of Chávez's UFW near Fresno.[142] Chávez delivered a reading at the episcopal ordination of Patrick Flores in San Antonio on May 5, 1970. Father Romero coordinated the Mass for Chávez's funeral in 1993.

Increasing Awareness

Over the years, with its Encuentros, national meetings, newsletters, and constant agitation, PADRES increased the church's awareness of the presence and rights of Latino Catholics in the United States.[143] This was acknowledged by an overwhelming majority of PADRES informants. The following statements are representative.

Fr. Roberto Flores:

> Creating an awareness among our people, among ourselves and Anglo clergy. We made them at least look at us as belonging to the whole administration of God's people and not a hierarchical church. I think we created an awareness of social justice but I think the church was already going there. A lot of Anglo priests were happy we did what we did because they knew that social justice had to be screamed out. . . . I think we created an awareness of any priest that was going to come into our community had to learn Spanish. We were no longer going to accept these damn Anglos who think they could come in and speak only English and be satisfied. MACC is a perfect example. . . . I think the biggest contribution of PADRES was the change in attitude of the Anglo clergy. They had to face the fact that they were no longer talking to the poor folk that was going to do anything you told them to do. But now they were talking to

the clergy that came from there and you were not going to put us down anymore. We're at your level, we've gone this far and we're not going to let you do this shit to our people anymore. Stop it. If you're going to come, learn, be aware of the culture, dare to learn what we have had to grow up with. We shook them up. We shook them up good. We made them wake up.[144]

Archbishop Patrick Flores:

I think we really opened the eyes of the bishops. . . . I think that in speaking to the bishops and other officials we made them realize, here's a big segment of the Catholic Church that needs attention in their way, in their style. And while they found it difficult, little by little a great number of bishops began to learn Spanish.[145]

Fr. Ramón Aragón:

I think the other thing PADRES accomplished was getting laypeople to understand who they were and that they had basic rights and that they were owners of the church. That it was legitimate for them to get involved in social issues. . . . I felt that very strongly. If it wouldn't have been for PADRES that wouldn't have happened in this diocese [Albuquerque]. . . . It was like, you people don't have anyone who is qualified to hold a high office. I think the pressure from PADRES and then the push and even some of the threats, like from Carrillo and Soriano, . . . about starting a Chicano church, which was all saber rattling, it had an effect of making people pay attention.[146]

Fr. Edmundo Rodríguez:

PADRES did a tremendous amount of *concientización* in the pueblo in many many places and left its imprint. A lot of things that developed later, like COPS in San Antonio and UNO in Los Angeles and whatever it's called in Houston, I think that a lot of *concientización* had gone on already, they just needed some way to organize that energy. There were a lot of experiments with *communidades de base*. There was a lot of support for organizing the farmworkers both in California and in South Texas. I know I and others participated in some of the *huelgas* [strikes] and things. And it became really important to have someone in the chancery office who could relate to the Mexicanos and that began to happen.[147]

Blanca García:

> PADRES made people aware that there are a lot of needs that priests have;
> that no one was addressing their needs. It was just a group of men that
> wanted the church to listen to their demands. And not so much demands
> but to recognize the potential, to recognize the talent, to recognize the
> leadership that these men have. These were grown men. I saw how the
> church still wanted to address grown men as children when they had very
> legitimate issues. What really impressed me about PADRES is they made
> the church aware of the discrimination with the illegal immigrants, with
> the farmworkers, all the groups that were being oppressed. And that's
> another thing that they did. They made the church become involved. The
> church at the time did not want to get involved with strikes, did not want
> to get involved with the government as far as INS and illegal aliens, and
> this is where the church needs to be. The church needs to be involved in
> the human rights of their congregation. The church got to a point where
> they were too involved in themselves; what part of town you lived; what
> kind of car you were driving; how many maids you had; they got involved
> in a status quo deal. How much status can one accomplish while being a
> priest? And they forgot about human rights, not only of the community
> but of their own priests. And I think PADRES gave them a very rude
> awakening. And a lot of people did object to it. And when I say a lot of
> people, I mean a lot of people within the church. The hierarchy. PADRES
> was a defender of human rights, not only just for Catholics but for every-
> one involved. And it's sad because everybody, like my generation, I grew
> up thinking that the church was fair and holy and a defender. It's not.[148]

The newly installed U.S. apostolic delegate, Archbishop Jadot, was made
aware of the plight of the Chicano-Latino people by PADRES. Jadot, a
Belgian who was a nuncio in Africa before coming to the United States
in winter 1973, had a direct line of communication with the Vatican
and thus had great influence. At the episcopal ordination of Archbishop
Roberto Sánchez in Santa Fe the following year, Jadot reportedly told
a PADRES official, "You are the first one to have told me about the
Hispanics in the United States. I knew about the blacks, but not the
Hispanics."[149]

PADRES also created awareness among otherwise conservative
Mexican American priests. Bishop Ramírez of Las Cruces, who was
ordained in 1966, recalls, "In those days my approach to ministry was,
I think, very narrow. It really didn't involve the social dimension. It was
more sacramental and familial. I didn't know what was happening in

the U.S. because I'd been away in Mexico so I didn't know very much about the Chicano movement. Certainly I didn't know what PADRES was all about. I barely knew about MACC. Then in 1976 I moved to San Antonio from Mexico to work for Father Elizondo at MACC and once there it was like hitting the ground running because a lot of things were happening and so I just ran with it and embraced the movement, especially on the part of the church, and became very supportive of PADRES."[150]

Fr. Ramón Aragón of the Santa Fe diocese said:

In the beginning I didn't see much of the social struggles of Hispanos. I think it was my contact with PADRES that made me aware of these things. I think for myself, I would have been very satisfied just being a sacramental priest. I think that PADRES created a tension within me that something had to happen in my own life, with my own vision, with my own attitude toward the church and to people, and that's what got me involved.[151]

SIX

SOCIAL ACTIVISM AND ITS COST

†

PAYING THE PRICE

Many PADRES members suffered personal consequences as a result of their activism on behalf of the oppressed. Father Romero suggests that some PADRES may have hurt their chances for advancement: "It costs. It costs people perceiving you as a radical or as a political priest. Saul Alinsky in his first book, *Rules for Radicals,* says if you want to be in this kind of stuff, and if you're a priest, you have to renounce explicitly and up front any hope of ever being a bishop. If it is in your plan, then you cannot play this game."[1]

For some, the experience was painful. Fr. Lonnie Reyes recalled: "It was kind of like you expected your mother was going to be there supporting you, understanding you if nothing else, but Mom wasn't there. Mom was castigating you for your sensitivities. It was a painful experience. . . . You trust that your mother is going to be there supportive and looking after you and being affirming, but you are virtually all alone."[2] Father Reyes said that some Anglo parishioners refused to shake his hand, which was "a painful experience."[3] To this day there are priests in the diocese who are still angry with him because of his activism. Father Ruiz said, "Here was an institution that we trusted, but which at the same time kept us down like second-class citizens. Perhaps if I had known how personally painful all this was going to be, I would have been more conservative."[4]

While few acknowledged this, all PADRES members, like all activist priests, faced the possibility of dismissal from the priesthood or forced relocation to some undesirable location that would inhibit their activism. This weighed heavily on the minds of some. Father Gallegos, who claims to have seen several Chicano priests forced out because of their activism, had this to say: "I was always concerned. I just wanted to be a priest, and they could take you out, man."[5]

PADRES members also faced risks outside the church because of their participation in various urban Mexican American communities and in farmworker movement activities. The risks both inside and outside the church were so great that, according to Father Gallegos, PADRES followed a policy whereby he and Father Casso, the two media specialists, were protected. They played discreet roles during protests and never signed their names to press releases and newsletters. This was seen as necessary because they were vital to the organization.

RESIGNATIONS

At least five of those who founded PADRES resigned from the priesthood. In the early seventies, these included Ralph Ruiz and Henry Casso, both of the San Antonio archdiocese; and Vincent Soriano and Alberto Carrillo, both of whom were Redemptorists. Significantly, these men were among the fiercest confrontationalists. Roberto Flores, a Franciscan, resigned in 1986.

Like all priests who resign, each of these men had a unique and complex reason for leaving. Alberto Carrillo, who was heavily involved in the movement against the racist educational system in Tucson, resigned soon after his famous speech on institutional racism at the PADRES National Congress in Los Angeles in October 1971. After the congress, he was told in no uncertain terms that he had angered many powerful people in the church and would not be able to function as a priest in California and several other states. Carrillo understood life as a priest would be made very difficult, so he left. He explained that he became extremely frustrated because change was not coming fast enough. Also, he decided that he could do more for the Mexican American people outside the church. Soon after, he married, and eventually he had two children. He has spent his post-PADRES years as an administrator and educator at the college level in Whittier, California. Over the years, he has taught Chicano studies to more than ten thousand Mexican American children. He and his wife, who is also a teacher, have been active for years in local politics.

Ralph Ruiz also resigned soon after the Los Angeles congress, but he gives a much more eclectic reason:

It wasn't that I was burned out or overworked. There is an identity that gives us purpose and a purpose that gives us meaning. When one's identity becomes muddled and the purpose becomes tainted, then you wonder about the meaning. When you begin to lose meaning, then you begin to wonder about your vocation. I began to look at my priesthood and to ask myself, What is this? Is this a plus or a minus? Questioning my place within the priesthood was not a result of overwork but a feeling of being alone after experiencing the cold shoulder of the power structure of the church. These are the kinds of mental gymnastics I went through at that time. I finally said to myself, Maybe my time is up.[6]

Ruiz's transition from priesthood to civilian life was difficult. For four months after he resigned he worked at a McDonald's in Washington, D.C. He said: "It was very difficult to go from being a priest to not being a priest, from being a general of PADRES to making hamburgers at McDonald's. Not even making them, just serving them. Hiding away from society, trying to get my gears going again. That transition was difficult. But, boy, I ate during those four months."[7] Ruiz has spent his post-PADRES life helping others. After his stint at McDonald's, he worked as an administrator in Washington, D.C. He married and in time became the father of three children. He worked as a union organizer in El Paso between 1974 and 1982 and then became a mission director for the Lutheran church.

Technically, Henry Casso did not resign from the priesthood. He simply left. In 1970, while still a priest, he joined the staff of the Mexican American Legal Defense Fund in California and began working on bilingual education policy. During this time, he received a Ford Foundation fellowship for doctoral studies, which he accepted. Soon after, he began his studies at the University of Massachusetts in Amherst. Casso explained what happened next: "In the meanwhile, I decided to get married, and the reason I decided to get married is that no one cared. I was involved in all this heavy stuff and no one really cared. So I guess instead of getting angry, I decided to get married. I got married in Los Angeles and decided to bring my wife to Amherst and there our first child was born." On graduation, he accepted a top position with the National Task Force de la Raza in New Mexico. Soon after, his wife gave birth to their second child. When asked about his relationship with the archdiocese of San Antonio during this period of his life, Casso responded: "Never even worried about it. And nobody ever said anything to me. . . . I just left."[8] Casso remained in New Mexico, where he successfully produced a weekly television program on an ABC affiliate on high-technology career preparedness. The program ran for twenty-five years. In addition, Casso founded Project Uplift, an organization that trains the state's young people for careers in high technology. In 2001 Casso was helping the government of Costa Rica to develop a national high-technology training program based on his New Mexico model. In addition, he is conducting research on the influence of the Catholic church and Our Lady of Guadalupe on the social development of the southwestern United States.

Roberto Flores explained his decision to leave the priesthood as follows:

> It was a process. I had left for a full year, I guess it was 1979 or 1980. I was exhausted. I was burned out. I had to take time off. I went and did some studying and reflecting, thinking whether I should leave, but I wasn't ready and I felt that the work that I had to do was pulling me too strongly. And then I finally said, you know, all this work and no progress. And no [progressive Mexican American] bishops and no more [Mexican American] vocations; we were seeing very few. And we didn't know whether there were just no vocations or if the vocations that were coming were being discouraged, which we suspected was happening. Well, I decided I better do something else.[9]

Flores currently works as a teacher and counselor for students with disabilities at San Antonio College in Texas.

Little is known about the post-priesthood path taken by Soriano, and I was not able to interview him.

THE END OF PADRES

In 1976 *Today's Catholic* interviewed PADRES' outgoing executive director, Fr. Juan Romero, and incoming executive director, Fr. Manuel Martínez. Both were firm in their belief that PADRES "must remain a movement, not an organization per se, if it is to continue to be an effective voice for Hispanics—and Hispanic leadership—in this country. And it must remain a people-oriented, grassroots movement to fulfill its goals."[10] This sentiment was repeated in a PADRES memorandum addressed to all PADRES members in September of that year that defined PADRES as a "*'movimiento'* . . . characterized by its cry for social justice" whose members have "maintained a constant struggle to be a visible and prophetic sign in the life of the Church and the advancement of the Hispanic community."[11] But by the early 1980s PADRES had taken on a more conservative tone; by the mid-1980s it was less active.[12] PADRES stopped meeting in 1989, although legally it still exists.[13] At that time, many PADRES members joined a newly formed clerical group composed primarily of foreign-born Latinos. The new group, Sacerdotes Hispanos, an umbrella group of Asociación Sacerdotes Hispanos of Miami and New York, functioned mainly as a fraternal support group for Spanish-speaking priests.[14] Sacerdotes Hispanos later changed its name to Asociación Nacional de Sacerdotes Hispanos (ANSH). Other PADRES members went their own way and became involved in various community-based efforts.

Explaining the Demise of PADRES

In the beginning, PADRES functioned outside formal church bureaucracy and therefore enjoyed a considerable degree of autonomy from the hierarchy. It could therefore act as advisor to the hierarchy and, through this advisory role, exert influence and advance its agenda within the church. By 1979, this advisory role was in the hands of the Secretariat for Hispanic Affairs, which PADRES helped create. But the Secretariat could not function as PADRES' arm of influence or advance the group's agenda because, as Father Romero writes, "One of the Secretariat's limitations is that it is, by definition, part of the institutional structure. Its members are employees of the bishops, and would therefore find it difficult to provide much real challenge to them."[15] This was one factor that contributed to the demise of PADRES. Another was PADRES' decision to give the chairmanship to Bishop Patrick Flores.

In 1972, soon after Fr. Flores became a bishop, he was made national chair of PADRES. Many thought PADRES would now have meaningful representation in the hierarchy. But in time they became disillusioned. At the PADRES National Congress in Los Angeles, Father Ruiz approached newly appointed Bishop Flores and asked him to be chairman of PADRES.

> He said, "I'll tell you tomorrow. Let me think about it." I think I knew what he was going to do—call Archbishop Furey, who was his boss, and ask for permission. Pat accepted the chairmanship. Our thinking was that if Pat becomes chair of PADRES, then PADRES would have

representation within the Council of Bishops. Now, you can see how naïve I was. How idealistic I was. Pat no longer belonged to PADRES. He had become part of the structural dragon. I am sure that in his heart and in his mind, Pat was a PADRES supporter. But little by little the inevitable happened. PADRES became more and more controlled by the structure. We trusted that by having one of our own within the structure, things would be better. But we shouldn't have been so naïve. The reality is that when you are swallowed up by the Church structure, you become part of it. . . . PADRES should have remained outside the structure because by becoming part of it, the structure began to control PADRES. Looking back, the one good thing about PADRES at the outset was that the Church did not control us because we were outside the structure as opposed to a committee of the Church or a department. It was a movement outside the structure. And PADRES was able to put pressure. And it would have grown, but what happened to us was that we became part of the structure. That was the end of PADRES.[16]

Ruiz, at the time working as a union organizer, recalled attending a PADRES conference in El Paso in the early 1980s:

I sat there throughout the proceedings, during which the members were trying to pass a resolution. A priest who was an assistant to Archbishop Patrick Flores got up and with much authority he warned the participants to vote down the resolution because it would not sit well with the archbishop. He must have been ordained four or five years. Yet he got up and spoke with the authority of the bishop. What was sad was that everybody just crumbled down. Hell, when I saw that, I knew that was the end of PADRES. In my time, if a cardinal had gotten up to speak in that manner we would have told him to go to hell. We were tired of top-down dictum. Figuratively speaking, PADRES was swallowed up by the dragon and it became part of the dragon.[17]

Trinidad Sánchez, who was a Jesuit brother and Executive Director of PADRES from 1978 to 1981 but who has since left the Jesuit community, said:

As Executive Director of PADRES the Hispanic seminarians [at Assumption Seminary in San Antonio] asked for our help, the PADRES organization, in organizing to have a Chicano director of the Seminary. I did so and of course we were organizing against Bishop Patrick Flores. After correspondence had been sent to Bishop Flores, the Reverend

David García, who was Flores's secretary at the time and a PADRES member, let me know in no uncertain terms that that was not what PADRES was about. That it was okay to be critical of Anglo bishops but not our own. That left a bad taste in my mouth.[18]

The election of Bishop Flores to the position of PADRES national chair was part of a gradual change in leadership. As mentioned, the group's leadership was dominated by the confrontational shock troops in the early years. They were slowly replaced by the conservative institutional guys. Leaders of a social movement organization are largely responsible for its overall character. Rex Hopper classifies leader types according to their prominence at certain stages in the development of movements.[19] In order, these types are agitator, prophet and reformer, statesman, and administrator-executive. The implication for PADRES is that the more conservative "institutional types"—Hopper's statesman or administrator-executive—were better suited and more willing to work within the system than the confrontational "shock troops"—Hopper's agitators. The institutional types may have inadvertently functioned as builders and facilitators of bureaucratic bridges between PADRES and formal church structures. "Bureaucratic bridge" refers to the connections PADRES established with the church hierarchy in the United States through Bishop Flores and the establishment of the Hispanic Secretariat. Through the reproduction of these bureaucratic bridges, PADRES gradually became more a part of the structure and thus lost much of its initial freedom to be critical of the church and carry out progressive actions.

PADRES' leadership change may have facilitated the co-optation of the group. Co-optation happens when the elites channel the energies and anger of the aggrieved insurgents into more legitimate and less disruptive forms of behavior.[20] The insurgent rabble are often encouraged to engage in dialogues with the elites, and insurgent leaders are often offered personal incentives, such as jobs, for their cooperation. In my research, PADRES leaders were not asked if they were ever offered special incentives to tone down their criticism. But there is reason to speculate that PADRES leaders were encouraged to and in fact did channel their anger and effort into legitimate church bureaucratic procedures, which may have had the effect of calming the movement. There are two facts that support this speculation. First, in letters between Cardinal Archbishop Bernardin, then secretary general of the USCC, and several other bishops, there was a stated desire to take the necessary steps to force PADRES to deal with the legitimate channels of grievances within the church. This is significant because it suggests intentionality on the part of the elites. Presumably, this meant that PADRES would lobby specific bishops' committees and maybe their demands would be forwarded to a higher authority, and so on. Second, after the "institutional guys" took over, PADRES's approach of working within the church system could have had the effect of pacification if in fact their energies were focused more on dealing with bureaucratic procedures and less on maintaining PADRES as a social movement. So perhaps it can be said that if there was co-optation of PADRES, it was partly the result of the efforts of the U.S. Catholic hierarchy and the approach to change taken by PADRES leaders.

LOSS OF CLEAR GOALS AND IDEOLOGY

When one or more forces that maintain the life of a social movement decline, so does the social movement. Among these forces are movement goals and movement ideology.[21] A goal is a clearly defined objective such as increasing the number of Chicano bishops. Ideology refers to a set of value-laden beliefs, such as "We believe that Latina/o Catholics should have meaningful decision-making power at the highest levels of the church." They are important in the life of a social movement because they act as its internal guidance. They answer the questions, "What do we believe and what are we trying to accomplish and why?"[22] In addition, they are used to enable solidarity and tenacity within the movement. They do so by helping to focus social unrest and activate "latent discontent by identifying a problem in terms that are meaningful and resonant for potential constituencies."[23] As a crucial point, "without a clear focus, individual discontent and social unrest continually shift from object to object so that energies are dissipated without altering the troublesome conditions."[24]

In the beginning, PADRES possessed a clear set of goals and a strong, coherent ideology. But in time, they declined as a result of two main developments. First, with the election of several Chicano bishops, the success of the National Encuentros, the establishment of MACC, and the success of the MTM, it can be argued that the hierarchy effectively took away enough of PADRES' key demands that it sapped the group of a clear set of goals.[25]

The second development deals with the issue of membership. When PADRES was first formed, the founders instituted a rule that only Chicano priests could be full voting members. And in the early years, most Chicano PADRES members agreed with the concept of open membership in principle and felt that such a thing would happen eventually. But they felt that the time was not right; it was most important first to speak to the bishops on behalf of Mexican American Catholics with a united voice. Also, Chicano-only membership, which brought together priests with similar ideologies from similar ethnic backgrounds, had the immediate consequence of facilitating the establishment of group identity, ideology, and clear goals. The result was a very focused, unified group that was very effective. This functioned as an added justification for exclusion and perhaps an incentive to maintain the policy.

The seemingly ever-present tension that existed within the organization in subsequent years reflected a battle between these practical members and the idealists who wanted to see the principle of open membership realized. At the Los Angeles congress of PADRES in October 1972 the bylaws were amended so that membership was open to Mexican American deacons. At this congress, like several times before, a move to open full membership to all priests working with Mexican Americans failed. In 1974 on a vote of 30 for, 9 against, and 1 abstention, membership was opened to all Latino priests, deacons, and religious brothers.[26] This move brought in several Puerto Rican American priests from the Northeast. Finally, in May 1981, at the PADRES National Congress in El Paso, the group voted to extend full membership to all priests, deacons, and religious brothers who minister to Latinos.[27] This infused the group with a greater variety of voices, which may have made the maintenance of a clear ideology difficult if not impossible.[28]

With several key goals seemingly accomplished, the PADRES movement lacked a clear answer to the question, What are we trying to accomplish? And without a common ideology, PADRES lacked a clear answer to the question, How do we accomplish it? These losses caused critical damage to PADRES' internal structure and contributed to its demise.

It should be noted that, while the national ideological climate was becoming increasingly conservative, Latino Catholicism was undergoing a similar shift. According to Stevens-Arroyo, between 1972 and 1977, battles were fought between Latino Catholics from two ideological camps—the pastoralists and the liberationists.[29] The pastoralists (analogous to the institutional guys) were the political moderates who emphasized institutional reform and the inclusion of Latino Catholics within Church structures. The liberationists (analogous to the shock troops) were more the hard-edged social-action types who felt the Church needed to be directly involved in social action at the grassroots level and within political organizations.

Of the two camps, the pastoralists had more success infiltrating Church structures and occupying positions of authority. They would eventually gain control of Latino Church structures. But they found it "increasingly difficult to maintain unity with the goals of the liberationists."[30] The two camps more and more were at odds. As the years progressed, ideological differences between them became quite pronounced and the liberationists were marginalized, gradually losing their influence on the national Church.[31]

Eventually, this marginalization of the liberationists extended to PADRES.[32] This was illustrated in 1977 when Fr. Roberto Peña, who was PADRES' national president at the time, tried to "issue a document holding the Latino bishops accountable to the goals of liberation," but the measure was opposed by the pastoralists on the grounds that it would "weaken the standing of Latino bishops before the Euro-American episcopacy."[33] Father Peña countered by arguing that, if such a measure were not carried out, "the Latino bishops would forfeit their base of support with the people and liberationist clergy in the parishes."[34] But Father Peña's argument failed.

CONCLUSION

For more than one hundred years, the U.S. Catholic Church had abused and neglected Mexican American Catholics. In 1969 a few dozen daring and courageous Mexican American priests had had enough. Hungry for justice, they called themselves "Chicanos" and began an insurgent movement in the U.S. Catholic Church on behalf of their ethnic kin. With its angry condemnation of the church and demands for change, PADRES was one of the nonsecular arms of the Chicano movement and a much-needed voice for the largely voiceless Mexican Americans. The emergence of PADRES, as well as Las Hermanas, was a damning indictment of the sins of the U.S. Catholic Church against its Mexican American members.

The birth of PADRES was of enormous significance. It marked the creation of the first national organization of Mexican American priests and the first time that a group of priests of any ethnicity organized nationally as a sustained movement in defense of Mexican American Catholics against both the Catholic Church and American society. Further, although more research is needed, it very well may have marked the start of the first national civil rights movement against the U.S. Catholic Church waged by priests in defense of their ethnic kin. Thus PADRES is a chapter of major importance in the history of both the church in the United States and Mexican Americans.

While the PADRES movement won many victories, it never realized its vision, at least not in terms of its original form. Today, the church can hardly be considered a space where Mexican American Catholics are respected. And it is not a tool for progressive social action. This conclusion is based on my observations and conversations with many Mexican American lay Catholics and PADRES founders. It can be tested by simply asking the right questions. For instance, to what extent does the church continue to reproduce the acquiescence and other forms of oppression among Mexican American Catholics that PADRES fought so hard to eradicate? Is the pain and isolation that PADRES founders felt in the 1960s being felt by Mexican American priests today? Do Catholic high schools with a high enrollment of Mexican American students offer Chicana/o studies courses?[35] And do these high schools discourage or encourage the formation of Chicana/o student organizations?[36] Do seminaries offer Chicana/o and Latina/o studies courses? To what extent have the progressive successes of PADRES been co-opted by the church? And how far have they strayed from PADRES' original vision?

More distressing, the lack of representation PADRES fought against still persists today. It is instructive to examine how African American Catholics enjoy relatively greater representation in the U.S. Catholic Church than do Latino-American Catholics. Of the approximately 62 million Catholics in the United States, approximately 50 percent are Latino-American (a conservative estimate), and 3 percent are African American.[37] Among 287 active U.S. bishops,[38] 25, or 8 percent, are Latino-American, and 13, or 4 percent, are African American.[39] Among 46,400 priests, 500, or 1 percent, are native-born Latino-American; and 300, or less than 1 percent, are African American.[40] Fr. Roberto Flores lamented, "Certainly we did not create more Chicano clergy, we did not create Chicano bishops in proportionate numbers. I don't think we're being served any better as a people than we were then. I don't think money is being poured in any more than it was then."[41] Similarly, Fr. Ralph Ruiz said: "I was naive. I think we all were. To think that we could radically change the church and make it more responsive to the social injustices afflicting the Chicano was an act of faith and hope, but naive nevertheless."[42]

Despite these shortcomings, PADRES must be given credit for trying to change the U.S. Catholic Church like never before for the benefit of their ethnic kin. Thus PADRES is a testament to human compassion and courage and an example of people's willingness to strive for basic human dignity for others despite impressive odds. The passion, vision, and hell-raising of PADRES and the still-active Las Hermanas offer many lessons on how to change the church from within. A thoughtful inquiry can unlock these lessons for a much-needed second wave.

SEVEN

THEORY AND ANALYSIS
The Emergence of PADRES

†

How and under what conditions did PADRES emerge? To answer this question, we must understand that PADRES was an intraorganizational social movement—that is, organized, sustained, collective action that sought to make meaningful changes to the social relations (e.g., laws, policies, and cultural practices) within a large organization having institutional status. The defining characteristic of this type of movement is that those who lead it are formal members of the organization and those for whom they struggle are the organization's clientele. One famous example is the Latin American liberation theology movement. During the late 1960s and early 1970s, several thousand leftist church insiders—bishops, priests, and nuns—began a movement within the Latin American church to transform it from a tool for the wealthy minority into a tool for advancing the welfare of the poor majority. Smith analyzed this movement by using the political process model, which previously had been used to analyze the black civil rights movement.[1] Despite the obvious differences, Smith proved that the political process model could be applied to such intraorganizational social movements.

In the years since it was proposed the political process model has been criticized, but some of its principles continue to play a prominent role in social movement theory.[2] One of these principles suggests that for social movements to emerge, the aggrieved must possess an action-oriented or insurgent state of being that increases the likelihood that collective action will happen. In what follows, I describe how this state of being was articulated in the emergence of PADRES among founding members based primarily on oral histories. These oral testimonies are supplemented by archival material from the first few years of PADRES' life.

PADRES' INSURGENT STATE OF BEING

The insurgent state of being as articulated in the PADRES case comprises several elements. The first involves the thinking of the founders. They were thinking that Mexican American Catholics were being treated unjustly by the church. This unjust treatment was neither isolated nor accidental but systematic. The nature of the causes of this treatment was structural and thus socially constructed. This is significant. If they had thought that the treatment was an unfortunate act of nature or God's will, then there would have been nothing they could have done aside from praying for things to get better. Further, they felt that the structures themselves, since they were causing the injustice, were wrong and had to be changed and that they were the ones who could change them. Thus PADRES founders justified their resistance.

The founders' views and ultimate judgments were based on two tacit frameworks. One was a normative framework, which can be understood as a set of principles that spelled out how the church should be treating Mexican American Catholics and what it should be doing for them. It was their conception of an ideal church. Briefly, these principles were as follows. The church should respect Mexican-American culture and make it an accepted part of church practices. The church should use its liturgy to uplift, not subjugate, Mexican Americans. The church should educate them to think critically about society rather than be gullible and fatalistic. The church should use its full strength to take care of their pressing social needs—education, labor, and civil rights—not with pious sermons but with substantive action such as organizing and leadership training among the poor and working class. This ideal church was based on the notion that it should treat Mexican American Catholics holistically, as both spiritual and material beings. This normative framework functioned as a standard with which PADRES judged the church's actual treatment of its Mexican American members, thus making it easy for them to identify the church's faults and suggest an alternative toward which to strive.

The second framework was analytical. This was a set of simple questions: who gets what, when, how, and why? These questions were used to analyze the church and secular institutions such as schools, local government, government agencies, and corporations. These institutions were analyzed in terms of their impact on the lives of Mexican American Catholics and how they related to one another. Thus it was determined that secular institutions were treating Mexican American Catholics unjustly. The church was likewise guilty, but it inadvertently went further: by holding back the Mexican American Catholics' social development, it reinforced secular oppression. The PADRES founders concluded that this web of institutional oppression stemmed from the fact that Mexican American Catholics lacked power in both church and society. The remedy was simple: they, PADRES founders, had to develop this power, and they believed they could.

The second element of this insurgent state of being is what PADRES founders were feeling. These were not men who simply philosophized about injustice. On the contrary, they did so with a "hot cognition"—one laden with emotion. These priests had fire in their bellies; they possessed a great sense of urgency and righteous anger over the injustices committed by the church against Mexican American Catholics, a people for whom they felt deep sympathy and love. These intense feelings facilitated the formation of PADRES by giving the founders the emotional motivation to act collectively. Crucially, they possessed a good deal of hope that they could change the mammoth church through collective action. If they had felt the situation was hopeless, it is unlikely they would have taken the initiative and organized PADRES. After all, who among PADRES founders would have wanted to do serious battle with the church knowing there was no possibility of winning? The answer is, no one.

The third element of this insurgent state of being is collective identity. The conception of collective identity associated with social movements is often framed in terms of some "we" in opposition to some "they" who have different values and agendas.[3] This identity can help movement participants to define themselves as members of the movement, can create a feeling of shared risk among them, and can be the basis for group solidarity. In addition, it can help movement participants to focus their energies on an oppositional target—some "they"—if the target is clearly defined. Thus it can facilitate social movement emergence and activities. This identity was definitely associated with the emergence of PADRES. Founders had a sense of "we"—Mexican American priests who were tired of church injustices—and this helped them to see themselves as members of a collectivity. This "we-ness" created a feeling of shared risk among them in the sense that it helped them feel as though they were not alone. They had a clearly defined "they"—specific structures of the U.S. Catholic Church. In these ways, a "we/they"-based collective identity was present and functioned as a vehicle for mobilization.

But this collective identity was not the only one in operation. There were two others, both constructed around founders' social locations as priests and as Mexican Americans. These constructions were based on commonly held meanings founders assigned to these social locations. For them, being a priest meant that you took care of both the spiritual and material conditions of the people you served; and if the material conditions in which the people live are unjust, then a priest should actively fight against the injustice. Their activism on behalf of Mexican American Catholics was therefore a logical extension of this activist priest identity.

As Mexican Americans, PADRES founders shared ethnic kinship with Mexican American Catholics. In addition, the founders possessed a distinct ethnic consciousness that facilitated a bond between them and Mexican American Catholics. This ethnic consciousness was noticed in the way founding members identified as "Chicano" and adopted the philosophy of Chicanismo. In doing so, they embraced a politically activist stance and strongly identified with the ideas of self-determination, ethnic solidarity, and the fight against cultural whitewashing and embraced their indigenous roots. In addition, they identified with Chicanismo's emphasis on activism and allegiance with the poor and working class. These commonly held meanings assigned to their position as priest and to their ethnic kinship relationship with Mexican American Catholics translated into binding solidarity among and between founders, built binding solidarity between founders and Mexican American Catholics, and motivated founders' decision to start PADRES and work together to change things.

How did PADRES priests negotiate their multiple identities, activist priest and Chicano? Some suggest that multiple identities are negotiated through a process by which people assign priority to their identities or choose a specific identity depending on the situation.[4] The latter has been written about quite eloquently by Chela Sandoval. Sandoval investigates the negotiation of multiple oppositional ideologies (MOIs) among women of color and other oppressed peoples.[5] She suggests that MOIs can facilitate opposition to the dominant structure if actors perform an activity whereby they weave between and among oppositional ideologies.[6] This is a process that "operates like the clutch of an automobile: the mechanism that permits the driver to select, engage and disengage gears in a system for the transmission of power . . . [and it] depends upon the ability to read the current situation of power and of self-consciously choosing and adopting the ideological form best suited to push against its configurations, a survival skill well known to oppressed peoples."[7]

I want to suggest that the negotiation between the identities of activist priest and Chicano was unlike Sandoval's model where identities are strategically and self-consciously chosen. In fact, there was no need to make such choices because these identities were consistent and mutually enhancing. For being an activist priest and Chicano meant that they felt it was their special duty to become personally involved in progressive social struggle; and it meant that they felt solidarity with the Chicano poor and working class. The negotiation was therefore a fusion of two dominant, mutually supportive identities nurtured by their hands-on involvement in Chicano communities and through interaction with other Chicano priests. As Fr. Juan Romero remarked, "There was no problem because we were Chicano priests, that's why. As integrated human beings it was part of our mission, part of being good priests, part of being in solidarity with the people that we were serving. These were our people. Mexicanos or Chicanos."[8]

These identities were not completely free from tension with competing identities. Activist priests were not in the majority in the church, and they were commonly at odds with priests and bishops who did not share their activist vision. Also, many were opposed by conservative Mexican American and white laity who viewed Chicanismo negatively. But these conflicts were resolved through a process of group nurturing.

Analysis of the Development
of PADRES' Insurgent State of Being

The insurgent state of being among founders did not happen overnight. Rather, it took years to develop; and it did so through a complex process. We can understand a lot about this process by looking at founders' common direct experiences during the period of formation—the 1950s, the decade in which most began seminary training; the 1960s, the decade in which most were ordained and began active ministry; and the very early 1970s, the years immediately following PADRES' official birth—and identifying patterns in the relationship between these experiences and the thoughts, feelings, emotions, and identities that were associated with them. From these patterns, we can suggest possible connections. In what follows, I review these experiences and suggest their possible connections to the components of the insurgent state of being. Moreover, I allow the history makers themselves to tell me if this or that experience influenced their thoughts, emotions, and actions—the components of their insurgent state of being—and I identify patterns in their responses. This will guard against, or at least help to reduce, the risk of what McAdam calls "structural conceit."[9] As I understand it, structural conceit refers to assuming that certain structural forces must have influenced the development of the components of an insurgent state of being. With oral testimonies and archival material, I do not have to assume.

Inside the church, founders had many bitter experiences. As seminarians, they faced cultural denigration and bigotry. As young priests, they faced more cultural denigration and bigotry and even job discrimination in terms of failure to receive promotions. But some of their experiences were inspiring. Vatican II filled them with optimism about the prospects for change within the church. Social justice teachings in the seminary helped them to set the foundation for an action-oriented conception of both the church and their priesthoods. As young priests, founders witnessed the church's cultural denigration and second-class treatment of Mexican American Catholics. Among founders, this caused a great deal of pain, anger, and frustration because, being victims themselves of cultural denigration and second-class treatment, they understood. In addition, it was their culture that was being denigrated and their ethnic kin who were enduring second-class treatment in front of their eyes. Thus righteous anger and activist mind-sets began to develop among founders.

Outside the church, founders spent much of their time working directly with their ethnic kin in poor and working-class barrios. While doing so, they became reacquainted with their culture and the Spanish language. This helped them to build a sense of unity between themselves and their people, and these common traits provided a foundation on which this unity was maintained. This unity became stronger with the founders' adoption of Chicanismo, which stressed ethnic pride and unity. Founders began to engage directly in grassroots struggles with their people on a daily basis. They became increasingly sensitive to and more able to identify with their people's plight. Further, this contact enhanced the development of the founders' sense of ethnic identification and unity as well as an activist mind-set, a mind-set that was strengthened by Chicanismo's emphasis on social justice activism and ethnic self-determination. The church for the most part was silent while these social struggles were going on. Founders noticed this. As a result, their righteous anger intensified. Meanwhile, activist role models, who were highly visible on a national scale, motivated founders to act boldly through the examples they set. And the Black Power movement led the founders to think about "brown power" and taking matters into one's own hands for the advancement of one's own people.

Founders were working independently of one another throughout the early and mid-1960s. But in the late 1960s, they started meeting in safe spaces that they created for themselves, free from the bishops and their cronies, in which they could speak freely and openly about the church. They started talking about their experiences and collectively making sense of them. They realized that the horrible things they were seeing and experiencing were not isolated but churchwide. They realized these problems were structural and had to be fixed. A we/they collective identity developed. Emotions ran high. The urgent feeling that something needed to be done, namely collective action, emerged. Meanwhile, through interaction on shared attributes such as language, culture, and political beliefs, they validated one another's normative conceptions of church and priesthood as well as one another's identities of activist priest and Chicano, making these conceptions and identities stronger and collectively held. Solidarity developed based on these shared attributes, which gave them a sense of shared risk and helped them to deal with their frustration and pain. Inspired now by each other, as well as by activist role models and the Black Power movement, they decided to act collectively. PADRES emerged. The more they met, the stronger their insurgent state of being became, and thus the more they agitated for change within the church.

FRAMEWORK UNDERLYING THE ANALYSIS OF INSURGENT STATE OF BEING

To analyze the development of the insurgent state of being in the PADRES case, I constructed a special framework, which is illustrated below. This framework is not meant as a general theory of intraorganizational social movements of PADRES' character. Certainly, a general theory cannot be built on a single case study with any appreciable degree of confidence. Rather, it is meant as a framework that helped me to analyze a specific case—the emergence of PADRES in terms of the ideational variable of social movements.

First, there are two interdependent realms that should be apparent— within the organization and outside the organization in the day-to-day lives of oppressed clientele. Thus the open organization approach seems to be appropriate. Put simply, the open organization approach views organizations as systems constituted by continuing exchanges between the environments in which they operate.[10] This implies that the practices inside the organization are influenced by the practices outside the organization and vice versa.

The insurgency that occurs within the organization is brought to pass in part by the change-minded organizational members who have experiences both inside the organization and outside the organization in the lives of the oppressed. We can think of these organizational members as dynamic mobile nodal points that act like channels through which intra- and extraorganizational experiences intersect in such a way that the possibility for resistance increases, even among those at the bottom of the power scale. Inside the organization, these change-minded organizational members have direct day-to-day contact with formal organizational practices, for example, training, day-to-day bureaucracy, and providing service to clientele. Outside the organization, they have direct, day-to-day contact with the practices of oppressed clientele, for example, their struggles with racism, discrimination, and poverty. They see the organization either not helping or in certain ways contributing to this oppression. And through various forms of media, they digest images of broad social events happening nationally and globally.

These experiences are translated into the components of the insurgent state of being among change-minded organizational actors within a third realm—small informal groups or "safe spaces" in which hard-edged, honest, and insightful criticism of the organization can take place in relative security. Within these spaces, change-minded organizational actors discuss and collectively make sense of their experiences in the other two dimensions and during the process develop their thoughts, feelings, emotions, identities—their insurgent states of being. Those who already possess these thoughts, feelings, emotions, and identities have these things magnified during the process. Crucially, during this process, they become aware of the organization's true role in this oppression. This is a necessary condition for social movement emergence because, as Weber argues, social movement emergence is "linked to the extent of the contrasts that have already evolved, and is especially linked to the transparency of the connections between the causes and the consequences of the . . . situation."[11] This serves the function of giving them a specific target for their collective efforts. This process within these small groups is similar to what happened during the emergence of Latin American liberation theology. The necessary consciousness among church insiders developed within small groups in which they made sense of their experiences inside and outside the church.[12] As Turner and Killian argue, "According to common sense, social movements result from grassroots collaboration," when "like-minded people begin urgent discussion of their grievances."[13]

Collective sense-making happens through interpersonal interaction and discussion. Through interpersonal interaction, a sense of group solidarity, accomplishment, and belonging develop which provide motivation for actors to make individual sacrifices to achieve collective goods. This is similar to the political process model's variable called "organizational strength."[14] Discussion, according to Turner and Killian, serves to "forge bonds that enable the discontented to work together as a dynamic unit."[15]

In analyzing the dynamics of social movement participation, Peter S. Bearman and Hyojoung Kim suggest that collective identity and solidarity among activists, which develops through commonalities among them, maintains and enhances their commitment against opposition.[16] Similarly, I argue that through interaction around commonalities among change-minded organizational actors, collective identity and solidarity among them develop, which in turn maintains and enhances their commitment against opposition. One of these commonalities is shared beliefs. Another is ethnic kinship. This, of course, is not always the case, but it does, I argue, increase the likelihood of such things happening by bringing into the relationship shared history, language, culture, and so on; and it is the interaction around these shared characteristics that empathy, solidarity, identity, and so on, can develop and become strong. And it seems that founding PADRES members had a great deal of this type of interaction both outside the church and within the small groups they created. This process is thematically similar to what some have called "cultural crystallization."[17] Stevens-Arroyo suggests that PADRES was made possible by this process.[18] But he does not substantiate his opinion with hard data; he relies on compelling historical narrative, but it lacks explanation and is too structural. This oral history project provides that substantiation and strengthens his opinion, with which I agree.

What if the change-minded organizational actors, in addition to sharing ethnic kinship with each other, share ethnic kinship with the oppressed? This can further enhance actors' commitment against opposition by facilitating the creation and reproduction of bonds—of solidarity, sympathy, mutual aid, support, and understanding—between themselves and the oppressed. This happens through interaction between change-minded organizational actors and the oppressed around commonly held ethnic kinship traits. And if the actors possess an ethnonationalistic ideology, the kind that emphasizes ethnic solidarity and support, these bonds can be even stronger, thus enhancing the actors' commitment even more.

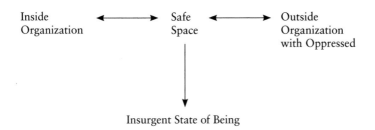

Insurgent State of Being

We can imagine the components that comprise the insurgent state of being as by-products of the practices of change-minded organizational actors that occur over time within an underlying terrain, a sublayer comprising three interdependent dimensions: inside the church, outside the church within the domain of the organization's oppressed clientele, and a safe space between the other two (see the figure above).

The components of the insurgent state of being can be clearly articulated, but they are always changing and always dependent for their reproduction on the practices of change-minded organizational actors within the three dimensions. Their development is not inevitable but contingent. Together, they represent a necessary sociopsychological variable for the emergence of intraorganizational social movements that seek to transform the organization for the benefit of oppressed clientele.

ORGANIZATIONAL ISSUES

✝

PADRES incorporated in April 1970, filing in Washington, D.C., to give the group national appeal in the eyes of the NCCB, which was also located there. It was structured vertically: board, national chairman, executive director, field director, regional directors, and local directors. Throughout its life, PADRES held annual national meetings with alternating emphases. One year the meeting would focus on action and strategic planning, the next year, on assessing the organization's successes and shortcomings. Always, valuable information was exchanged. Father Carrillo talked about the meetings: "When we got together we would ask each other, how did you handle this one? What did you do? I'd get a call: how did you gain the support of the Department of Health, Education and Welfare? Or I'd call someone: how did you guys handle the Safeway boycott? What do you do? And so we were helping one another because we were all doing the same things."[1]

By October 1971 PADRES had organized itself nationally into seven regions, each managed by a regional director. The national office was housed in three locations in San Antonio between 1969 and 1974. The fourth location was a small single-family house located across the street from the headquarters of the archdiocese of San Antonio. PADRES moved into the house in April 1975. PADRES Frs. Raúl Luna and Juan Romero converted part of the house into office space. It became known as PADRES House and was made available to PADRES who were traveling and needed a place to stay.

PADRES intended to form a network of action groups throughout the nation that would function as semiautonomous arms of PADRES. Ideally, these groups would be composed of people from all walks of life dedicated to the advancement of Mexican Americans and would be controlled by their own leadership but in coordination with local PADRES members. The action groups would develop their own programs based on the specific needs of Mexican Americans in their area. As of 1971 four action groups were organized, three in Texas and one in New Mexico.

The task of setting up these action groups was given to Fr. Joe López of the Kansas City archdiocese. Father López joined the PADRES staff in July 1970 after Frs. Ruiz and Rodríguez made a request to Archbishop Ignatius J. Strecker to allow Father López to leave the Kansas City archdiocese and work with PADRES full time. The archbishop could have refused, and he had at least one credible reason for doing so. In a letter to PADRES, he wrote that he felt Father López was needed to "serve our Mexican-American peoples within our own Archdiocese." But instead he graciously agreed to "provide Fr. López with our customary priestly pastoral salary of the Archdiocese" in the form of a "check" that "will be sent to him each month." He added that PADRES was a "most deserving apostolate . . . at the national level" that was sincere in its efforts "to further the cause of more than one-fourth of the Catholics of the United States whom at this time constitutes the most dispossessed Catholic minority in our country."[2] Father Ruiz had this to say about Archbishop Strecker's support: "The Archbishop was committed enough to allow Joe to work for PADRES full-time. That in itself demonstrated not only commitment, but also a lot of guts!"[3] Father Rodríguez added: "Bishops don't easily release priests to do work full-time in other dioceses and organizations. Bishop Strecker did release Joe López to work full time with PADRES and was genuinely supportive of PADRES. Strecker had an organization which worked on developing leadership in local churches. He knew that was one of the purposes of PADRES in the Hispanic community."[4]

Father López's title was PADRES national field director and his formal job description included visiting bishops and priests throughout the country to garner support for PADRES and recruit new members, organize PADRES diocesan offices, form action groups, and coordinate workshops. He seems to have worked for PADRES in this capacity at least through 1971. In 1973 he became the first Mexican American vocational director in the history of the San Antonio archdiocese.[5] Regrettably, Father López passed away in March 2001, before I had the opportunity to interview him.

Practically, PADRES' initial success as an organization was attributed to the exceedingly talented and motivated group of Chicano priests who were its founding members. Father Ralph Ruiz was the fiery, charismatic organizer. Fr. Edmundo Rodríguez was the cool-headed thinker and widely considered the intellectual strategist. Fr. Luciano Hendren was a financial wizard. Fr. David Durán was a certified public accountant before he became a priest. Fr. Alberto Carrillo and several others were experienced agitators and fearless confronters willing to take risks. Frs. Albert Gallegos and Henry Casso were writers and savvy media specialists. Father Gallegos had been formally trained in journalism at Northwestern University. All had strong leadership abilities, and all understood the issues and agreed on what needed to be done. In addition, a few dozen others were willing and able to attend meetings and function as foot soldiers.

The original, core group was composed of about 30 Chicano priests, and according to Father Rodríguez, it was "very focused and thus had the strongest impact."[6] As of October 16, 1974, there were 95 dues-paying Chicano members.[7] It is not known exactly how many PADRES members made up the organization during its entire twenty-year existence. Conservative estimates suggest that the number of full and associate dues-paying members hovered at about 80. According to Father Carrillo, during the early 1970s, there were "probably about 50 or 60 members, but . . . [the hierarchy] didn't know whether [there were] 1,000 or 2,000."[8] In 1975 the *Catholic Almanac* reported that PADRES possessed a nationwide membership of 1,113, including 256 Latino priests. In 1977 these numbers changed to 2,000 and 200, respectively. Despite being asked on several occasions, PADRES leadership kept the actual number of members a secret. This security measure was an effort to keep the hierarchy guessing about its real strength. Whether PADRES was successful or not is not known.

In April 1971 PADRES welcomed the formation of Las Hermanas, most of whose founding members were Chicanas. The group as a whole had a strong feminist orientation. According to Lara Medina, the founding of Las Hermanas marked the first time Chicana sisters collectively challenged discrimination in the church.[9] Throughout the years, PADRES and Las Hermanas worked together on a wide variety of projects. Although the relationship was often fraught, it continued until PADRES' demise in 1989. To its credit, Las Hermanas is still active today.

FUNDING

In addition to membership dues, which amounted to little more than $1,000 per year, PADRES received funding from a variety of sources.

A partial list is $500 from the Southwest Council of La Raza in October 1969; a $7,000 grant received on March 20, 1970, from the Inter-Religious Foundation for Community Organization, a Protestant organization, for the Mobile Team Ministry; and a $15,000 grant received on June 3, 1970, from the NCCB to conduct a mobile team feasibility study for 1970. In December 1970 PADRES requested $125,000 from NCCB for the Mobile Team Ministry but was granted only $39,400. On September 20, 1971, PADRES was awarded a $100,000 grant from the Campaign for Human Development (CHD) for development of its programs, especially the Mobile Team Ministry. At this time Father Ruiz and Bishop Patrick Flores sat on the board of the CHD. In 1974 the Jesuits loaned PADRES $5,000, and collections from various U.S. bishops totaled $6,000.[10] Also in 1974 PADRES received $1,000 from CHD to set up workshops for Comunidades de Base, grassroots Christian communities designed to help people organize to solve their social problems. In 1975 PADRES received $10,000 from the American Board of Catholic Missions and $5,000 from the Catholic Church Extension Society of the USA.

It should be noted that during this time PADRES expended more effort soliciting monies from sources other than the Catholic Church. These sources include the Ford Foundation, individuals such as Delores Hope, Bob Hope's wife, who was active in Catholic charities, and numerous Protestant churches in Texas. Solicitation of Protestant churches was aided by Lutheran pastor Jack O'Donnell of the Lutheran Church of America, who was hired by PADRES as a full-time staff member in March 1971 and worked for PADRES for five years as the "Protestant Liaison." Father Ruiz explained the rationale for hiring Reverend O'Donnell: "It was determined that PADRES needed to be more ecumenical because Protestants were increasingly evangelizing Latinos and because it was felt that the top-down efforts toward ecumenism were not moving fast enough. So we needed to determine which denomination is closest to the Catholic Church in terms of theology and liturgy and which denomination has done more for the Catholic Church. It was determined that Lutherans fit the bill."[11] Soon after this decision was made, Father Ruiz met with Bishop Philip Wahlburg, head of the Texas-Louisiana Synod, and explained what PADRES wanted and why. Bishop Wahlburg recommended Reverend O'Donnell, who was hired soon after. It should also be noted that the Lutheran church paid Reverend O'Donnell's salary and pension and covered housing and medical insurance expenses for him and his family. According to Father Ruiz, in addition to Reverend O'Donnell and Father López, during at least the first two years of

PADRES' life, full-time paid staff included Executive Director Fr. Roberto Flores, Secretary Blanca García, a layperson, and Fr. Richard Eustice, who wrote grant applications and organized the newsletter. Father Eustice was ordained in the Brownsville, Texas, diocese under Bishop Madeiros and came to work for PADRES with the bishop's blessing.

All monies received by PADRES were important for maintaining the organization. But some funding sources had special implications. The monies from sources outside the church helped to increase the group's independence from the church. And, as Father Ruiz explained: "[Monies from the USCC] translated into legitimacy in the eyes of the laity and inside the church. So when we went from parish to parish the pastors could see us as more legitimate."[12]

Although PADRES received some funding from the USCC, it was never without a struggle. For instance, in 1970 PADRES requested $125,000 but was granted $39,400. Meanwhile, the Black Caucus requested $650,000 but was granted $150,000. Sensing a double standard, PADRES held a press conference to complain that the bishops showed a lack of concern about the organization's agenda. PADRES also expressed dissatisfaction in its newsletter: "Is PADRES realizing the cliche, 'If you're black, please come back; if you're brown, don't stick around'?"[13]

By 1973 PADRES, Las Hermanas, and the National Office of Black Catholics were actively seeking regular funding commitments from the NCCB, but only the NOBC was successful. The funding came from a national collection. A special Episcopal liaison committee, which had been created to deal with the NOBC, stated in one of its reports to the USCC/NCCB that "the annual collection offers the best possible means of supporting NOBC on a continuous basis thus avoiding a consistent financial crisis that have developed tension over the past few years."[14] This added to the tensions between PADRES and the NCCB that had arisen when the NCCB had refused to set up a special liaison committee for PADRES, even though it had done so for the NOBC. Many PADRES members interpreted this as a double standard. In newsletters, PADRES was openly critical of the NCCB and continued to agitate for a national collection, to which the NCCB responded coldly.[15]

METHODOLOGY

†

I interviewed thirty-one people: nineteen Chicano priests who were PADRES members, a Puerto Rican priest who was a PADRES member, one white priest who was a PADRES associate member, two white priests who were not PADRES members but who recall its formation, one member of Las Hermanas, and seven laypersons who collaborated with PADRES. Since PADRES essentially began as a Chicano priest movement and because my central question deals with its formation, I focused on the original founding Chicano members who actually started PADRES. These founding members include Frs. Ralph Ruiz, Henry Casso, Edmundo Rodríguez, Alberto Carrillo, Albert Gallegos, Lonnie Reyes, Patrick Flores, Manuel Martínez, Vicente López, Roberto Peña, Roberto Flores, and Juan Romero. Ruiz is credited with being the progenitor of PADRES. Fathers Ruiz, Casso, Carrillo, and Roberto Flores, who resigned from the priesthood, were generally more candid about the past than were the active priests. Further, the higher the status within the church of an active priest, the more conservative were his responses.

Leaders were identified by examining the organizational documents. The individuals were then located with the aid of the *U.S. Catholic Directory* and by word-of-mouth. I contacted them and asked them to participate. If a person seemed unsure about participating or said no, I dropped the issue and responded with, "Thank you. Please contact me if you change your mind." This is the policy I use when trying to secure an interview. It reflects the respect I have for people and their stories. With very few exceptions, everyone I asked was happy to talk to me.

I conducted person-to-person interviews with informants in San Antonio, Austin, Las Cruces, Albuquerque, Belem, and the Los Angeles greater metropolitan area. I conducted several follow-up interviews by telephone and e-mail. I conducted one interview with an informant in Denver exclusively by e-mail.

Each priest was asked the same series of questions, but I allowed them flexibility to speak tangentially or talk about the issues they thought were important even if they were not on the list of questions. Without listing them verbatim, questions on this list asked them to reflect on their childhood, their seminary experience, their lives as young Chicano priests, and their involvement with PADRES. They were asked to reflect on what they were thinking, feeling, and experiencing and how they viewed both themselves and Mexican American Catholics during these periods. And they were asked to reflect on the social changes (e.g., Vatican II and the UFW) that influenced their thoughts and feelings and views of themselves and their people during these periods. The interviews lasted about an hour and a half, but I imposed no time limit. The same holds true for the nonpriests I interviewed. Laypersons interviewed were asked general questions about PADRES and their personal involvement with PADRES, and they were asked to confirm the stories of other informants and to share whatever stories they wished, but these informants play a largely peripheral role.

The main archive source is the Archive Department of the Archdiocese of San Antonio, Texas. This department is in possession of several files of PADRES material in addition to more than four hundred pages of PADRES material on microfilm. I obtained personal archive material (papers and documents owned by individual informants) by simply asking for them, then photocopying them at my expense.

NOTES

†

CHAPTER 1

1. See, e.g., Acuña 1988; Gómez-Quiñones 1990; Martínez and Vásquez 1974; Montejano 1999; Muñoz 1989; Navarro 1995, 2000; Rodríguez 1977; Rosales 1996; *Viva la causa* 1995.

2. See "Pope Apologizes for Catholic Sins Past and Present," *Los Angeles Times,* March 13, 2000. See also *Guardian,* Internet ed., March 13, 2000; Associated Press, March 13, 2000; CNN.com, March 13, 2000.

3. Sandoval 1983d, 439.

4. Díaz-Stevens and Stevens-Arroyo 1998.

5. The first book on Las Hermanas, by Lara Medina (2004), is an excellent companion to this book.

CHAPTER 2

1. Mirandé 1985: 135. See also Beal 1994: 30.

2. See Cadena 1987: 53. For support of this claim, see Beal 1994.

3. See Cadena 1987: 59–60. See also Lampe 1994; Sandoval 1983d.

4. Fr. Edmundo Rodríguez, interview by author, October 19, 2000.

5. See Acuña 1988; Mirandé 1985.

6. Cadena 1987: 66–67.

7. See Sandoval 1983a.

8. See Cadena 1987; Sandoval 1990.

9. Medina 1998: 20.

10. Blanca Romo García, interview by author, November 13, 2000.

11. See Gutiérrez 1983.

12. See, e.g., Guerrero 1987; Elizondo 1983.

13. See Cone 1982; Deck 1986.

14. See Cadena 1987.

15. Fr. Ralph Ruiz, interview by author, September 28, 2000.
16. Roberto Piña, interview by author, September 28, 2000.
17. Medina 1998: 19.
18. See Hendren 1983.
19. See also Engh 1994.
20. See Cadena 1987: 65–68.
21. See Grebler, Moore, and Guzmán 1970. See also Sandoval 1983a. Cadena (1987: 65–68) mentions that the church promoted Americanization through building schools in barrios and Catholic youth clubs. In these settings, as well as during Sunday sermons, the church disseminated, among other things, anti-Communist propaganda.

García (1991) argues that the church in San Antonio accommodated the Spanish language and other cultural practices of Mexicans and Mexican Americans from 1929 to 1941. It did so because it was competing with an emerging Pentecostal movement, which may have been friendly to the Spanish language and Mexican culture. I do not know whether the church in San Antonio continued this policy or how widely it was applied in the San Antonio Archdiocese, but it is reasonable to hypothesize that the church tailored its efforts to annihilate the Spanish language and other Mexican cultural traits to fit its own interests. It can also be hypothesized that San Antonio was a special case, given its large Mexican immigrant and Mexican American populations, and thus concessions by the church were appropriate. This is an area for future research.

22. Burns 1994a: 150.
23. Sandoval 1990: 92.
24. See Mirandé 1985. See also Pulido 1991; McNamara 1973.
25. Levy 1975: 84, cited in Burns 1994a: 149.
26. Cadena 1987: 65.
27. Burns 1994a: 149.
28. Pattillo-McCoy (1998) argues that cultural ownership of the black church by blacks facilitates organizing for change, building and maintaining a positive sense of self, and building unity among members.
29. "Report of the Subcommittee for the Spanish-speaking of the Minorities Committee of the Los Angeles Priests' Senate," 1971.
30. See Cabral 1973.
31. See Gaventa 1980.
32. Cadena 1987: 55. There are numerous examples of foreign priests and bishops being imposed on the Mexican American people. See Sandoval 1983c, cited in Medina 1998: 18.
33. Lamy, Letter, 1 February 1852, Archives of the Archdiocese of Santa Fe, Folio No. 1; cited in Hendren 1983: 198.
34. Cadena 1987: 60.
35. See Sandoval 1983a: 368.
36. U.S. Catholic Almanac 1971, 511. See also Cadena 1989: 109.
37. Cadena 1989: 109, cited in Medina 1998: 17.
38. "PADRES," National Catholic Reporter, April 2, 1971.
39. Official Catholic Directory, 1970. This number includes archbishops and auxiliary bishops.

40. Matovina 1999: 221.
41. Carrillo n.d.
42. Hendren 1983: 205.
43. See Cone 1982; see also McAdam 1982.
44. See Mirandé 1985.
45. Cadena 1987: 95.
46. Carrillo 1971.
47. This quote comes from p. 2 of a hard copy of Carrillo 1971a given to me by Alberto Carrillo.
48. See Burns 1994b. See also Servín 1970: 148; Monroy 1978: 223; Romo 1976: 188; Vargas 1997; Mirandé 1985.
49. Fr. Virgil Elizondo, interview by author, February 12, 2000.
50. See Dolan and Hinojosa 1994. See also Burns 1994b; Medina 1998; Beal 1994; Grebler, Moore, and Guzmán 1970; Leininger 1979.
51. Sandoval 1994: 133–134. See also Cadena 1987: 69.
52. Sandoval 1990: 92; see also Sandoval 1983b: 413–414.
53. Sandoval 1990: 92.
54. Medina 1998: 174. This view of the Bishop's Committee is widely shared by PADRES informants. In addition, many indicated that this was a typical feature of church social welfare efforts aimed at Mexican Americans before 1970. Medina (1998: 16) notes that "the Victorynoll sisters were established principally to work in Mexican American communities and thus had a larger percentage of Chicana sisters. Victorynoll leadership, however, remained dominated by Euro-American sisters."
55. Mirandé 1998: 114.
56. See Grebler, Moore, and Guzmán 1970. See also Woods 1967; Bronder 1982; Privett 1988; Colaianni 1968; Meconis 1979; LaLonde 2000.

CHAPTER 3

1. Ruiz interview.
2. Ruiz interview.
3. Ruiz interview.
4. Fr. Alberto Carrillo, interview by author, October 29, 2001.
5. Fr. Roberto Peña, interview by author, November 23, 2000.
6. Fr. Lonnie Reyes, interview by author, October 19, 2000.
7. Fr. Juan Romero, interview by author, February 13, 2002.
8. Peña interview.
9. Peña interview.
10. "PADRES," *National Catholic Reporter*, April 2, 1971.
11. Rodríguez interview.
12. Ruiz interview.
13. Fr. Albert Gallegos, interview by author, January 21, 2001.
14. Romero interview.
15. Fr. Manual Martínez, interview by author, March 30, 2001.
16. Rodríguez interview.

17. Fr. Vicente López, interview by author, February 19, 2002.
18. Rodríguez interview.
19. Fr. Roberto Flores, interview by author, February 16, 2002.
20. Martínez interview.
21. Ruiz interview.
22. Romero interview.
23. Romero interview.
24. Romero interview.
25. Romero interview.
26. Romero interview.
27. Carrillo interview.
28. Carrillo interview.
29. Fr. Henry Casso, interview by author, January 23, 2001.
30. Grebler, Moore, and Guzmán 1970: 106.
31. Grebler, Moore, and Guzmán 1970: 113.
32. Grebler, Moore, and Guzmán 1970: 197–200. See also Rochin 1974. Rochin documents high poverty rates among Chicanos in the Southwest.
33. Statistics on low educational attainment are reviewed in Grebler, Moore, and Guzmán 1970. See also Cardenas 1974.
34. See, e.g., Estrada et al. 1981; Rivera 1973.
35. Many scholars have analyzed these issues. See, e.g., Acuña 1988; Almaguer 1971, 1974; Cotrell 1975; Brischetto, Cotrell, and Stevens 1983; García 1978; G. G. González 1974.
36. For these movements, see, respectively, Goines 1993; Small 1994; Piven and Cloward 1979; Stern 1994.
37. Gómez-Quiñones 1990: 103.
38. See, e.g., Gómez-Quiñones 1990. See also Acuña 1988; Martínez and Vásquez 1974; Muñoz 1989; Rosales 1996.
39. PASSO was a coalition comprising the League of United Latin American Citizens (LULAC), GI Forum, and other organizations. It formed after the 1960 presidential elections from the Viva Kennedy clubs in Texas. MAYO was formed by several Chicano students at St. Mary's University in San Antonio in 1967. MAYO was instrumental in organizing more than fifty high school walkouts. See Rosales 2000.
40. Fr. Ralph Ruiz, Letter to Archbishop Furey, San Antonio, Texas, October 15, 1969.
41. Rodríguez interview.
42. Rodríguez interview.
43. Rodríguez interview.
44. Peña interview.
45. Ruiz n.d.
46. Ruiz interview.
47. Ruiz interview.
48. Ruiz interview.
49. Ruiz interview.
50. Carrillo interview.

51. Carrillo interview.
52. Carrillo interview.
53. Carrillo interview.
54. Ruiz interview.
55. See Rodríguez 1994: 216.
56. Rodríguez 1994: 216.
57. Rodríguez 1994: 217.
58. See Sandoval 1990.
59. Gallegos interview.
60. Gallegos interview.
61. Fr. Balthasar J. Janacek, interview by author, October 2, 2000.
62. Sandoval 1990: 65.
63. Archbishop Patrick Flores, interview by author, October 15, 2000.
64. Romero interview.
65. P. Flores interview.
66. Carrillo interview.
67. Romero interview.
68. Juan Romero, Letter to Most Rev. Sylvester Trinan, December 14, 1972.
69. Janacek interview.
70. Elizondo interview.
71. Ruiz interview.
72. Anonymous PADRES founder interview.
73. Reyes interview.
74. R. Flores interview.
75. Gallegos interview.
76. R. Flores interview.
77. García interview.
78. See Sandoval 1990; Hurtado 1978.
79. Sandoval 1990: 64.
80. Sandoval 1990: 64.
81. See Sandoval 1983d; Lucas 1981; Alurista 1972; del Grito 1972; Isais-A. 1979; Mosqueda 1986.
82. Pulido 1991.
83. Isais-A. 1979.
84. Pulido 1991: 17.
85. Pulido 1991.
86. Pulido 1991.
87. Pulido 1991.
88. Pulido 1991.
89. Pulido 1991.
90. Burns 1994b: 129.
91. Elizondo interview.
92. Romero interview.
93. Ruiz interview.
94. Privett 1988.

95. Rice 1991.
96. Ruiz interview.
97. Anonymous PADRES founder interview.
98. Reyes interview.
99. Sandoval 1990: 65.
100. Anonymous PADRES founder interview.
101. See Alarcón 1990; Acuña 1988; Muñoz 1989; Rodríguez 1977.
102. Alarcón 1990; Acuña 1988; Muñoz 1989; Rodríguez 1977. See also Gómez-Quiñones 1990; *El Plan de Santa Barbara* 1970.
103. *El Plan de Santa Bárbara,* 9.
104. *El Plan de Santa Bárbara,* 9.
105. See Gómez-Quiñones 1990.
106. Muñoz 1989: 63.
107. Mirandé 1985: 2–3.
108. Salazar 1970; Murrillo 1971.
109. Gutiérrez and Hirsh 1973.
110. Lampe 1977.
111. R. Flores interview.
112. Gallegos interview.
113. Romero interview.
114. Ruiz interview.
115. Roberto Flores interview.
116. Rodríguez interview.
117. Peña interview.
118. Romero interview.
119. Romero interview.
120. Colaianni 1968.
121. Many PADRES founders also enjoyed close working relationships with local activists. For instance, in San Antonio, Father Ruiz collaborated with Judge Albert Pena, state senator Joe Bernal, and Congressman Henry B. González.
122. Ruiz interview.
123. See Rodríguez 1994.
124. Ruiz interview.
125. See Rodríguez 1994.
126. Ruiz interview.
127. Rodríguez interview.
128. Carrillo interview; Carrillo n.d.
129. Carrillo interview.

CHAPTER 4

1. Ruiz interview.
2. Ruiz interview.
3. Ruiz interview.

4. Sandoval 1990 reports that 50 people attended. According to the *San Antonio Express News,* October 9, 1969, there were 30. The *San Antonio Express News,* October 12, 1969, reported "some 50." Medina 1989 says 25.

5. PADRES Press Release, October 9, 1969. See also *San Antonio Express News,* October 9, 10, and 12, 1969; *San Antonio Light,* October 10, 1969; *Catholic Almanac 1977.*

6. Father Ruiz was 33; Father Carrillo, 30; Father Gallegos, 33; and Fathers Rodríguez and Roberto Flores, 34.

7. Gallegos interview.

8. Ruiz interview.

9. Rodríguez interview.

10. Martínez interview.

11. Casso interview.

12. R. Flores interview.

13. R. Flores interview.

14. PADRES Press Release, October 9, 1969.

15. PADRES Press Release, October 9, 1969.

16. Carrillo n.d. This sentiment was confirmed by Carrillo during the interview with the author.

17. *San Antonio Light,* October 10, 1969; *San Antonio Express News,* October 10, 1969; PADRES Press Release, October 9, 1969.

18. Casso interview; Ruiz interview.

19. Ruiz interview.

20. *San Antonio Light,* October 10, 1969.

21. The *Sun,* a supplement to the *San Antonio Express News,* October 16, 1969.

22. *San Antonio Light,* October 10, 1969.

23. PADRES Press Release, October 9, 1969.

24. PADRES Press Release, October 9, 1969.

25. PADRES Press Release, October 9, 1969.

26. Ralph Ruiz, Letter to Archbishop Furey, October 9, 1969, Archive of the Archdiocese of San Antonio.

27. Ralph Ruiz, Letter to Archbishop Furey, October 9, 1969.

28. *San Antonio Light;* October 10, 1969; *San Antonio Express News,* October 10, 1969.

29. Frs. Edmundo Rodríguez and Ralph Ruiz, Letter to Archbishop Dearden, October 15, 1969, Archive of the Archdiocese of San Antonio.

30. PADRES Letter to Bishops of United States, November 11, 1969, Archive of the Archdiocese of San Antonio.

31. PADRES, Letter to Bishops of United States, November 11, 1969.

32. Facts largely quoted from PADRES, Letter to Bishops of United States, November 11, 1969.

33. PADRES, Letter to Bishops of United States, November 11, 1969.

34. PADRES, Letter to Bishops of United States, November 11, 1969.

35. PADRES, Letter to Bishops of United States, November 11, 1969.

36. PADRES, Letter to Bishops of United States, November 11, 1969.

37. PADRES, Letter to Bishops of United States, November 11, 1969.

38. PADRES, Letter to Bishops of United States, November 11, 1969.

39. PADRES, Letter to Bishops of United States, November 11, 1969.

40. PADRES, Letter to Bishops of United States, November 11, 1969.

41. Bishop Bernardin, Letter to Bishops Furey, Manning, Buswell, Green, and Medeiros, December 6, 1969, Archive of the Archdiocese of San Antonio.

42. Bishop Bernardin, Letter to Bishops Furey, Manning, Buswell, Green, and Medeiros, December 6, 1969.

43. Letter from Bishop Bernardin to Bishops Furey, Manning, Buswell, Green, and Medeiros, December 6, 1969.

44. Joseph L. Bernardin, Letter to Bishop Thomas J. McDonough, January 10, 1970, Archive of the Archdiocese of San Antonio.

45. *San Antonio Light,* February 8, 1970. The number of attendees is not clear. The *San Antonio Light* and *San Antonio Express News,* February 5, 1970, both report that about two hundred people were in attendance. But in interviews PADRES founders suggest the number was much larger. Ruiz: 400; Carrillo: 500; V. López: 700.

46. See Carrillo n.d.

47. Janacek interview.

48. Janacek interview. See also Carrillo n.d.

49. *San Antonio Light,* February 5, 1970. See *also Tucson Daily Citizen,* February 5, 1970.

50. Ruiz interview. Ruiz's account is consistent with those of several other PADRES founders. A note on the walk-out: According to the *San Antonio Light,* February 5, 1970, "about 25" priests walked out. And according to *the Tucson Daily Citizen,* February 5, 1970, "the 43 members of PADRES announced they agreed to restrict membership," suggesting that 43 priests, both Chicano and white, were in the room into which Father Ruiz and others walked and subsequently agreed with Ruiz's vision.

51. Janacek interview.

52. Janacek interview; Carrillo n.d.

53. Carrillo n.d.

54. V. López interview.

55. See Matovina 1999.

56. Carrillo interview.

57. Rodríguez interview. This sentiment is shared by PADRES informants. See also Matovina 1999.

58. Anonymous PADRES founder interview.

59. See Medina 1998.

60. PADRES Press Release, February 7, 1970, "Chicano Priests Move with the People," Archive of the Archdiocese of San Antonio.

61. PADRES Press Release, February 7, 1970, "Chicano Priests Move with the People."

62. Carrillo n.d.

63. Romero interview.

64. Reyes interview.

65. Gallegos interview.

66. Hector Madrigal, interview by author, February 16, 2001.
67. Romero interview.
68. Romero interview.
69. Ruiz interview.
70. See PADRES Newsletters, 1969–1972.
71. PADRES Newsletter, March 1973; Romero interview.
72. Romero interview; Carrillo interview.
73. Taylor and Whittier 1995: 173.
74. PADRES Resolutions, National Meeting, 1971.
75. Anonymous PADRES founder interview.
76. Romero interview
77. Roberto Flores interview.
78. Fr. Ramón Aragón, interview by author, January 23, 2001.
79. Romero interview.
80. Roberto Flores interview.
81. "PADRES Organizes for Chicano Power," *National Catholic Reporter,* April 2, 1971.
82. Carrillo interview.
83. Carrillo interview.
84. Carrillo 1971a.
85. Carrillo 1971a.
86. Carrillo 1971a.
87. Carrillo interview.
88. Carrillo 1971a.
89. Carrillo 1971a.
90. In his paper, Carrillo (1971a) also quotes the pope: "If the Redemptive of Christ is a value that must reach our people, we must then heed the words of Pope Paul 'to take up a double task of inspiring and of innovating in order to make structures evolve, so as to adapt them to the real needs of today.'"
91. Romero interview.
92. Carrillo interview.
93. Patrick Flores interview.
94. Ruiz interview.
95. Peña interview.
96. V. López interview.
97. Carrillo interview.
98. Taken largely from PADRES Newsletter, 1970.
99. Rodríguez interview.
100. Peña interview.
101. Aragón interview.
102. Romero 1994: 77.
103. Letter to Ralph Ruiz, November 18, 1969. At the request of Ralph Ruiz, the name of this bishop will be kept confidential. Actually, for reasons that are unclear, in his letter the bishop asked Ruiz to tell no one about it. It is worth speculating that some of the more progressive U.S. bishops wanted to jump on the PADRES bandwagon but were afraid of reprisals from conservative U.S. bishops or the Vatican.

104. PADRES Newsletter, 1975, Archive of the Archdiocese of San Antonio.
105. PADRES Newsletter, 1975.
106. Carrillo n.d.; see also PADRES Newsletter, 1975, Archive of the Archdiocese of San Antonio.
107. Carrillo n.d.
108. Carrillo n.d.
109. R. Flores interview.
110. Aragón interview.
111. Carrillo interview.
112. Gallegos interview.
113. Archbishop Furey of San Antonio, Letter to Rev. Joseph Bernardin, General Secretary of USCC, December 11, 1969, Archive of the Archdiocese of San Antonio.
114. Archbishop Furey of San Antonio, Letter to Apostolic Delegate Rev. Luigi Raimondi, November 4, 1969, Archive of the Archdiocese of San Antonio.
115. Archbishop Furey of San Antonio, Letter to Fr. R. V. Monticello, Associate General Secretary, USCC, April, 1974, Archive of the Archdiocese of San Antonio.
116. PADRES Second Annual Congress Program, October 11–13, 1971, Archive of the Archdiocese of San Antonio.
117. Romero interview. See also Carrillo n.d.
118. Carrillo n.d.
119. Romero interview.
120. Carrillo n.d. Confirmed in Romero interview.
121. Romero interview.
122. Ernesto Calderón, Waco, Texas, Autobiography, unpublished manuscript, Reyes Papers, Austin, Texas.
123. PADRES Newsletter, July 1971, Archive of the Archdiocese of San Antonio.
124. Reyes interview.
125. PADRES Memo to the Executive Board, June 29, 1971, Archive of the Archdiocese of San Antonio.
126. Reyes interview.
127. PADRES Memo to the Executive Board, July 2, 1971, Archive of the Archdiocese of San Antonio.
128. PADRES Memo to the Executive Board, July 2, 1971.
129. Juan Romero, Letter to Most Rev. Sylvester Trinan, December 14, 1972, Archive of the Archdiocese of San Antonio.
130. Juan Romero, letter to Most Rev. Sylvester Trinan, December 14, 1972.

CHAPTER 5

1. Rodríguez interview.
2. Romero interview.

3. R. Flores interview.

4. P. Flores interview.

5. Carrillo interview.

6. Carrillo 1971a.

7. Carrillo interview.

8. Romero interview.

9. R. Flores interview.

10. Carrillo interview.

11. This is an understatement. Burns (1994a: 151) refers to the loss of Mexican Catholics to Protestantism as a "perennial fear" of the U.S. Catholic Church.

12. R. Flores interview.

13. Ruiz interview.

14. Fr. Ralph Ruiz, Letter to Archbishop Furey, San Antonio, Texas, October 15, 1969, Archive of the Archdiocese of San Antonio.

15. Carrillo interview.

16. Ruiz interview.

17. Carrillo interview.

18. Janacek interview.

19. PADRES Internal Memo, November 23, 1971, Archive of the Archdiocese of San Antonio.

20. Carrillo n.d.

21. Ruiz interview.

22. R. Flores interview.

23. Casso interview.

24. Carrillo interview.

25. Carrillo interview. Overall, Carrillo's account was confirmed by several others. One fact, however, remains uncertain. According to Carrillo, then-Father Patrick Flores was present at the confrontation and he was one of the good cops. This was not confirmed by others due to lack of recollection.

26. P. Flores interview.

27. Sandoval 1994: 149.

28. McMurtrey 1987: 81.

29. Janacek interview.

30. Cadena 1987: 77.

31. PADRES Pamphlet, distributed at the Second National PADRES Congress, October 11–13, 1971, Archive of the Archdiocese of San Antonio.

32. Ruiz interview.

33. Romero 1974.

34. Romero 1974.

35. Romero 1974.

36. Romero 1974.

37. Juan Romero, Letter to PADRES National Office, September 5, 1977, Archive of the Archdiocese of San Antonio.

38. Romero 1986.

39. Carrillo n.d.

40. Carrillo n.d.
41. Carrillo n.d.
42. Carrillo n.d.
43. See Stevens-Arroyo 1994: 109.
44. Medina 1998: 168.
45. Rodríguez 1994: 225.
46. Romero 1994.
47. Gallegos interview.
48. Casso interview.
49. Sandoval 1990: 78.
50. Romero 1994: 85.
51. Romero interview.
52. Matovina 1999: 229. See also Romero 1994.
53. Romero 1994: 85.
54. Romero 1994: 85.
55. Romero 1994: 85.
56. Sandoval 1990: 73.
57. Sandoval 1990: 73.
58. V. López interview. See also Romero 1990.
59. Romero 1994: 84.
60. Reyes interview.
61. V. López interview.
62. Ruiz interview.
63. Ruiz n.d.
64. Romero interview.
65. Rodríguez interview.
66. Romero interview.
67. Rodríguez 1971.
68. Romero interview.
69. Rodríguez 1971.
70. Romero interview.
71. Romero interview. Details about how the MTM was administered and its impacts on leadership development among the poor and working class are discussed in later sections.
72. PADRES handout, "PADRES National Congress," October, 1971, Los Angeles, Archive of the Archdiocese of San Antonio.
73. Elizondo n.d.
74. Romero interview.
75. Carrillo interview.
76. See Matovina 1999.
77. PADRES Proposal, December 16, 1972, Archive of the Archdiocese of San Antonio.
78. PADRES Proposal, December 16, 1972.
79. Medina 1998: 164.
80. Romero interview.
81. Leonard Anguiano, interview by author, December 21, 2000.

82. Juan Romero, Letter to Virgil Elizondo, 1972, Archive of the Archdiocese of San Antonio.
83. PADRES Newsletter, June 1972, Archive of the Archdiocese of San Antonio.
84. Romero interview.
85. Rodríguez interview.
86. Rodríguez interview.
87. Rodríguez interview.
88. Sandoval 1983c.
89. Anguiano interview.
90. Antonio C. Cabral, interview by author, December 15, 2000. Cabral's accounts are supported by two former members of CASA of San Antonio, Manuel Vázquez and Chavel López, who were interviewed by telephone by the author on February 23, 2001.
91. Cabral interview.
92. Cabral interview.
93. Cabral interview.
94. Cabral interview.
95. Medina 1998: 274–275.
96. Medina 1998: 279–280.
97. Fr. Ralph Ruiz, Letter to Bishop Bernardin, March 11, 1970, Archive of the Archdiocese of San Antonio.
98. Bishop Joseph Bernardin, Letter to Ralph Ruiz, March 16, 1970, Archive of the Archdiocese of San Antonio.
99. Fr. Ralph Ruiz, Letter to Bishop Bernardin, March 21, 1970, Archive of the Archdiocese of San Antonio.
100. Ruiz interview.
101. Ruiz interview.
102. Ruiz interview.
103. Sandoval 1983b: 427.
104. Sandoval 1983b: 427.
105. Sandoval 1983b: 427.
106. Romero interview.
107. P. Flores interview.
108. Madrigal interview.
109. Romero interview.
110. Romero interview.
111. Sandoval 1994: 145.
112. Fr. Vicente López, quoted in Carrillo n.d.
113. According to Sandoval (1990), the heated exchange went something like this. Krol said: "While in God's providence there are people of many different racial, ethnic, and national origins in our Church in the United States, and while each group has something distinctive and very precious to offer to the life of the total community out of its respective heritage, in the final analysis there is among us neither Jew nor Greek, neither Irishman nor Pole, nor German, nor Italian, nor Anglo, nor Spanish-speaking, nor Black, nor white—but all of us

one in Christ Jesus, all are descendants of Abraham" (p. 80). To which Bishop Flores responded: "From us have been stolen our lands, our language, our culture, our customs, our history and our way of religious expression. We have also been victims of oppression, discrimination, semi-slavery. We have been poorly paid for our work; we have lived in housing worse than that of monkeys in a zoo; we have not been admitted to some schools" (p. 80). Sandoval continues: "In the face of all that, he [Bishop Flores] charged, the Church had been silent. That was the tone of the presentations. It was a time to air grievances stored over many generations" (p. 80).

114. Sandoval 1994: 143.
115. Quoted in Sandoval 1994: 143.
116. Quoted in Sandoval 1994: 143.
117. Rodríguez interview.
118. Sandoval 1994: 146.
119. Carrillo interview.
120. Aragón interview.
121. Rodríguez interview.
122. Rodríguez interview.
123. Romero interview.
124. Rodríguez interview.
125. Stevens-Arroyo interview.
126. PADRES Newsletter, November 1974.
127. PADRES Newsletter, November 1974.
128. Stevens-Arroyo interview.
129. Díaz-Stevens and Stevens-Arroyo 1998: 176.
130. "PADRES Organizes for Chicano Power," *National Catholic Reporter,* April 2, 1971.
131. PADRES, "Resolutions of PADRES National Congress," October 1971, Los Angeles, Archive of the Archdiocese of San Antonio.
132. PADRES, "To the Catholic Bishops of the United States: Seminary Training for the Mexican-American Candidate for the Priesthood" (ca. 1971), Archive of the Archdiocese of San Antonio.
133. PADRES, "To the Catholic Bishops of the United States."
134. See Sandoval 1994.
135. PADRES Newsletter, December 1971, Archive of the Archdiocese of San Antonio.
136. Carrillo interview.
137. Medina 1998: 84.
138. Romero n.d.
139. Romero interview.
140. Romero interview.
141. Romero interview.
142. PADRES Newsletter, September 1973, Archive of the Archdiocese of San Antonio.
143. Romero 1994.
144. Roberto Flores interview.
145. Patrick Flores interview.

146. Aragón interview.
147. Rodríguez interview.
148. García interview.
149. Carrillo n.d.
150. Ricardo Ramirez, interview by author, February 2, 2001.
151. Aragón interview.

CHAPTER 6

1. Romero interview.
2. Reyes interview.
3. Reyes interview.
4. Ruiz interview.
5. Gallegos interview.
6. Ruiz interview.
7. Ruiz interview.
8. Casso interview.
9. R. Flores interview.
10. *Today's Catholic,* January 14, 1976.
11. Rafael Jiménez, First Vice President, PADRES Memorandum, September 27, 1976.
12. See Matovina 1999.
13. Matovina 1999; see also Romero 1994.
14. See Matovina 1999.
15. Romero 1992.
16. Ruiz interview.
17. Ruiz interview.
18. Trinidad Sánchez, interview by author, October 20, 2001.
19. Hopper 1950; cited in Turner and Killian 1987: 379.
20. Piven and Cloward 1979: 30.
21. Turner and Killian 1987: 262–278. Turner and Killian refer to the combination of goals and values within a movement as the movement's value orientation (p. 278).
22. Turner and Killian 1987: 278.
23. Turner and Killian 1987: 278.
24. Blumer 1978: 1.
25. In his influential work on community organizing, Alinsky (1971:161) wrote, "There is a way to keep the action going and to prevent it from being a drag, but this means constantly cutting new issues as the action continues, so that by the time the enthusiasm and the emotions for one issue have started to de-escalate, a new issue has come into the scene with a consequent revival." Following this line of reasoning, one could argue that in part PADRES's demise was a result of its failure to formulate new goals.
26. PADRES Board Meeting Minutes, July 1974, Archive of the Archdiocese of San Antonio.
27. *Today's Catholic,* May 8, 1981.

28. It's a reasonable question to ask: did the "institutional guys" who replaced the "shock troops" influence the selection of goals in such a way that the new goals became a reflection of the new leadership? As of now, I have not found enough data to answer, so it will have to wait for future research.

29. Stevens-Arroyo 1994: 113.

30. Ibid., 114.

31. Ibid.

32. Ibid.

33. Díaz-Stevens and Stevens-Arroyo 1998: 201.

34. Ibid.

35. Teaching Chicana/o studies to Mexican American youth was a priority for PADRES in the early years.

36. This was a conclusion from the PADRES El Paso group that came out of discussions in preparation for a PADRES national congress circa 1970.

37. For numbers on black Catholics, see *Official Catholic Directory* 2000; and *U.S. Catholic Almanac* 2001. For numbers on U.S. Latino Catholics, see *Official Catholic Directory* 2000; based on Latino-American population of 35 million, U.S. Census Bureau 2000.

38. See U.S. Catholic Conference, Office of the Executive, 2000. This number includes active archbishops and auxiliary bishops.

39. *Los Angeles Times,* June 1, 2000, lists 24 Latino-American bishops. Bishop Gómez was named number 25 in February 2001. It is unknown how many of these are native-born Latino-Americans. For black bishops, see *Catholic Almanac* 2001.

40. For the total number of priests, see *Catholic Almanac* 2001. A study by the National Association of Hispanic Priests (NASH) in 1999 found that the number of U.S.-born Latino priests (i.e., from all Latino subgroups) in the United States is about 500. Sandoval (1990) uses the estimate of 200 native-born Mexican American priests in 1989.

41. R. Flores interview.

42. Ruiz interview.

CHAPTER 7

1. Smith 1991.

2. See McAdam 1999.

3. See, e.g., McAdam 1999; Gamson 1992; Gamson 1995; Della Porta and Diani 1999; Turner and Killian 1987.

4. See Moor 1990.

5. Sandoval 1991: 1–24.

6. Sandoval 1991: 14.

7. Sandoval 1991: 14, 15.

8. Romero interview.

9. McAdam 1999.

10. See Scott 1987.
11. Weber 1968: 184.
12. Smith 1991.
13. Turner and Killian 1987: 231.
14. McAdam 1982.
15. Turner and Killian 1987: 231.
16. Bearman and Kim 1997.
17. Stevens-Arroyo 1994.
18. Stevens-Arroyo 1994.

APPENDIX I

1. Carrillo interview.
2. Archbishop Ignatius J. Strecker, Letter to Fr. Ralph Ruiz, July 27, 1970; Archive of the Archdiocese of San Antonio.
3. Ruiz interview.
4. Rodríguez interview.
5. PADRES Newsletter, July 1973, Archive of the Archdiocese of San Antonio.
6. Rodríguez interview.
7. PADRES Meeting Notes, October 16, 1974, Archive of the Archdiocese of San Antonio.
8. Carrillo interview.
9. Medina 1998: 142.
10. Juan Romero, Letter to J. Rausch, General Secretary, USCC, April 5, 1974, Archive of the Archdiocese of San Antonio.
11. Ruiz interview.
12. Ruiz interview.
13. PADRES Newsletter, December 1970.
14. USCC/NCCB, "Agenda Report," Documentation for General Meeting of NCCB and USCC, 1973, 93, Archive of the Archdiocese of San Antonio.
15. See Juan Romero, Letter to Rev. J. Rausch, General Secretary, USCC, Archive of the Archdiocese of San Antonio. See also PADRES Board Meeting Agenda, October 16, 1974, Archive of the Archdiocese of San Antonio.

GLOSSARY

†

With a few exceptions (i.e, Chicano, Encuentro, Latino, Mexican American), these definitions are taken from the *Official Catholic Directory*, 2000.

Apostolate: The mission of Christ and participation in it. Its object is to bring Christ to others.

Archbishop: A bishop of a main or metropolitan diocese in an ecclesiastical province.

Bishop: A priest who becomes a bishop is responsible for the pastoral care of his diocese. In addition, bishops have the responsibility to act in council to guide the church.

Brother: A man who is a member of a religious order but is not ordained or studying for the priesthood.

Chicano/a: A self-identification. In this study, this term denotes a progressive political identity and class among those Mexican Americans who literally call themselves Chicano/a.

Cursillo: The Cursillo de Cristianidad, or Little Course in Christianity, is a three-day program for achieving spiritual renewal or spiritual awakening. It seeks to convey a new sense of individual and organized political action.

Diocese: The standard term for a territorial division of the church entrusted to the bishop who rules in his own name as local ordinary and not as a delegate to another. The chief diocese of a province is an archdiocese, which is headed by an archbishop. A diocese is usually limited to a definite territory so that it comprises all the faithful who inhabit that territory.

Encuentro: The Encuentro is a traditional nationwide gathering of the U.S. Latino Catholic community that began in the 1970s where Latinos discuss critically their relationship with the U.S. Catholic Church and celebrate their cultures and faith. However, the fourth nationwide Encuentro in 2000 included representatives of all sectors of the Catholic community, aiming to be a celebration of the rich cultural, ethnic, and linguistic diversity which marks the Catholic Church in the United States.

Hierarchy: In general, the term refers to the ordered body of clergy, divided into bishops, priests, and deacons. In Catholic practice, the term refers to the bishops of the world or of a particular region.

Hispanic: In this study, this term refers to a person of Hispanic descent who resides in the United States. Note that persons of Mexican descent comprise the largest Hispanic subgroup. "Hispanic" is used interchangeably with "Latino."

Latino/a: In this study, the term means a person of Latin descent who resides in the United States. "Latino" is used interchangeably with "Hispanic."

Mexican American: A nationality. An American of Mexican descent. Synonyms: Raza, Mexicano.

Mexicano: In this study, this term means Mexican American or Mexican immigrant.

National Conference of Catholic Bishops (NCCB): The episcopal conference of U.S. bishops. The membership is composed of diocesan bishops and their associate bishops. The conference decides matters of ecclesiastical law and issues policy statements on political and social issues.

Nuncio: In the United States, the papal representative is sent by the pope to both the local church and to the government. His title is Apostolic Pro-Nuncio.

Ordinary: Diocesan bishops, religious superiors, and certain other diocesan authorities with jurisdiction over the clergy in a specific geographic area or the members of a religious order.

Ordination: The sacramental rite by which a sacred order is conferred (diaconate, priesthood, episcopacy).

Parish: A specific community of the Christian faithful within a diocese, which has its own church building, under the authority of a pastor who is responsible for providing them with ministerial service. Most parishes are formed on a geographic basis, but they may be formed along national or ethnic lines.

Pastor: A priest in charge of a parish or congregation. He is responsible for administering the sacraments, instructing the congregation in the doctrine of the church, and other services to the people of the parish.

Personal Prelature: In addition to the territorial arrangement of the church into particular or local churches or dioceses, canon law provides for nonterritorial areas of religious jurisdiction, incorporating secular clergy and deacons. Membership is also open to laypersons. These prelatures are established to meet specific pastoral or missionary needs at the regional, national, or international level without infringing on the rights of the local bishops. A prelature is presided over by a personal prelate, who is an ordinary with the right to establish seminaries and ordain priests as members of the prelature.

Propagation of the Faith: An organization, headquartered in Rome, which distributes aid to Catholic missions and organizes the work of missionaries all over the world. The organization has responsibility for fostering missionary vocations, assigning missionaries to fieldwork, defining ecclesiastical boundaries and assigning clergy to them, and encouraging training and installation of native-born clergy.

Provincial: The superior (quasi-bishop) of the communities of a religious order that constitutes a province.

Raza: In this study, this term means Mexican American.

Religious Priest, Diocesan Priest: Religious, or regular, priests are those who are professed members of a religious order (e.g., the Jesuits). Religious clergy live according to the rule of their respective orders. In pastoral ministry, they are under the jurisdiction of their local bishop, as well as the superiors of their order. Diocesan, or secular, priests are under the direction of their local bishop. They commit to serving their congregations and other institutions.

Seminary: An educational institution for men preparing to become a priest. A school for the spiritual, academic, and pastoral education and formation of priesthood candidates is known as a major seminary, in which the focus is on philosophical and theological education. To prepare for entrance into a major seminary, a period of study is set aside for the required courses in the humanities and the sciences in institutions called minor seminaries.

Sister or nun: Women in religious orders who belong to institutes that have professed simple vows.

Spanish speaking: Latino American.

Superior: The head of a religious order or congregation. He or she may be the head of a province or an individual house.

United States Catholic Conference (USCC): The civil corporation and executive agency of the National Conference of Catholic Bishops. The USCC acts as the national public policy organization of the NCCB. Its purpose is to organize and promote Catholic activity in the United States and abroad and to carry out the religious and social action of the Catholic Church in the United States. The major departments are education, communication and social development, and world peace.

BIBLIOGRAPHY

†

ARCHIVAL COLLECTIONS

PADRES Files. Department of Archives, Chancery Office, Archdiocese of San Antonio, Texas.

Alberto Carrillo Papers. Files in possession of Alberto Carrillo, Whittier, California.

Ramón Gaitán Papers. Files in possession of Gilbert R. Cadena, Pasadena, California.

Roberto Peña Papers. Files in possession of Roberto Peña, Eagle Pass, Texas.

Lonnie Reyes Papers. Files in possession of Lonnie Reyes, Austin, Texas.

Juan Romero Papers. Files in possession of Juan Romero, Santa Monica, California.

Ralph Ruiz Papers. Files in possession of Ralph Ruiz, San Antonio, Texas.

SECONDARY SOURCES

Abbott, Walter M., ed. 1966. *The Documents of Vatican II*. London: Geoffrey Chapman.

Acuña, Rodolfo. 1988. *Occupied America: A History of Chicanos*. 3d ed. New York: HarperCollins.

Alarcón, Norma. 1990. "Chicana Feminism: In the Tracks of the Native Woman." *Cultural Studies* 4 (3): 248–56.

Albrow, Martin. 1970. *Bureaucracy*. London: Pall Mall.

Alinsky, Saul D. 1971. *Rules for Radicals: A Practical Primer for Realistic Radicals*. New York: Random House.

Almaguer, Tomás. 1971. "Toward the Study of Chicano Colonialism." *Aztlán* 2 (spring): 7–22.

———. 1974. "Historical Notes on Chicano Oppression: The Dialectics of

Radical and Class Domination in North America." *Aztlán* 5 (spring–fall): 27–56.

Alurista, Alberto. 1972. "Campo Cultural de la Raza." In *Anthology of Mexican-American Literature,* ed. Stan Steiner and Luis Valdez. New York: Alfred A. Knopf.

Aminzade, Ron, and Doug McAdam. 2001. "Emotions and Contentious Politics." In *Silence and Voice in the Study of Contentious Politics,* ed. Ron Aminzade, Jack Goldstone, Doug McAdam, Elizabeth Perry, William Sewell, Sidney Tarrow, and Charles Tilly, 14–50. Cambridge: Cambridge University Press.

Anzaldúa, Gloria. 1987. *Borderlands: La Frontera, The New Mestiza.* San Francisco: Aunt Lute Books.

Arendt, Hannah. 1951. *The Origins of Totalitarianism.* New York: Harcourt Brace.

Ashby, William Ross. 1968. "Principles of the Self-Organizing System." In *Modern Systems Research for the Behavioral Scientist,* ed. Walter Buckley, 108–118. Chicago: Aldine.

Bailey, Kenneth D. 1994. *Methods of Social Research.* 4th ed. New York: Free Press.

Beal, Tarcisio. 1994. "Hispanics and the Roman Catholic Church in the United States." In *Hispanics in the Church: Up from the Cellar,* ed. Philip E. Lampe, 25–52. San Francisco: Catholic Scholars Press.

Bearman, Peter S., and Hyojoung Kim. 1997. "The Structure and Dynamics of Movement Participation." *American Sociological Review* 62 (February): 70–93.

Bennis, Warren G. 1959. "Leadership Theory and Administrative Behavior." *Administrative Science Quarterly* 4 (December): 259–301.

Berryman, Phillip. 1987. *Liberation Theology: Essential Facts about the Revolutionary Movement in Latin America.* Philadelphia: Temple University Press.

Beverley, John. 1989. "The Margin at the Center: On Testimonial Narrative." *Modern Fiction Studies* 35 (1): 11–28.

Billington, Ray Allen. 1938. *The Protestant Crusade.* New York: Macmillan.

Blumer, Herbert. 1978. "Social Unrest and Collective Protest." In *Studies in Symbolic Interaction,* ed. Norman K. Denzin, 1–54. Greenwich, Conn.: JAI Press.

Breiter, Toni. 1977a. "Hispanic Priest Joins National Conference of Catholic Bishops." *Agenda* 7, no. 4 (July–August): 43–44.

———. 1977b. "Second National Pastoral Meeting of US Catholic Spanish Speaking to Be Held." *Agenda* 7, no. 3 (May–June): 41.

Briggs, Kenneth A. 1992. *Holy Siege: The Year That Shook Catholic America.* San Francisco: HarperSan Francisco.

Brischetto, Robert, Charles L. Cotrell, and Michael Stevens. 1983. "Conflict and Change in the Political Culture of San Antonio in the 1970s." In *The Politics of San Antonio,* ed. David R. Johnson, John A. Booth, and Richard J. Harris, 75–113. Lincoln: University of Nebraska Press.

Brockett, Charles D. 1991. "The Structure of Political Opportunities and Peasant Mobilization in Central America." *Comparative Politics* 24: 253–274.

Bronder, Saul E. 1982. *Social Justice and Church Authority*. Philadelphia: Temple University Press.

Brubaker, Rogers. 1996. *Nationalism Reframed: Nationhood and the National Question in the New Europe*. New York: Cambridge University Press.

Buckley, Frederick W. 1967. *Sociology and Modern Systems Theory*. Englewood Cliffs, N.J.: Prentice-Hall.

Burawoy, Michael. 1991. "The Extended Case Method." In *Ethnography Unbound: Power and Resistance in the Modern Metropolis*, ed. Michael Burawoy et al., 271–287. Berkeley: University of California Press.

Burns, Gene. 1992. *The Frontiers of Catholicism: The Politics of Ideology in a Liberal World*. Berkeley: University of California Press.

Burns, Jeffrey M. 1994a. "Catholic Ministry in the Era of the 'Mexican Problem,' 1910–1943." In *Mexican Americans and the Catholic Church, 1900–1965*, ed. Jay P. Dolan and Gilberto M. Hinojosa, 148–175. Notre Dame: University of Notre Dame Press.

———. 1994b. "Establishing the Mexican Catholic Community in California: A Story of Neglect?" In *Mexican Americans and the Catholic Church, 1900–1965*, ed. Jay P. Dolan and Gilberto M. Hinojosa, 129–148. Notre Dame: University of Notre Dame Press.

Cabral, Amílcar. 1973. *Return to the Source: Selected Speeches*. Ed. Africa Information Service. New York: Monthly Review Press.

Cadena, Gilbert R. 1987. "Chicanos and the Catholic Church: Liberation theology as a Form of Empowerment." Ph.D. diss., University of California, Riverside.

———. 1989. "Chicano Clergy and the Emergence of Liberation Theology." *Hispanic Journal of Behavioral Science* 11, no. 2 (May): 107–121.

———. 1995. "Religious Leaders as Organic Intellectuals: Activist Priests and Sisters in the Chicano Community." *Religioni e Societa* 10, no. 22–23 (May–December): 195–207.

Calderón, Ernesto. n.d. "Autobiography." Unpublished manuscript.

Calhoun, Craig. 1993. "Nationalism and Ethnicity." *Annual Review of Sociology* 19: 211–240.

Cardenas, B. 1974. "Defining Equal Access to Educational Opportunity for Mexican American Children: A Study of Three Civil Rights Actions Affecting Mexican American Students and the Development of a Conceptual Framework for Effecting Institutional Responsiveness to the Educational Needs of Mexican American Children." Ed.D. diss., University of Massachusetts.

Carrillo, Alberto. 1971a. "A Chicano Critique of the U.S. Catholic Church." Paper presented at PADRES National Congress, Los Angeles, October. Alberto Carrillo Papers.

———. 1971b. "The Sociological Failure of the Catholic Church toward the Chicano." *Journal of Mexican American Studies* 1, no. 2 (winter): 75–83.

———. n.d. "History of PADRES." Unpublished manuscript. Alberto Carrillo Papers.

Carpio, Patricia. 1972. "Church Revolt in Colorado: Mexicano Catholics Say No to Catholic Authorities." *La Luz* 1, no. 1 (April): 46.

Casanova, José. 1994. *Public Religions in the Modern World.* Chicago: University of Chicago Press.

Castells, Manuel. 1977. *The Power of Identity.* Malden, Mass.: Blackwell.

Catholic Almanac. 1971. Paterson, N.J.: St. Anthony's Guild, 1971.

Catholic Almanac. 1977, 2001. Huntington, Ind.: Our Sunday Visitor.

Cerulo, Karen A. 1977. "Identity Construction: New Issues, New Directions." *Annual Review of Sociology* 23: 385–409.

"'Chicano' Priests Meet in S.A., May Organize." 1969. *San Antonio Express,* October 9.

Clegg, Stewart. "Foucault, Power and Organization." 1998. In *Foucualt, Management and Organization Theory,* ed. Alan McKinlay and Ken Starkey. Thousand Oaks, Calif.: Sage.

Colaianni, James F. 1968. *The Catholic Left: The Crisis of Radicalism Within the Church.* Philadelphia: Chilton.

Cone, James H. 1982. *My Soul Looks Back.* Nashville: Abingdon.

Costain, Anne W. 1992. *Inviting Women's Rebellion: A Political Process Interpretation of the Woman's Movement.* Baltimore: Johns Hopkins University Press.

Cotrell, C. L. 1977. "Municipal Services Equalization and Internal Colonialism in San Antonio, Texas: Explorations in Chinatown." Paper presented at the Rocky Mountain Social Services Convention, April.

Cruz, David V. 1977. "Raised Eyebrows and No Crucifixes." *Nuestro* 1, no. 7 (October): 52–53.

Curran, Charles E. 1986. *Faithful Dissent.* Kansas City, Mo.: Sheed & Ward.

D'Antonio, William V. 1994. "Autonomy and Democracy in an Autocratic Organization: The Case of the Roman Catholic Church." *Sociology of Religion* 55, no. 4 (winter): 379–396.

Dahm, Charles W. 1981. *Power and Authority in the Catholic Church: Cardinal Cody in Chicago.* Notre Dame, Ind.: University of Notre Dame Press.

Davidoff, Paul. 1965. "Advocacy and Pluralism in Planning." *Journal of the American Institute of Planners* 31 (4): 331–338.

Day, Mark R. 1984. "San Bernadino Hispanic Meeting Latest Step in Encuentro Process." *National Catholic Reporter* 21 (December): 1, 20.

Deck, Allan Figueroa. 1989. *The Second Wave: Hispanic Ministry and the Evengelization of Cultures.* Mahwah, N.J.: Paulist Press.

———, ed. 1992. *Frontiers of Hispanic Theology in the United States.* Maryknoll, N.Y.: Orbis Books.

Della Porta, Donatella, and Mario Diani. 1999. *Social Movements: An Introduction.* Malden, Mass.: Blackwell.

Díaz-Stevens, Ana Maria, and Antony M. Stevens-Arroyo. 1998. *Recognizing the Latino Resurgence in U.S. Religion.* Boulder, Colo.: Westview Press.

Dolan, Jay P. 1975. *The Immigrant Church: New York's Irish and German Catholics, 1815–1865.* Baltimore: Johns Hopkins University Press.

————. 1985. *The American Catholic Experience: A History from Colonial Times to the Present.* New York: Doubleday.

Dolan, Jay P., and Gilberto M. Hinojosa, eds. 1994. *Mexican Americans and the Catholic Church, 1900–1965.* Notre Dame, Ind.: University of Notre Dame Press.

Dussel, Enrique D. 1981. *A History of the Church in Latin America: Colonialism to Liberation, 1492–1979.* Grand Rapids, Mich.: Eerdmans.

El Plan de Santa Barbara. 1970. Santa Barbara, Calif.: La Causa.

Elizondo, Virgil. 1983. *Galilean Journey: The Mexican-American Promise.* Maryknoll, N.Y.: Orbis Books.

————. n.d. "Mexican American Cultural Center Proposal." Unpublished manuscript [February 1971].

Engh, Michael E. 1994. "From Frontera Faith to Roman Rubrics: Altering Hispanic Religious Customs in Los Angeles, 1855–1880." *U.S. Catholic Historian* 12, no. 4 (fall): 85–105.

Estrada, L., F. C. García, R. F. Macías, and L. A. Maldonado. 1981. "Chicanos in the United States: A History of Exploitation and Resistance." *Daedalus* 110 (2): 103–131.

Etzioni, Amitai. 1964. *Modern Organizations.* Englewood Cliffs, N.J.: Prentice-Hall.

Eyerman, Ron, and Andrew Jamison. 1991. *Social Movements: A Cognitive Approach.* University Park: Pennsylvania State University Press.

Fichter, Joseph Henry. 1977. "Restructuring Catholicism." *Sociological Analysis* 38: 154–166.

Flores, María Eva. 1999. "PADRES." In *The Handbook of Texas Online.* Austin: Texas State Historical Society.

Flores, Patrick. 1980. "The Church Must Liberate." In *Prophets Denied Honor: An Anthology on the Hispano Church of the United States,* ed. Antony M. Stevens-Arroyo, 220–225. Maryknoll, N.Y.: Orbis Books.

Friedrich, Carl. 1952. "Some Observations on Weber's Analysis of Bureaucracy." In *Reader in Bureaucracy,* ed. Robert K. Merton, 27–33. Glencoe, Ill.: Free Press, 1952.

García, M. T. 1978. "Internal Colonialism: A Critical Essay." *Revista Chicano-Riqueña* 6 (3): 38–41.

García, Richard A. 1991. *Rise of the American Middle Class: San Antonio, 1929–1941.* College Station: Texas A&M University Press.

Gamson, William A. 1992. *Talking Politics.* New York: Cambridge University Press, 1992.

————. 1995. "Constructing Social Protest." In *Social Movements and Culture,* ed. Hank Johnston and Bert Klandermans, 85–106. Minneapolis: University of Minnesota Press.

Gamson, William A., Bruce Fireman, and Steven Rytina. 1982. *Encounters with Unjust Authority.* Chicago: Dorsey Press.

Garvey, Gerald. 1993. *Facing the Bureaucracy: Living and Dying in a Public Agency.* San Francisco: Jossey-Bass.

Gastón, María Luisa. 1978. "Renaissance of Hispanic Participation in the U.S. Catholic Church." *La Luz* 7, no. 10 (October): 8–10.

Gaventa, John. 1980. *Power and Powerlessness: Acquiescence and Rebellion in an Appalachian Valley.* Urbana: University of Illinois Press.

Giddens, Anthony. 1979. *Central Problems in Social Theory: Action, Structure and Contradiction in Social Analysis.* New York: Basic Books.

Goffman, Ervin. 1974. *Frame Analysis: An Essay of the Organization of Experience.* Cambridge, Mass.: Harvard University Press.

Goines, David L. 1993. *The Free Speech Movement: Coming of Age in the 1960s.* Berkeley, Calif.: Ten Speed Press.

Gómez-Quiñones, Juan. 1990. *Chicano Politics: Reality and Promise, 1940–1990.* Albuquerque: University of New Mexico Press.

González, David. 1974. "Padres Unidos." *La Raza* 2 (3): 12–13.

González, G. G. 1974. "A Critique of the Internal Colony Model." *Latin American Perspectives* 1 (1): 154–161.

Grabow, Stephen, and Allan Heskin. 1973. "Foundations for a Radical Concept of Planning." *Journal of the American Institute of Planners* 39: 106–114.

Gramsci, Antonio. 1957. *The Modern Prince and Other Writings.* Trans Louis Marks. New York: International.

———. 1971. *Selections from the Prison Notebooks of Antonio Gramsci.* Ed. and trans. Quintin Hoare and Geoffrey Nowell Smith. New York: International.

———. 1995. *Further Selections from the Prison Notebooks.* Ed. and trans. Derek Boothman. London: Lawrence & Wishart.

Grebler, Leo, Joan W. Moore, and Ralph C. Guzmán. 1970. *The Mexican-American People.* New York: Free Press.

Greeley, Andrew M. 1966. *The Hesitant Pilgrim: American Catholicism after the Council.* New York: Sheed & Ward.

———. 1972. *Priests in the United States.* Garden City, N.Y.: Doubleday, 1972.

———. 1979. *Crisis in the Church.* Chicago: Thomas More Press.

———. 1982. "The Failures of Vatican II after Twenty Years." *America* 146 (February 6): 86–96.

———. 1988. "Defection among Hispanics." *America* 159, no. 3 (July 30): 61–62.

———. 1998. "The Revolutionary Event of Vatican II." *Commonweal* 125, no. 15 (September 11): 14–21.

Grito, Dolores del. 1972. "Jesus Christ as a Revolutionary." In *Anthology of Mexican-American Literature,* ed. Stan Steiner and Luis Valdez, 393–394. New York: Alfred A. Knopf.

Guerrero, Andres G. 1988. *A Chicano Theology.* Maryknoll, N.Y.: Orbis Books.

Gutiérrez, Armando, and Herbert Hirsh. 1973. "The Militant Challenge to the American Ethos: Chicanos and Mexican Americans." *Social Science Quarterly* 54: 830–845.

Gutiérrez, Gustavo. 1983. *The Power of the Poor in History: Selected Writings.* Trans. Robert R. Barr. Maryknoll, N.Y.: Orbis Books.

———. 1990. *A Theology of Liberation.* Ed. and trans. Caridad Inda and John Eagleson. Maryknoll, N.Y.: Obis Books.

Gutiérrez, José Angel. 1998. *The Making of a Chicano Militant: Lessons from Crystal City.* Madison: University of Wisconsin Press.

Hammersley, Martyn. 1984. "Some Reflections upon the Macro-Micro Problem in the Sociology of Education." *Sociological Review* 32, no. 2 (May): 316–324.

Hammersley, Martyn, and Paul Atkinson. 1983. *Ethnography: Principles in Practice.* London: Tavistock.

Harrison, Michael I., and John K. Maniha. 1978. "Dynamics of Dissenting Movements within Established Organizations: Two Cases and a Theoretical Interpretation." *Journal for the Scientific Study of Religion* 17 (3): 207–224.

Harvey, David. 1996. *Justice, Nature, and the Geography of Difference.* Cambridge, Mass.: Blackwell.

Hasenfeld, Yeheskel, ed. 1992. *Human Services as Complex Organizations.* Newbury Park, Calif.: Sage.

Hendren, Luciano C. 1983. "The Church in New Mexico." In *Fronteras: A History of the Latin American Church in the USA since 1513,* ed. Moises Sandoval, 195–207. San Antonio, Tex.: Mexican American Cultural Center.

Hoffer, Eric. 1951. *The True Believer: Thoughts on the Nature of Mass Movements.* New York: New American Library.

Hollis, Christopher. 1967. *The Achievements of Vatican II.* New York: Hawthorn Books.

hooks, bell. 1990. *Yearning: Race, Gender, and Cultural Politics.* Boston: South End Press.

Hopper, Rex D. 1950. "The Revolutionary Process: A Frame of Reference for the Study of Revolutionary Movements." *Social Forces* 28 (March): 270–279.

Hurtado, Juan. 1978. "An Attitudinal Study of Social Distance between the Mexican-American and the Church." Ph.D. diss., United States International University.

———. 1979. "The Social Interaction between the Chicano and the Church: An Historical Perspective." *El Grito del Sol* 4, no. 1 (winter): 25–45.

Isaac, Jeffry C. 2001. "The Road Not Taken: Anthony Giddens, the Third Way and the Future of Social Democracy." *Dissent* (spring): 61–70.

Isais-A., Raoul. 1979. "The Chicano and the American Catholic Church." *El Grito del Sol* 4, no. 1 (winter): 9–24.

Jasper, James. 1997. *The Art of Moral Protest.* Chicago: University of Chicago Press.

Jenkins, J. Craig, and Bert Klandermans, eds. 1995. *The Politics of Social Protest: Comparative Perspectives on States and Social Movements.* Minneapolis: University of Minnesota Press.

Johnston, Hank, and Bert Klandermans, eds. 1995. *Social Movements and Culture.* Minneapolis: University of Minnesota Press.

Kassimir, Ronald. 1996. "The Social Power of Religious Organization: The Catholic Church in Uganda, 1955–1991." Ph.D. diss., University of Chicago.

Kaufman, Philip S. 1989. *Why You Can Dissent and Remain a Faithful Catholic.* Bloomington, Ind.: Meyer-Stone.

Kerr, Louise Ano Nuevo. 1976. "The Chicano Experience in Chicago: 1920–1970." Ph.D. diss., University of Illinois at Chicago Circle.

Kornhouser, William. 1959. *The Politics of Mass Society.* Glencoe, Ill.: Free Press.

Kosmin, Barry A. 1993. *One Nation Under God: Religion in Contemporary American Society.* New York: Harmony Books.

Krumholz, Norman. 1994. "Advocacy Planning: Can it Move the Center?" *Journal of the American Planning Association* 60 (2): 150–152.

LaLonde, Kristine Lynn. 2000. "Transformation of Authority: Reform, Rebellion and Resistance in the Catholic Church in the 1960." Ph.D. diss., University of Virginia.

Lampe, Philip E. 1977. "Ethnic Identity among Minority Groups in Public and Parochial Schools." *Ethnic Group* 12: 193–196.

———. 1994. "Hispanic Heterogeneity." In *Hispanics in the Church: Up from the Cellar,* ed. Philip E. Lampe, 7–24. San Francisco: Catholic Scholars Press.

Lara-Braud, Jorge. 1971a. "The Status of Religion among Mexican-Americans." In *La Causa Chicana: The Movement for Justice,* ed. Margaret M. Mangold, 87–94. New York: Family Service Association of America.

———. 1971b. "The Status of Religion Among the Mexican Americans." Paper presented at Joint Meeting of American Academy of Religious and the Society of Biblical Literature, Southwest Region, Fort Worth, Texas, March 19.

Lasswell, Harold D., and Abraham Kaplan. 1950. *Power and Society: A Framework for Political Inquiry.* New Haven: Yale University Press.

Levy, Jacques. 1975. *César Chávez: Autobiography of la Causa.* New York: Norton.

Lipsky, Michael. 1970. *Protest in City Politics.* Chicago: Rand-McNally.

"Los Padres: Hispano Priests Organize." 1973. *La Luz* 2, no. 2 (May): 6–10.

"Los Padres: Hispano Priests Organize." 1977. *La Raza Habla* 2, no. 2 (March): 1–4.

Lucas, Isidro. 1981. *The Browning of America.* Chicago: Fides Claretian.

Lynn, Dumenil. 1991. "The Tribal Twenties: Assimilated Catholics' Response to Anti-Catholicism in the 1920s." *Journal of American Ethnic History* 11, no. 1 (fall): 21–50

Marcoux, Marcene. 1982. *Cursillo: Anatomy of a Movement.* New York: Lambeth Press.

Martínez, Elizabeth S., and Enriqueta Vásquez. 1974. *Viva la Raza! The Struggle of the Mexican-American People.* Garden City, N.Y.: Doubleday.

Marx, Karl. 1976. *Capital: A Critique of Political Economy.* Vol. 1. Trans. Ben Fowkes. New York: Vintage Books.

Matovina, Timothy. 1999. "Representation and the Reconstruction of Power: The Rise of PADRES and Las Hermanas." In *What's Left? Liberal American Catholics,* ed. Mary Jo Weaver, 220–237. Bloomington: Indiana University Press.

McAdam, Doug. 1982. *Political Process and the Development of Black Insurgency, 1930–1970.* Chicago: University of Chicago Press.

———. 1999. *Political Process and the Development of Black Insurgency 1930–1970.* 2d ed. Chicago: University of Chicago Press.

McAdam, Douglas, John D. McCarthy, and Mayer N. Zald, eds. 1996. *Comparative Perspectives on Social Movements.* New York: Cambridge University Press.

McCall, George J., and J. L. Simmons. 1966. *Identities and Interactions.* New York: Free Press.

McCarthy, J. D., and Mayer Zald. 1977. "Resource Mobilization and Social Movements: A Partial Theory." *American Journal of Sociology* 82: 1212–1241.

McCormick, Richard A. 1998. "The Church & Dissent: How Vatican II Ushered in a New Way of Thinking." *Commonwealth* 125, no. 4 (February 27): 15–21.

McGreevy, John T. 1997. "Thinking on One's Own: Catholicism in the American Intellectual Imagination, 1928–1960." *Journal of American History* 84, no. 1 (June): 97–131

McGovern, Arthur F. 1989. *Liberation theology and Its Critics: Toward an Assessment.* Maryknoll, N.Y.: Orbis Books.

McLoughlin, Emmett. 1968. *Famous Ex-Priests.* New York: L. Stuart.

McMurtrey, Martin. 1987. *Mariachi Bishop: The Life Story of Patrick Flores.* San Antonio, Tex.: Corona.

McNamara, Patrick H. 1973. "Catholicism, Assimilation, and the Chicano Movement: Los Angeles as a Case Study." In *Chicanos and Native Americans: The Territorial Minorities,* ed. Rudolph O. de la Garza, Z. Anthony Kruszewski, and Tomas A. Arciniega, 124–130. Englewood Cliffs, N.J.: Prentice-Hall.

Meconis, Charles A. 1979. *With Clumsy Grace: The American Catholic Left, 1961–1975.* New York: Seabury Press.

Medina, Lara. 1998. "Las Hermanas: Chicana/Latina Religious-Political Activism, 1971–1997." Ph.D. diss., Claremont Graduate University.

Melucci, Alberto. 1989. *Nomads of the Present: Social Movements and Individual Needs in Contemporary Society.* Ed. John Keane and Paul Mier. Philadelphia: Temple University Press.

"Mexican American Cultural Center Opens under Leadership of Bishop Patrick F. Flores." 1972. *La Luz* 1, no. 3 (June): 38–39.

"Mexican American Priests Group Forms." 1969. *San Antonio Light,* October 10.

Meyer, David S. 1993. "Peace Protest and Policy: Explaining the Rise and Decline of Antinuclear Movements in Postwar America." *Policy Studies Journal* 21: 35–56.

Mirandé, Alfredo. 1985. *The Chicano Experience: An Alternative Perspective.* Notre Dame, Ind.: University of Notre Dame Press.

Monroy, Douglas. 1978. "Mexicans in Los Angeles, 1930–1941." Ph.D. diss., University of California, Los Angeles.

Montejano, David. 1987. *Anglos and Mexicans in the Making of Texas, 1836–1986.* Austin: University of Texas Press.

———. 1999. *Chicano Politics and Society in the Late Twentieth Century.* Austin: University of Texas Press.

Moore, Barrington. 1978. *Injustice: The Social Bases of Obedience and Revolt.* White Plains, N.Y.: M. E. Sharpe.

Morris, Aldon D., and Carol McClurg Mueller, eds. *Frontiers in Social Movement Theory.* New Haven: Yale University Press.

Mosqueda, Lawrence. 1986. *Chicanos, Catholicism and Political Ideology.* Lanham, Md.: University Press of America.

Muñoz, Carlos. 1989. *Youth, Identity, Power: The Chicano Movement.* London: Verso, 1989.

Murillo, Nathan. 1971. *The Mexican American Family.* St. Louis: V. C. Mosby.

"National Conference of Catholic Bishops Report: More Hispano Bishops Needed." 1973. *La Luz* 2, no. 6 (October): 28–29.

Navarro, Armando. 1995. *Mexican American Youth Organization: Avant-garde of the Chicano Movement in Texas.* Austin: University of Texas Press.

———. 2000. *La Raza Unida Party: A Chicano Challenge to the U.S. Two-Party Dictatorship.* Philadelphia: Temple University Press.

Neuman, Lawrence. 1994. *Social Research Methods: Qualitative and Quantitative Approaches.* 2d ed. Needham Heights, Mass.: Allyn and Bacon.

O'Brien, John A., ed. 1969. *Why Priests Leave: The Intimate Stories of Twelve Who Did.* New York: Hawthorn Books.

Oberschall, Anthony. 1973. *Social Conflict and Social Movements.* Englewood Cliffs, N.J.: Prentice-Hall.

Official Catholic Directory. 1970. New York: P. J. Kenedy & Sons.

Official Catholic Directory. 2000. New Providence, N.J.: P. J. Kenedy & Sons.

Olson, Marcus. 1965, *The Logic of Collective Action.* Cambridge, Mass.: Harvard University Press.

"PADRES." 1978. *La Luz* 7, no. 10 (October): 44.

"PADRES and LAS HERMANAS." 1980. *La Luz* 8, no. 6 (February–March): 18, 44.

"PADRES Organizes for Chicano Power." 1971. *National Catholic Reporter,* April 2, p. 18.

PADRES Pamphlet. 1971. "The Second National PADRES Congress." Distributed at the Second National PADRES Congress, October 11–13. Archive of the Archdiocese of San Antonio, Texas.

"PADRES to Seek Action by Church." 1969. *San Antonio News,* October 10.

Parenti, Michael. 1970. "Power and Pluralism: A View from the Bottom." *Journal of Politics* 32 (3): 501–530.

Pattillo-McCoy, Mary. 1998. "Church Culture as a Strategy of Action in the

Black Community." *American Sociological Review* 63, no. 6 (December): 767–784.

Petal, Marla. 1988. "Counter-Hegemonic Culture and Prefigurative Politics in an Emerging Social Movement: A Case Study of LA Jobs with Peace." Ph.D. diss. proposal, University of California, Los Angeles.

Pfeffer, Jeffrey, and Gerald R. Salancik. 1978. *The External Control of Organizations.* New York: Harper & Row.

———. 1974. "Organizational Decision-making as a Political Process: The Case of a University Budget." *Administrative Science Quarterly* 19 (June): 135–151.

Piven, Frances Fox, and Richard A. Cloward. 1979. *Poor People's Movements: Why They Succeed, How They Fail.* New York: Vintage Books.

Pondy, Louis R., and Ian I. Motroff. 1979. "Beyond Open System Models of Organization." In *Research in Organizational Behavior,* vol. 1, ed. Barry M. Staw, 3–39. Greenwich, Conn.: JAI Press.

"Pope Apologizes for Catholic Sins Past and Present." 2000. *Los Angeles Times,* March 13.

Powers, William F. 1992. *Free Priests: The Movement for Ministerial Reform in the American Catholic Church.* Chicago: Loyola University Press.

"Priests Organization to 'Speak for People.'" 1969. *San Antonio Express,* October 10.

"Priests to Hold News Conference." 1969. *San Antonio News,* October 9.

Privett, Stephen A. 1988. *The U.S. Catholic Church and Its Hispanic Members: The Pastoral Vision of Archbishop Robert E. Lucey.* San Antonio, Tex.: Trinity University Press.

Pulido, Alberto L. 1991. "Are You and Emissary of Jesus Christ? Justice, the Catholic Church, and the Chicano Movement." *Explorations in Ethnic Studies* 14, no. 1 (January): 17–34.

Pycior, Julie Leininger. 1979. "La Raza Organizes: Mexican American Life in San Antonio, 1915–1930 as Reflected in Mutualista Activities." Ph.D. diss., University of Notre Dame.

"Radical Priests Challenge Pope." 1969. *San Antonio Light,* October 8.

Raven, Bertram H. 1983. "Interpersonal Influence and Social Power." In *Social Psychology,* 2d ed., ed. Bertram H. Raven and Jeffrey Z. Rubin, 399–443. New York: Wiley.

———. 1990. "Political Applications of the Psychology of Interpersonal Influence and Social Power." *Political Psychology* 11 (3): 493–520.

———. 1992. "Power/Interaction Model of Interpersonal Influence." *Journal of Social Behavior and Personality* 7 (2): 217–244.

Report of the Subcommittee for the Spanish-speaking of the Minorities Committee of the Los Angeles Priests' Senate. 1971. Archive of the Archdiocese of San Antonio, Texas.

Rivera, Julius. 1973. "Justice, Deprivation and the Chicano." *Aztlán* 4 (spring): 123–136.

Rochin, Refugio I. 1974. "Economic Deprivation of Chicanos: Continuing Neglect in the Seventies." *Aztlán* 4 (1): 85–102.

Rodríguez, Edmundo. 1971. "The Mobile Team Ministry." Paper presented at PADRES National Congress, Los Angeles, October. Archive of the Archdiocese of San Antonio, Texas.

———. 1994. "The Hispanic Community and Church Movements: Schools of Leadership." In *Hispanic Catholic Culture in the U.S.: Issues and Concerns,* ed. Jay P. Dolan and Allan Figueroa Deck, 206–239. Notre Dame, Ind.: University of Notre Dame.

Rodríguez, Olga, ed. 1977. *The Politics of Chicano Liberation.* New York: Pathfinder Press.

Romero, Juan. 1973. "Letter to the Editor." *La Luz* 2, no. 3 (June): 4.

———. 1974. "PADRES and the Selection of the Bishop." *PADRES Newsletter,* May. Archive of the Archdiocese of San Antonio, Texas.

———. 1980. "PADRES: Who are They and Where Are They Going?" In *Prophets Denied Honor: An Anthology on the Hispano Church of the United States,* ed. Antonio M. Stevens-Arroyo, 139–140. Maryknoll, N.Y.: Orbis Books.

———. 1988. "History of PADRES." Paper presented at CEHILA-U.S.A. Symposium, Las Cruces, New Mex., January. Romero Papers.

———. 1990. "Charism and Power: An Essay on the History of PADRES." *U.S. Catholic Historian* 9, nos. 1–2 (winter–spring): 147–163.

———. 1992. "Tension between Cross and Sword: A Profile of Father Luis Olivares." Paper presented at CEHILA Symposium, Los Angeles. Romero Papers.

———. 1994. "Mexican American Priests: History of PADRES 1969–1989." In *Hispanics in the Church: Up from the Cellar,* ed. Philip E. Lampe, 71–94. San Francisco: Catholic Scholars Press.

———. n.d. "The San Bernadino Affair." Unpublished manuscript. Romero Papers.

Romo, Richard. 1976. "Mexican Workers in the City: Los Angeles, 1915–1930." Ph.D. diss., University of California, Los Angeles, 1976.

Rosales, F. Arturo. 1996. *Chicano! The History of the Mexican- American Civil Rights Movement.* Houston: Arte Publico Press.

Rosales, Rodolfo. 1991. "The Rise of Chicano Middle Class Politics in San Antonio, 1951 to 1985." Ph.D. diss., University of Michigan.

———. 1999. "Personality and Style in San Antonio Politics." In *Chicano Politics and Society in the Late Twentieth Century,* ed. David Montejano, 3–30. Austin: University of Texas Press, 1999.

———. 2000. *The Illusion of Inclusion: The Untold Political Story of San Antonio.* Austin: University of Texas Press.

Roybal, Rose Marie. 1974. "Paul Sedillo, Jr.: A Profile of the Spanish Speaking within the Hierarchy of the Catholic Church." *La Luz* 3, no. 2 (May): 24–25.

Ruether, Rosemary Radford. 1992. "Spirituality and Justice: Popular Church Movements in the United States." In *A Democratic Catholic Church: The Reconstruction of Roman Catholicism,* ed. Eugene C. Bianchi and Rosemary Radford Ruether, 189–206. New York: Crossroad.

Ruiz, Ralph. 1968. Unpublished manuscript. Ralph Ruiz Papers.

Rule, James, and Charles Tilly. 1975. "Political Process in Revolutionary France: 1830–1832." In *1830 in France*, ed. John Marrinman, 44–86. New York: New Viewpoints.

Russell, James. 1980. *Marx-Engels Dictionary*. Westport, Conn.: Greenwood Press.

Salazar, Rubén. 1970. *Chicanismo*. Crystal, Tex.: El Distrito Escolar Independencia de Crystal.

Sandoval, Chela. 1991. "U.S. Third World Feminism: The Theory and Method of Oppositional Consciousness in the Postmodern World." *Genders* 10 (spring): 11–15.

Sandoval, Moisés. 1978. "The Latinization of the Catholic Church." *Agenda* (November–December).

———. 1983a. "The Church and El Movimento." In *Fronteras: A History of the Latin American Church in the USA since 1513*, ed. Moises Sandoval, 377–412. San Antonio, Tex.: Mexican American Cultural Center.

———. 1983b. "Church Structure for the Hispanics." In *Fronteras: A History of the Latin American Church in the USA since 1513*, ed. Moises Sandoval, 413–438. San Antonio, Tex.: Mexican American Cultural Center.

———. 1983c. "Effects of World War II on the Hispanic Peoples." In *Fronteras: A History of the Latin American Church in the USA since 1513*, ed. Moises Sandoval, 341–376. San Antonio, Tex.: Mexican American Cultural Center.

———, ed. 1983d. *Fronteras: A History of the Latin American Church in the USA since 1513*. San Antonio, Tex.: Mexican American Cultural Center.

———, ed. 1983e. *The Mexican American Experience in the Church: Reflections on Identity and Mission*. San Antonio, Tex.: Mexican American Cultural Center Tenth Anniversary Forum.

———. 1990. *On the Move: A History of the Hispanic Church in the U.S.* Maryknoll, N.Y.: Orbis Books.

———. 1994. "Organization of a Hispanic Church." In *Hispanic Catholic Culture in the U.S.: Issues and Concerns*, ed. Jay P. Dolan and Allan Figueroa Deck, 131–165. Notre Dame, Ind.: University of Notre Dame.

Sandoval, Moises, and Salvador E. Alvarez. 1983. "The Church in California." In *Fronteras: A History of the Latin American Church in the USA since 1513*, ed. Moises Sandoval, 209–221. San Antonio, Tex.: Mexican American Cultural Center.

Schall, James V. 1982. *Liberation Theology in Latin America*. San Francisco: Ignatius Press.

Scott, Richard W. 1987. *Organizations: Rational, Natural, and Open Systems*. 2d ed. Englewood Cliffs, N.J.: Prentice-Hall.

"Seek Commitment: 50 Priests Organize." 1969. *San Antonio Express*, October 12.

Seidler, John. 1986. "Contested Accommodation: The Catholic Church as a Specific Case of Social Change." *Social Forces* 64, no. 4 (June): 847–874.

Seidler, John, and Katherine Meyer. 1989. *Conflict and Change in the Catholic Church.* New Brunswick, N.J.: Rutgers University Press.

Seligmann, Irving S. 1968. "The Political Alienation of the Mexican American in San Antonio, Texas." Thesis, St. Mary's University, San Antonio.

Servín, Manuel P. 1970. *The Mexican Americans: An Awakening Minority.* Beverly Hills: Glencoe Press.

Shaw, Stephen J. 1991. *The Catholic Parish as a Way-Station of Ethnicity and Americanization: Chicago's Germans and Italians, 1903–1939.* New York: Carlson.

Small, Melvin. 1994. *Covering Dissent: The Media and the Anti-Vietnam War Movement.* New Brunswick, N.J.: Rutgers University Press.

Smith, Christian. 1991. *The Emergence of Liberation Theology: Radical Religion and Social Movement Theory.* Chicago: University of Chicago Press.

Snow, David A., and Robert D. Benford. 1992. "Master Frames and Cycles of Protest." In *Frontiers of Social Movement Theory*, ed. Aldon Morris and Carol Mueller, 133–155. New Haven: Yale University Press.

Snow, David A., Burke Rochford, Steven Worden, and Robert Benford. 1986. "Frame Alignment Processes, Micromobilization, and Movement Participation." *American Sociological Review* 51, no. 4 (August): 464–481.

Soja, Edward W. 1996. *Thirdspace: Journeys to Los Angeles and Other Real-and-Imagined Places.* Cambridge, Mass.: Blackwell.

Steele, Jay. 1976. "Hispanics Protest Racism: Boycott Boston School." *Guardian* 28, no. 16 (January 28): 4.

Stern, Kenneth S. 1994. *Loud Hawk: The United States versus the American Indian Movement.* Norman: University of Oklahoma Press.

Stevens-Arroyo, Anthony M. 1994. "The Emergence of Social Identity among Latino Catholics." In *Hispanic Catholic Culture in the U.S.: Issues and Concerns*, ed. Jay P. Dolan and Allan Deck, 77–129. Notre Dame, Ind.: University of Notre Dame Press.

———, ed. 1980. *Prophets Denied Honor.* Maryknoll, N.Y.: Orbis Books.

"Study Finds Segregation of Latinos in Catholic Church." 2000. *Los Angeles Times*, March 1.

Sylvest, Edwin. 1983. "Hispanic American Protestantism in the United States." In *Fronteras: A History of the Latin American Church in the USA since 1513*, ed. Moises Sandoval, 279–338. San Antonio, Tex.: Mexican American Cultural Center.

Tafolla, Carmen. 1983. "The Church in Texas." In *Fronteras: A History of the Latin American Church in the USA since 1513*, ed. Moises Sandoval, 183–194. San Antonio, Tex.: Mexican American Cultural Center.

Tarrow, Sidney. 1989. *Democracy and Disorder: Protest and Politics in Italy, 1965–1975.* Oxford: Oxford University Press.

Taylor, Verta. 1996. *Rock-a-bye Baby: Feminism, Self-Help and Postpartum Depression.* New York: Routledge.

Taylor, Verta, and Nancy Whittier. 1995. "Analytical Approaches to Social Movement Culture: The Culture of the Women's Movement." In *Social*

Movements and Culture, ed. Hank Johnston and Bert Klandermans, 163–
187. Minneapolis: University of Minnesota Press.
"Teaching about the Holocaust." 2000. *Los Angeles Times,* March 13.
Tilly, Charles. 1975. *The Rebellious Century, 1830–1930.* Cambridge, Mass.:
Harvard University Press.
"Time for Action Is Now!" 1967. *La Raza,* October 29.
Torre, Aurelio de la. 1978. "Catholic Leaders Approached for Updated
Changes." *Somos* 1, no. 6 (November): 8–9.
Turner, Ralph H. 1969. "The Theme of Contemporary Social Movements."
British Journal of Sociology 20: 390–405.
Turner, Ralph H., and Lewis M. Killian. 1987. *Collective Behavior.* 3d ed. En-
glewood Cliffs, N.J.: Prentice-Hall.
"United Hispanic Catholic Leaders Form the Hub of the Hispanic Apostolate."
1978. *La Luz* 7, no. 10 (October): 24–25.
"U.S. Catholic Conference Secretariat for Hispanic Affairs." 1980. *La Luz* 8,
no. 6 (February–March): 18.
Vargas, Zaragosa. 1997. "Tejana Radical: Emma Tenayuca and the San Anto-
nio Labor Movement during the Great Depression." *Pacific Historical Re-
view* 66, no. 4 (November): 553–580.
Viva la causa: 500 Years of Chicano History. The Complete Teaching Kit. 1995.
Albuquerque: Southwest Organizing Project.
Wartenberg, Thomas E., ed. 1992. *Rethinking Power.* Albany: State University
of New York Press.
Weber, Max. 1958. *From Max Weber: Essays in Sociology.* Ed. and trans. H. H.
Gerth and C. Wright Mills. New York: Oxford University Press.
———. 1978. *Economy and Society: An Outline of Interpretive Sociology.* Ed.
Guenther Roth and Claus Wittich; trans. Ephraim Fischoff. Berkeley: Uni-
versity of California Press.
Weick, Karl E. 1979. *The Social Psychology of Organizing.* Reading, Mass.:
Addison-Wesley.
Wolin, Sheldon S. 1960. *Politics and Vision: Continuity and Innovation in
Western Political Thought.* Boston: Little, Brown.
Woods, Frances Jerome. 1967. *Mexican Ethnic Leadership in San Antonio,
Texas.* New York: Arno Press.
Yin, Robert K. 1994. *Case Study Research Design and Methods.* 2d ed. Thou-
sand Oaks, Calif.: Sage.
Zajonc, Robert B. 1980. "Feeling and Thinking: Preference Needs No Infer-
ences." *American Psychologist* 35: 151–175.

PERSONAL INTERVIEWS

Anguiano, Leonard. December 21, 2000. Interview by the author.
Aragón, Ramón. January 23, 2001. Interview by the author.
Bernal, Joe. December 12, 2000. Interview by the author.

Cabral, Antonio. December 15, 2000. Interview by the author.

Carrillo, Alberto. October 29, 2001. Interview by the author.

Casso, Henry. January 23, 2001. Interview by the author.

Elizondo, Virgil. February 12, 2002. Interview by the author.

Flores, Patrick. October 15, 2000. Interview by the author.

Flores, Roberto. February 16, 2001. Interview by the author.

Gallegos, Albert. January 21, 2001. Interview by the author.

García, Blanca Romo. November 13, 2000. Interview by the author.

Garza, David. December 15, 1999. Interview by the author.

Henke, Raymond. November 2, 2000. Interview by the author.

Janacek, Balthasar J. October 2, 2000. Interview by the author.

López, Chavel. February 23, 2001. Interview by the author.

López, Vicente. February 19, 2002. Interview by the author.

Madrigal, Héctor. February 16, 2001. Interview by the author.

Martínez, Manuel. March 30, 2001. Interview by the author.

Matula, Lawrence. May 3, 2001. Interview by the author.

Piña, Roberto. December 18, 2000. Interview by the author.

Peña, Roberto. November 23, 2000. Interview by the author.

Ramírez, Ricardo. February 2, 2001. Interview by the author.

Reyes, Lonnie. October 19, 2000. Interview by the author.

Rodríguez, Edmundo. January 23, 2001. Interview by the author.

Romero, Juan. February 13, 2002. Interview by the author.

Ruiz, Ralph. September 28, 2000. Interview by the author.

Sánchez, Trinidad. October 20, 2001. Interview by the author.

Tarango, Yolanda. October 31, 2000. Interview by the author.

Vázquez, Manuel. February 23, 2001. Interview by the author.

INDEX

†

Furey, Francis James, 22, 25, 51, 54,
59, 79, 80, 88, 89, 92
Gallegos, Albert, 15, 16, 32, 35, 43,
45, 52, 66, 67, 79, 89, 96, 127,
150, 153; photos of, 63, 64
García, Blanca Romo, 6, 36, 124,
152
García, Genaro, 31
García, Peter E., 114
García, Rubén, 83
Garza, David, 132
Gaventa, John, 9
Germans, and their influence and
representation in the U.S. Catholic
Church, 4, 11, 32, 33, 39, 49, 72,
73, 85
Gómez-Quiñones, Juan, 21
González, Corky, 26, 106
Gortaire, Alfonso, 102
Green, Francis J., 59, 79
Guara, Alexander, 72
Gutiérrez, Armando, 44
Gutiérrez, Gustavo, 102, 105
Gutiérrez, José Angel, 39, 92

Hendren, Luciano C., 11, 150
Hirsh, Herbert, 44
Hopper, Rex, 132
Hunger Hearings Conference, 25
Hunger in America, 25

IAF. See Industrial Areas Foundation
Industrial Areas Foundation (IAF),
84, 112, 115, 116
Inner City Apostolate, 23, 27
Instituto de Pastoral en Latino
América (IPLA), 102–103
Insurgent state of being, 139–147
IPLA. See Instituto de Pastoral en
Latino América
Irish, and their influence on and
representation in the U.S. Catholic
Church, 4, 5, 9, 11, 32, 35, 65,
72–74, 76, 78–81, 85, 86, 79,
91, 94

Jackson, Jesse, 27
Jadot, Jean, 95, 124
Janacek, Balthasar "Balty," 32, 34,
60, 61, 63, 89, 92, 113
Jocist Cell Movement, 98

Kelly Air Force Base (San Antonio),
23
Killian, Lewis M., 146
Killian, William, 40
Kim, Hyojoung, 146
King, Martin Luther, Jr., 26, 45, 48
Krol, John, 112

Lampe, Philip E., 44
Lamy, Jean-Batiste, 8, 10
Las Hermanas, 1, 2, 102–104, 106,
111, 112, 120, 121, 150, 152, 153
Levin, Bishop, 25
Liberation Theology, 6, 102, 103,
112, 145
Linskens, John, 105
López, Joe, 108, 109, 110, 149, 151
López, Patricio, 14, 72
López, Vicente, 17, 63, 77, 78, 98,
112, 153; photo of, 64
Lucey, Robert E., 12, 16, 26, 40
Luna, Raúl, 148
Luna, Roger, 5

MACC. See Mexican American
Cultural Center
Madrigal, Héctor, 67, 111
MALDEF. See Mexican American Le-
gal Defense and Educational Fund
Manning, Timothy, 59, 80, 81, 89
Marins, José, 105
Martínez, Manuel, 16, 19, 52, 129,
153; photo of, 64
Matovina, Timothy, 97
MAYO. See Mexican-American
Youth Organization
McAdam, Douglas, 11
McAllister, Walter, 25
McDonough, Thomas Joseph, 59
McElwain, Hugh, 16